# MODERNISM, NARRATIVE
# AND HUMANISM

In *Modernism, Narrative and Humanism*, Paul Sheehan attempts to re-define modernist narrative for the twenty-first century. For Sheehan modernism presents a major form of critique of the fundamental presumptions of humanism. By pairing key modernist writers with philosophical critics of the humanist tradition, he shows how modernists sought to discover humanism's inhuman potential. He examines the development of narrative during the modernist period and sets it against, among others, the nineteenth-century philosophical writings of Schopenhauer, Darwin and Nietzsche. Focusing on the major novels and poetics of Conrad, Lawrence, Woolf and Beckett, Sheehan investigates these writers' mistrust of humanist orthodoxy and their consequent transformations and disfigurations of narrative order. He reveals the crucial link between the modernist novel's narrative concerns and its philosophical orientation in a book that will be of compelling interest to scholars of modernism and literary theory.

PAUL SHEEHAN is a Sydney-based writer and researcher. He studied at Birkbeck College, London, and has published articles on Dickens and Beckett.

# MODERNISM, NARRATIVE AND HUMANISM

PAUL SHEEHAN

CAMBRIDGE
UNIVERSITY PRESS

PUBLISHED BY THE PRESS SYNDICATE OF THE UNIVERSITY OF CAMBRIDGE
The Pitt Building, Trumpington Street, Cambridge, United Kingdom

CAMBRIDGE UNIVERSITY PRESS
The Edinburgh Building, Cambridge CB2 2RU, UK
40 West 20th Street, New York, NY 10011-4211, USA
477 Williamstown Road, Port Melbourne, VIC 3207, Australia
Ruiz de Alarcón 13, 28014 Madrid, Spain
Dock House, The Waterfront, Cape Town 8001, South Africa

http://www.cambridge.org

First published 2002

Printed in the United Kingdom at the University Press, Cambridge

*Typeface* Baskerville Monotype 11 / 12.5 pt     *System* LaTeX 2$_\varepsilon$   [TB]

*A catalogue record for this book is available from the British Library*

ISBN 0 521 81457 x hardback

*For G. R. and J. S. Sheehan*

*homó sum: humani níl a me aliením puto.*
(I am a man, I count nothing human foreign to me.)

Terence, *Heauton Timorumenos*

Nothing human is foreign to us, once we have digested the racing news.

Samuel Beckett, *Texts for Nothing*

# Contents

# *Preface*

> To have humanism we must first be convinced of our humanity. As
> we move further into decadence this becomes more difficult.
>
> Thomas Pynchon[1]

The decades since the end of the Second World War have been notable for precipitating, among other radical changes, a thoroughgoing
reappraisal of what it means to be human. Changes in political practice
and intellectual rationale, and recent scientific endeavours such as the
Genome Project and embryonic-stem-cell research, have raised serious
doubts as to how secure that elusive category, the 'human', really is. And
as the measure of these changes is still being taken, postwar theoretical
discourse has transformed the human from a discrete, intuitively understood idea (or ideal) into a site of contention, where notions of hybridity,
contradiction and dispersion circulate freely and abundantly. The more
knowledge we have of the human, it now seems, the more it slides from
our grasp.

Since the Renaissance first brought the notion into modern
Western consciousness, the various humanisms that have burgeoned –
Enlightenment, liberal, existential – have assumed a degree of certainty
about what it means to be human. In most instances this is supported
by appeals to intrinsic rational, moral and axiological dimensions, and
a belief in a universal human nature and/or condition. A major reper-
cussion of the *Shoah* in the decades since it became public knowledge –
and probably for a long time still to come – has been a foreclosure of
that certainty, a breakdown of the categories of rationality, morality, etc.,
laying them open to sustained critical scrutiny and revalencing. Thus the
Kantian stress on the free use of reason ('The *public* use of one's reason
must always be free, and it alone can bring about enlightenment among
human beings')[2] is, within the purview of such iconoclasts as Zygmunt
Bauman, a significant contributor to the ideology that made the death

camps possible.³ But if one certainty has been shaken – the certainty of what is irreducibly human – its place has been taken by a different kind of certainty: that we know what the *in*human is, and what it does (it constructs our understanding of the 'human'). This is the bailiwick of theoretical and philosophical antihumanism, whose replacement categories betoken a diversity that hides their common certitude: language, discourse, desire, being, *natura*, the unconscious, social formation, and technology, to cite some of the more prominent and widely disseminated.

The present project aims to show that this concern with the human, though quickened by the theoretical and philosophical response to the unprecedented horrors of the *Shoah*, has its roots in the earlier decades of the twentieth century. Specifically, it emerges from the cultural upheavals that have been historicised as the 'crises of modernism'. Thus the misology of critical commentators such as Bauman has its pre-Holocaust counterparts in a number of modernist avatars. This is not, however, to impute any ethical parity to Bauman's critique of the discourses of reason and, say, D. H. Lawrence's perorations of misanthropy. It is rather to illustrate two things. First, to show that the critical engagement with the concept of the human is not an exclusively postwar skirmish, but a century-long project, whose roots are concealed by the shifting cultural formations of the late nineteenth and early twentieth centuries. And second, to demonstrate that this earlier engagement was crucial, not incidental, in establishing the conditions of possibility for the postwar antihumanism dominating continental theory and philosophy in its various present-day guises.

The name I have given this critical engagement is 'anthropometric' – literally, the measure of the size and proportions of the human body, adapted here to mean the taking of the measure of the 'human': as transcendental category, empirical reality, or malleable, indeterminate becoming. An anthropometric tradition can be identified because the taking of this measure – in the terms I am about to sketch out – has, over the past 150 years, become increasingly problematic.

The defining feature of anthropometric thought is a bifurcation: the human no longer possesses an *a priori* connection to humanism. Formerly, there was an unspoken agreement, a commensurability, between the naming of the human and the doctrine(s) of humanism. To speak of or to write about the human was, perforce, to assume particular modes of conduct, embodied in a clutch of political and ethical guidelines befitting such a noble being. Similarly, any doctrine identifiable as humanist invoked a knowable entity, a possessor of certain endemic, existential attributes. As Emmanuel Levinas has observed: 'In a wide sense, humanism signified the recognition of an invariable essence named "Man".'[4] The anthropometric philosophers and writers at the heart of the discussion abjure this congenital human-humanism connection.

On the one hand, 'humanism without the human' is evident in the work of Schopenhauer. For him, the absence of a given being identifiable as 'human' is no obstacle to his prescribing doctrines for appropriate ethical and political behaviour, or what might be summed up as ethics without metaphysics. On the other hand, 'the human without humanism' (or 'the human without the "human"'), takes apart the metaphysical and axiological assumptions that have accreted around the term (category, concept) 'human'. Its chief exponents are Nietzsche and Heidegger, who both evinced either a frustrating vagueness or a wily reticence in establishing a blueprint for appropriate human conduct. Their works display, indeed, a notorious absence of any specific prescription for social, political or ethical renewal – despite the fact that both have at various times inspired, if that is the right word, socio-political commentary. This could be described as being without metaphysics, attempting as it does to break with the humanist figure of 'metaphysical man'.

These two strands are not intended to exhaust all anthropometric thought in the past 150 years. The four novelists under consideration – Conrad, Lawrence, Woolf and Beckett – though undeniably anthropometric, fall outside both lines of enquiry. Part of their purpose within this project, therefore, is to comment on these lines, to establish the boundaries between humanist and counterhumanist attitudes of mind. Beyond the role played by these four writers, the chief purpose in identifying an anthropometric tradition in nineteenth- and twentieth-century thought is to delineate a coherent genealogy, a process whereby these often diverse critics of the 'human' can be seen to possess certain affinities.

A parallel might be made with the argument Margot Norris mounts in *Beasts of the Modern Imagination*. Attacking the traditional separation of animal and human, of 'creatural and cultural man',[5] she brings to life a biocentric era spanning the years from 1830 to 1930. The biocentric art that emerged during this period 'required an unromantic, unsentimental (although not entirely unsympathetic) fidelity to the animal's alien otherness'.[6] There are significant differences from the anthropometric era, however, and they are threefold. Firstly, and most obviously, the dates are slightly later, beginning in the mid-nineteenth century and ending in the mid-twentieth. Secondly, the animal is only one category of anthropometrism (the mechanical and the transcendent are equally as important). Thirdly, Norris assays artists as well as writers and philosophers, whereas the present argument focuses purely on literary modernism, and how narrative is manifested and deformed by novelists and philosophers. Nevertheless, *Beasts of the Modern Imagination* is an important precedent for the anthropometric genealogy, in its recognition that some drastic rethinking of human and inhuman has taken place.

As with much discussion of philosophy and literature, there are border crossings between the two territories. The major prose works of Conrad, Lawrence, Woolf and Beckett are treated with philosophical seriousness, to explore their reflections on human being within the constellation of their narrative poetics. And the converse also applies. The key figures of post-Kantian continental philosophy are examined for their dispositions towards narrative, and for the inevitable 'aesthetic' effect – performative, poetic, nondiscursive – produced by their revocation of the *diktats* of reason. No claim is made that these very different thinkers are bound together by some profoundly common essence. Although they all address what is other than human, the modalities of that address are for the most part diverse, and the differences cannot be ignored; indeed, they are used here to give form and substance to the imaginary anthropometric tradition I have sketched out. The complexity of thought underlying the hundred-year-long development of the human problematic, from the 1850s to the 1950s, cannot be neatly contained in a single narrative thread, nor followed through a single historical modality. The issues that are raised do, finally, dovetail into one another, but only after they have undergone comparative analysis with different lines of thought and cultural forms in different eras.

# Acknowledgments

Thanks are due first and foremost to Steven Connor, whose expert commentary and advice dispensed for an earlier incarnation of this work, as a doctoral thesis, was incalculable. I also benefited enormously from his and Isobel Armstrong's Graduate Theory Seminars, which managed to cover many of the issues addressed herein. Among my colleagues at Birkbeck College, Joe Brooker was the most attentive and perspicuous critic of the various drafts. I also owe a debt of gratitude for spirited and articulate discussion, both in and out of reading groups and seminars, to David Deeming, Eliane Glaser, Nattie Golubov, Phyllis James, Ulrika Maude, Julian Sheather and Amrita Sidhu. Finally, for advice and information on publishing, not to mention unfailing support, I wish to thank Daniela Caselli, Ana Parejo Vadillo and Bob Eaglestone.

# INTRODUCTION

## *The anthropometric turn*

Formal realism, in fact, is the narrative embodiment of a premise that Defoe and Richardson accepted very literally, but which is implicit in the novel form in general: the premise, or primary convention, that the novel is a full and authentic report of human experience . . .

Ian Watt[1]

What relation does the novel have to human being, human life, human-ism? Its most obvious characteristic is the ability to encode life into text, by drawing on the conventions of 'formal realism'. Compared with epic poetry and literary ballads, the novel has a greater purchase on mimesis, and against the short story and the novella it has the potential breadth to convey a life, a saga, a tradition.[2] The novel, of all literary forms, can most comfortably contain the arc of history, from the personal to the global. By these lights, the *roman fleuve* is perhaps the epitome of the form.

Ian Watt maps the origins of the novel on to the beginning of modern philosophy. It was in his method, writes Watt, that Descartes attained greatness. In contrast with his predecessors, the French philosopher's pursuit of truth was conceived as a wholly individual matter, as a clean break with precedent and tradition. The literary form of the novel re-capitulates these interwoven notions of individualism and innovation. In its aim, 'truth to individual experience', the novel could not help but strike a unique chord. Defoe's procedure reveals this Cartesian analogue: '[Defoe's] total subordination of the plot to the pattern of the autobio-graphical memoir is as defiant an assertion of the primacy of individual experience in the novel as Descartes's *cogito ergo sum* was in philosophy.'[3]

The novel has ties not only with individualism and innovation, but with the quintessentially human attribute of logic. The novel, writes Hugh Kenner, is 'the bastard son begotten by empirical science upon a dormant Muse, and it has been cursed with logical crosses from the day it learned to talk'.[4] But does this make it a specifically *humanist* modality, the literary form of humanism? The clearest link between the humanist tradition and the novel is the *Bildungsroman*. Humanism's central theme, established during the Renaissance, was human potentiality. Man pos-sessed latent powers of creativity, which could only be released through formal education. In German letters humanism is associated with *Bildung*, the tradition of education through self-cultivation. But this association is not unequivocal. On the one hand, it was Wilhelm von Humboldt, the architect of the Prussian education system, who did more than anyone else to establish the concept of *Bildung* in an institutional context.[5] But on the other, *Bildung* in general is a much more diffuse process of individual growth and evolution, an expression of bourgeois humanism rather than a narrow marker of educational accomplishment.[6]

The novelistic genre that emerges bears this out. The typical *Bildungs-roman* plot begins with the protagonist's childhood in the country or the provinces, a childhood marred by paternalistic constraint. To free his imagination from these fetters, the protagonist must escape to the city.

Significantly, traditional pedagogy has failed him by this point, left him frustrated rather than fulfilled. It is experience of urban life that furnishes him with real 'education'. Sexual encounters stimulate soul-searching and value-reappraisal, marking his rite of passage to the modern world and to maturity. Once this has been achieved he can return to the family home, to put in relief the success of his entry into modern life. Jerome H. Buckley summarises this journey as 'childhood, the conflict of generations, provinciality, the larger society, self-education, alienation, ordeal by love, the search for a vocation and a working philosophy'.[7]

Education, then, is not outwardly imparted to the individual through humanistic pedagogy, but wrested into shape inwardly as the self struggles to take shape, to become fully integrated, under the pressure of urban social encounter both physical (sexual) and mental (philosophical). So although the *Bildungsroman* draws heavily on the Renaissance model of humanism as *potentiality*, of the self awaiting instruction in order to come into its own, the way in which this happens resembles a proto-Romantic self-forging. It is no surprise to recall that Goethe, who established the *Bildungsroman* in 1795–6 with *Wilhelm Meister's Apprenticeship*, had already engendered the prototype for the Byronic hero some two decades earlier in *The Sorrows of Young Werther*.

Georg Lukács defines *Wilhelm Meister*'s theme (and, by extension, the quintessential shape of the *Bildungsroman*) as 'the reconciliation of the problematic individual, guided by his lived experience of the ideal with concrete social reality'.[8] This is the tradition of *Bildung*, of self-development or self-culture, transplanted to the arena of societal encounter. Yet unlike the Romantic paradigm – which also focused intently on the inner life – society is not an abiding impediment to self-realisation. Indeed, social experience is crucial for the hero properly to develop and integrate his powers; it is self-cultivation that is the goal, not self-transcendence.[9] Thus the *Bildungsroman* is concerned not with self *per se* but with transformation of self – by family, by bourgeois society, by history. The difference is not a negligible one. It finally serves to close the gap (opened up by the Romantic analogue) between the *Bildungsroman* and humanistic *Bildung*.

However, at the very inception of the genre – encoded in its DNA, as it were – is a recessive chromosome. Thirty years before *Wilhelm Meister* the generic paradigm for the *Bildungsroman* took shape with C. M. Wieland's *History of Agathon*. Michael Beddow describes its emergence as a response to a perennial dilemma: the Enlightenment inability to reconcile the Cartesian coordinates of mind and extension.

Like so many of his European contemporaries, Wieland was troubled by the implications of mechanistic explanations of the physical world for traditional views about the nature and status of man. He had himself strongly felt the plausibility of each of two incompatible extreme positions: assimilation of human consciousness to the mechanical laws of the physical world, and the strict separation of human spirituality from material reality. Unable to give singleminded assent to either of these positions, but unable either to find any discursive philosophy that resolved the conflict between them to his satisfaction, he turned to a type of imaginative literature of his own devising. Through prose fiction of the kind he created in *Agathon*, he hoped to engage his readers' imaginative powers in the task of establishing a true picture of human nature, such as strictly philosophical reflection could not, in his view, provide.[10]

If Cartesian individualism gave to the novel a model of subjectivity, Cartesian dualism provided the dilemma that only the *Bildungsroman* could overcome: Enlightenment frustration with the relationship between *res cogitans* (rational human subjects) and *res extensa* (lifeless objects, including animals). The 'solution' proffered was to see discursive philosophy as a kind of category mistake. It is *fiction* that can perform this task, not philosophy. But the problem nonetheless remains, as a kind of 'philosophical unconscious' within the genre, an epistemological conundrum that can only be addressed by adopting a different set of terms. The Cartesian dilemma, therefore, is not so much a staging device as a congenital condition, immanent rather than epigenic.

Franco Moretti's designation of the *Bildungsroman* as 'the "symbolic form" of modernity' takes on a different cast in this context.[11] Moretti argues that Europe is plunged into modernity, in the wake of the Industrial and French Revolutions, so unexpectedly that European culture lags behind. Europe's experience of modernity is therefore premature, even illegitimate. The *Bildungsroman* conveys this illegitimacy in two ways. The peregrinations of its protagonist describe a forging of values on the hoof, as it were, in the absence of a suitable mentor or pedagogue (actual father or father-figure). There is no 'great system' for acquiring knowledge that the protagonist can participate in. He becomes educated under adversarial circumstances – not from the measured pedagogy of the university, but through self-forged learning on the streets, living by his wits. Formally, too, the *Bildungsroman* is, in its inaugural state, a miscegenated, 'illegitimate' form. Though *Wilhelm Meister* is ostensibly a novel, literary debate rubs shoulders with criticism, poetry with song. The *Bildungsroman* – the 'bastard' form – survives 'because of its ability to accentuate modernism's dynamism and instability'.[12] This instability is present in the genre, as we

have just seen, almost before it comes into being. Its congenital uncertainty will become more pronounced as the novel is reshaped by modernity, mutating to accommodate itself to modernity's diversifying energies.

Although the *Bildungsroman* stresses the protagonist's moral destination,
the narrative's teleology is questionable. Individual inclination comes up
against social necessity, resulting in the hero's achieving a different goal
from the one expected.[13] Human agency is not ruled out entirely, but the
vicissitudes of social formation serve to *ironise* it. Writ large, it echoes a
particular view of history, as Arthur Danto observes:

> But Vico really required reference to human intentions in his historical explana-
> tions, and so do all philosophies of history which pretend to interpret history as
> *irony*, where men not only make their history and in ways they never intended:
> but where what they bring about rather is *counter* to their intentions. Vico for
> one, and Hegel and Marx for others, suppose history globally to exhibit irony
> in this sense.[14]

'Outcome' as an ironical consequence of 'intention' is symptomatic of
agential dispersal, between human and nonhuman. Systems and structures exceed the controlling power underwritten by the *cogito*, claiming
for themselves a degree of autonomous self-persistence.[15] In Chapter 2
this dialectical process of human-nonhuman interaction is discussed in
relation to forms of technology.

The *Bildungsroman*, the genre of fiction supposedly existing as a shining
example of integrated selfhood, had a troubled inception and contains,
as we have just seen, the seeds of philosophical uncertainty. It is not just
formal realism, Cartesian individualism and *Bildung* that authorise the
shift from philosophical thinking to imaginative involvement, but something much more fundamental to the novel, to *all* novels: narrative logic.
It is narrative that enables the temporal dimension of human nature to
be expressed, making it possible to demonstrate the growth of subjectivity without confronting the impasse of Cartesian dualism. 'To raise the
question of the nature of narrative', writes Hayden White, 'is to invite
reflection on the very nature of culture and, possibly, even on the nature
of humanity itself.'[16] Thus narrative can serve as the structuring principle linking the human to the novel, to modernism, and to philosophical
reflection.

The genre of the *Bildungsroman*, it seems clear from the above, is essential to an emplotment of the transactions between the human (humanism, *humanitas*) and the novel. Its antagonist is the experimental, formally
diverse modernist novel, with its fraught negotiations between *anthropos*

and narrative. This literary form offers a powerful commentary on the various struggles to break free of narrative – or at least to find a different order for its particular conventions. In doing so it illuminates the persistent fixation on the 'human', and the ways in which it is implicated within narrative understanding and orientation, through the hundred-year anthropometric era, from the 1850s to the 1950s.

### GROUNDWORK: SOME TERMS AND TENETS

It is necessary at this point to outline some of the key terms for the argument that follows. This does not, perforce, include the 'human'; its undefinability is the starting point of the discussion. (It will be more pertinent to consider what has been done in the name of the human, or better, what has been done as a result of the inability to name, i.e., coherently account for the human.) Nevertheless, 'humanism', the 'inhuman' and 'narrative' can be adumbrated, to prepare the ground for what ensues.

Richard Etlin's recent book, *In Defense of Humanism*, makes the claim that 'the divine spark which gives and sanctifies creativity and genius in the domain of art is comparable to the natural law that gives and sanctifies the rights of man'.[7] It is *humanism* that underwrites this 'natural law'. Philosophically, humanism is that discourse of the modern subject derived from the Cartesian tradition of reason, logic, cognition, reflexivity; and its Kantian moral affiliates of responsibility, duty, respect, self-sovereignty, agency. In this tradition a reasoning being is also a moral being.

Implicit in humanism is the idea of *autonomy*, the belief that 'man is the measure of all things' and the maker of all meanings; and *mastery*, that he has dominion over himself and his world. These two axioms, which become less defensible as the anthropometric turn unfolds, are mutually supporting. Self-sovereignty provides a precedent for sovereignty (i.e., over nature), and the latter permits the nonhuman world to be appropriated by and incorporated into the human world, by means of (for example) anthropomorphisation. Three humanistic tenets in particular will reappear in later chapters: scale, value and soul.

Scale prepares the ground for anthropocentrism. For man to be the measure of all things, he must place himself at the centre of the world and make it 'his'. Once at the centre, everything from subatomic particles to the deepest reaches of space can be subjected to an anthroponomic scale. However, since Copernicus, Darwin and Freud have shown the untenability of this claim cosmologically, biologically and psychologically – each administering a great blow to 'human mega-lomania'[18] – *humanitas* must be defined in terms more rarefied, albeit no less dogmatic. What these terms amount to is a metaphysical essence too singular to register on any instruments of measurement.

Robert C. Solomon notes how 'the boundaries of the "human" shift so easily from biology to morality...What is called "humanity" thus becomes a wholly *moral* term.'[19] In the argument I mount, this shift is identified in terms of *value*: humanism as a belief in the inherent value of that abstract entity, humanity. Theoretical and philosophical antihumanism criticise man for his self-importance, for overvaluing himself and his achievements. But it would be wrong to conclude from this that they disparage *anthropos*, or endorse misanthropy. Martin Heidegger writes:

Because we are speaking against 'humanism' people fear a defense of the in-human and a glorification of barbaric brutality. For what is more 'logical' than that for somebody who negates humanism nothing remains but the affirmation of inhumanity? [...] It ought to be somewhat clearer now that opposition to 'humanism' in no way implies a defense of the inhuman but rather opens other vistas.[20]

Though such a claim is clearly open to dispute, it is important to recognise the difference between antihumanist and antihuman.[21]

Implicated in the belief in value is humanism's greatest determinant, the notion of the *soul*. Chapter 1 explores some of the soul's conceptual history. In determining the course of modern humanism Descartes considered the soul to be the seat of reason, the *âme raisonnable*, famously located in the pineal gland. In the Kantian component of the humanist tradition this becomes 'free will', the capacity to choose to be a moral being, in keeping with one's inbuilt sense of virtue. Defying this tradition, Schopenhauer turned Kant's internal sense into the seat of unreason, a malevolent force not restricted just to human beings; in the process he formulated something like the Freudian unconscious. Similarly, D. H. Lawrence uses terms such as 'soul', 'heart' and 'being' to describe the metaphysical essence of man, when what he really meant was 'unconscious'. One of the processes taking place in literary modernism, then, is the transformation of the soul into the unconscious, a new metaphysic for man's nonphysical essence.

In postwar antihumanism the unconscious is an abiding means of de-centring *anthropos*. It is no accident that Jean-Paul Sartre, the great renovator of the humanist tradition, identified the unconscious with *mauvaise foi*. Psychoanalysis, he wrote incredulously, is 'the idea of a lie without a liar; it allows me to understand how it is possible for me to be lied to without lying to myself'.[22] What for Sartre is the classic instance of *mauvaise foi* becomes, for Lacan, the basis whereby human autonomy is resolutely undermined. Decreeing the unconscious to be the discourse of the other, he identifies it as the place where language – and the possibility of coherent communicative exchanges between people – is dislocated and dispersed. Unintended meanings proliferate, and humanistic self-understanding is revealed to be based on self-deceit.[23]

The scale-endorsing logic of anthropocentrism – according to which man is the measure of all things – is thus maintained first by appealing to the human as a 'moral' category, and then by positing the soul as proof of this appeal. Scale, value and soul are deep-seated organising principles, put under sustained scrutiny in the chapters that follow.

To examine the human and its others is not just to address those critical programmes describing how the human is ostensibly constructed from without (language, discourse, desire and so forth). The human's 'others' are also those categories perennially associated with the human but which humanist philosophy has attempted, with varying degrees of success, to exclude. These are the subhuman, the parahuman and the preterhuman. Or, as they are formulated below, the categories of, respectively, the animal, the mechanical and the transcendent.

Animals, machines and transcendents are not in themselves inhuman, but rather nonhuman. They become *in*human only by dint of their proximity to the human. To invoke the human-as-animal or the human-as-machine is to affirm the cohabitation of human and inhuman. Historically, the animal inhuman enters the popular consciousness with the evolutionary mechanism of natural selection. Based on chance and necessity rather than divine guidance, evolution naturalised the human being by emphasising its animal origins. The arrival of the mechanical inhuman is less definitive. On the one hand, La Mettrie's *L'Homme Machine*, published in 1748, depicted man as an automatistic being, whose behaviour was determined by mechanical laws; eighty years later, machine anxiety is vividly apparent in Thomas Carlyle's 'Signs of the Times'.[24] On the other hand, the dissolution of the so-called 'fourth discontinuity' is still being predicted, and its imminent arrival has become a perennial subject for postmodern thinking.[25]

The human-as-transcendent is more anomalous, in that its historical manifestations are split between humanism and antihumanism. Deriding man for his frailties and yearning for something more rarefied is evident in certain forms of Romanticism – even though, as T. E. Hulme pointed out, Romantic ideology could also be invoked to exalt human potential. Deriving from Rousseau's conception of man as 'possessor of unlimited powers', this notion prompted Hulme to submit a corrective: 'We introduce into human things the *Perfection* that properly belongs only to the divine, and thus confuse both human and divine things by not clearly separating them.'[26] For Hulme humanist arrogance emerged when man seized for himself the role of surrogate divinity. The notion of human being as transcendent being provides the focus for the discussion in Chapter 3.

The third of my key terms, narrative, poses difficulties by its very ubiquity. If literary texts, and their hermeneutic precursors, biblical texts, were once the 'natural' sites for studying narrative (i.e., fiction, biography and autobiography) their domain has been invaded by a diversity of paraliterary forms: historiography, philosophy, psychology, sociology and anthropology. This explosion of narrativity can be gauged by the contents of a recent anthology, *Narrative in Culture*, which extends narrative discussion to such areas as economics, legal discourse and genetics.[27]

Given such an expansive, and expanding, discursive field, I will begin with a simple proposition. Narrative, the process of storymaking and storytelling, is language arranged meaningfully over time. The interrelation of time, meaning and language is a complex one. Duration is bound up with *seriality*, with the organising of the temporal; it is temporal succession that transforms a group of events into a story.[28] The 'meaning' emitted by a group of events lies in their *causal connection*. Events are joined in series, by a process of *mutual implication*: one event implies the next, which is (retrospectively) implied by all that has gone before. So it could be said that events in series owe their existence to each other.[29] If events thrive on meaning, so, too, does plot – the most essential and least variable aspect of narrative.[30] Plot imposes a meaning on the events through an *immanent structure* that, though only revealed at the end, has been present all along.[31] (Paul Ricoeur's work on the experience of temporality in narrative discourse will be discussed in the final section of this chapter.)

Frank Kermode defines plot as 'an organization that humanizes time by giving it form'.[32] Narrative, that is to say, is *human-shaped*. It is a uniquely human way of making order and meaning out of the raw material of existence. It is also, more importantly, a way of carving necessity from the uncertainty and potential chaos of personal experience. Put simply, we tell stories about ourselves to give our lives meaning and purpose, and about our kind to maintain the crucial human/inhuman distinction. This is a twofold process: the mere existence of narrative suggests *difference*, a separation from nature (which does not, needless to say, manifest narrative order); and the kinds of narratives that are produced have supported that separation.

Narrative production thus plays a fundamental role in defining our humanity and, as it were, keeping us human. Ontogenetically, myths and folktales work to give a deep-historical perspective on our cultural inheritance. Phylogenetically, we live 'immersed in narrative, recounting and reassessing the meaning of our past actions, and anticipating the outcome of our future projects, situating ourselves at the intersection of several stories not yet completed.'[33]

But crucial to the working of narrative is that it must suppress contingency. The (retrospective) formation of an immanent structure transforms uncertainty into inevitability. That something is narrativised *this* way, rather than any other, effectively drives out the competition. Daniel O'Hara notes that all grand narratives come to seem like coercive myths – an authoritative means of 'explain[ing] everything totally'.[34] In the novel narrative development has a tendency to totalise events by sublating them: novels require 'the liberty to return to whatever has already passed over in the narrative sequence.'[35] Or in more recent vernacular, there must always be sufficient links to the home page.

I noted earlier that narrative has traditionally been regarded as human-shaped – made by and for human beings, to consolidate their humanness. But in masking contingency and totalising event-series, narrative logic – encoded in the terms raised earlier, of seriality, causal connection, mutual implication, immanent structuration – cannot be entirely human-shaped. It has the potential to exceed the limits of anthropological mastery, just as language has this potential. Indeed, literary narrative is composed from the impersonal, indifferent, recalcitrant archive that is language, a labyrinthine network that, without ever being entirely present to consciousness, offers and structures the materials for all our thoughts and statements (Edward Said refers to 'man's unhappy historical insertion into a language game that he can barely understand').[36] Yet narrative still bears a human countenance, as it is language organised, aestheticised, arranged into patterns of meaningful development. What role, then, might the nonhuman determinant of language play for the human-inflected phenomenon that is narrative?

THE VOICE-MACHINE COMPLEX

Configuring human and nonhuman claims, I suggest that (literary) narrative is a composite of voice and machine. 'Voice' is inescapable at the start, no matter how dispassionate or detached it may seem. We pay attention to the 'grain' of language, the texture of the word, alert to potential emphases, ironies and (so to speak) sleights of hand. 'Machine' begins with the recognition that a story-type is being played out or performed, making reference to a generic code; but the *specificity* of this playing out is nuanced by the ways in which it departs from this type. Voice is subsumed in the process of storytelling mechanics – a process that relies on responsiveness to convention (tropes, motifs, stylistic devices). It could be said that the more 'successful' a narrative is – the closer it comes to pure story, to chains of events that compel and that stimulate anticipation – the less 'human' it becomes, evacuating voice from its mechanical performance.

What does it mean, to say that narrative is 'machinelike'? This is, of course, a figuration, based on the observation that narrative follows a causal pattern, like a mechanism. The narrative voice as metaphor is an accepted part of storytelling poetics. As Paul de Man has noted: 'The term *voice*, even when used in a grammatical terminology as when we speak of the passive or interrogative voice, is, of course, a metaphor inferring by analogy the intent of the subject from the structure of the predicate.'[37] It is, in fact, a particularly humanistic metaphor, suggesting the presence of, and direct one-to-one contact with, a narrating entity.

It is a necessary task of readerly praxis that some kind of textual 'voice' be imagined. Rather than struggle with its abandonment, then, I have augmented it with another kind of imagining, narrative as a machinelike operation. The narrative machine is just as metaphoric as the narrative voice, but it works the other way. Where the reader brings into being, in a sense, a 'voice' as part of the reading process, it is the machine that makes the reader into a particular kind of observer, a respondent to certain typological cues. Machine, in short, is one of the prior conditions for making narrative comprehensible, whereas voice offers the chance for difference, variation and irregularity, pulling against narrative's machinelike precision. Other writers have deployed this metaphor. Harold Bloom, for example, adopting Kenneth Burke's terminology, has referred to his writing as a 'machine for criticism'.[38]

Narrative works to the extent that it can replace contingency and uncertainty with necessity and inevitability. It must establish plot immanence and serial necessity. Yet it needs both sets of terms, chance *and* design, to work, for 'narratives that entirely fit expectations are not really narratives at all'.[39] Narrative compels initially through the creation of expectation, the production of possibility. It compels ultimately through what we might think is the opposing experience: the sense that its resolution, its final shape, could not be other than it is. These two sets of terms – chance, surprise, unlikeliness, on the one hand, and expectation, predictability, inevitability, on the other – are mapped, respectively, on to the modalities of voice and machine. By apprehending narrative, human and machine become interfused in the same process.

Yet despite narrative's nonhuman – i.e., machinelike – action, we still apprehend our lives according to its strictures. Frank Kermode accounts for this, in *The Sense of an Ending*, in terms of its ability to be consonant with our needs. He stresses concordance as a feature of all literary texts: the end harmonises with the beginning, the middle concords with the beginning and end (6). This formal self-consistency also occurs within our experience of ourselves, in the self-narratives of human beings, linking origins with ends. At the heart of such concordances is consolation, 'the power of form to console' (151). Kermode defines form as the 'interconnexion of parts all mutually implied' (123). Mutual implication, as we have seen, is integral to plot (the end as immanent, the parts as concordant) and event causation (events in series owing their existence to each other).

Challenging Kermode's view is D. A. Miller's avowal that narrative closure is not 'end-oriented'. Since the model of narrative dynamics I am drawing on owes a great deal to Kermode, it is pertinent to address Miller's chief criticism. He sees accounts of narrative procedure such as Kermode's as 'based on the tyranny of a narrative' that is 'thoroughly predestined', propounding the idea that 'all novels are completely legislated in advance, according to an identical general pattern'. In addition, 'closure never has the totalizing powers of organization that these critics claim for it', because novels 'are never fully or finally governed' by closure.[40]

I have two responses to these objections. In the first place, Miller elides the distinction between narrative and the novel. The latter, of course, deploys the former, but is not interchangeable with it. One of the key points of the present study is to see narrative at work in philosophical texts. The exemplars are Hegel (in Chapter 1) whose *Phenomenology of Spirit* I show to be the most narrativistic of works, insofar as it appropriates the narrative mechanics of the *Bildungsroman*; and Schopenhauer (in Chapter 2) whose *The World as Will and Representation* I regard as novelistic. Hegel's *Phenomenology* is formidably dense and recondite, yet oddly poetic, too; steered by a narrative voice that is all but submerged, the work adheres to the dynamics of narrative by rigorously organising events into causally related series, which then secrete a particular kind of meaning.

Schopenhauer's *The World as Will* features a philosophical voice as insistent and omnipresent as a nineteenth-century novelist's, effortlessly sustaining the illusion of his presence, and keeping at bay the tide of pessimism that governs his philosophical concerns. The novelistic aspect is, then, architectural rather than dynamic. If there is a kind of nineteenth-century philosophy that resembles the novel, Schopenhauer's *meisterwerk* epitomises it.

Secondly, the emphasis on narrative closure I wish to adopt is structural rather than event-oriented. This kind of closure, which lends structural integrity to a narrative, can only be retrospective. It can further be explained in terms of the difference between narrative change as it unfolds, and narrative change in retrospect. Miller's 'tyranny of narrative' is not evident as narrative unfolds – on the contrary, it appears uncertain and contingent. Once narrative culmination has occurred, these changes appear inevitable; an immanent structure has been brought into being via this culmination, and uncertainty has been transformed into surety. Thus if the 'end' is contained in the 'beginning' – in the manner of Hegelian totalisation – it is only apparent *at* the end. The so-called 'tyranny of narrative closure' is retrospective, reflective, an afterthought rather than a guiding impetus. As I have already suggested, a successful narrative configuration depends on the movement from contingency to inevitability – or from the transformation of time, change and chance into time, change and necessity. It is this very process, of course, that comes under increasing strain with modernist reworking.

### MAPPING MODERNISM: CRISIS IN FORM

It could be argued that the novel is the predominant expressive form of literary modernism. The major modernist productions of Musil and Mann, Proust and Joyce, and (to a lesser extent) Lawrence and Woolf, feed promiscuously on their literary predecessors. Their delineations of consciousness provide a display of interiority more immediate than drama, and more intensely intimate than the poetic subjectivity of the lyric. In addition, the modernist novel's concern (to different degrees) with the external world – the mores and manners of the various classes, the materiality and minutiae that encompass them – reveals both an encyclopedic attentiveness to behaviour and material phenomena, and a doublecoded concern with diachrony, registering history even as it attempts to transcend it. If modernism is too diverse, too contradictory, too multifarious to be contained within any one particular form of literature, the novel's protean ability to reappropriate the literary technique of the past and 'make it new' promotes it to the forefront of the modernist endeavour.

All of this is, as I have suggested, arguable. Immediately prior to the modernist sense of crisis, the novel served as the great Whig book of progressive history. As Malcolm Bradbury remarks, it was 'the novel in its traditional form as the burgher epic, the novel of social reality, moral assessment, direct representation of life and history'.[41] Such a form was incapable of accommodating, in the twentieth century, the sense of rupture and disjunction, the dissolution of certainties and terrifying losses of faith. A different kind of great prose book became an imperative. Yet despite its far-reaching technical reappropriation and innovation, the modernist novel does not quite fulfil that brief. To establish just how continuous (or discontinuous) it was with the novel tradition of the past, let us consider some particularities of modernist narrative.

The fundamental difference between traditional (i.e., premodernist) narrative and modern (i.e., modernist and after) narrative is the difference between the plot of resolution and the plot of revelation. In the traditional mode problems are solved, situations are worked out; there is a kind of 'emotional teleology' at work. The modern mode, conversely, abjures the question of 'what will happen?', and refuses even to acknowledge it. Events are not resolved; instead, a state of affairs is revealed. Thus plot development in traditional narrative is an 'unraveling', and in modern narrative it is a 'displaying'.[42] A similar distinction lies behind Brecht's conception of epic theatre. He contrasts it with 'Aristotelian drama', observing that whereas the latter proceeds via one thing *out of* another, epic drama operates on the principle of one thing *after* another.[43] It uses seriality, but resists the causality that makes events interdependent and transforms seriality into necessity, into the immanent structure constituting plot. In Brechtian theory there is an evident political purpose to the distinction. History is not written in advance, it depends upon human participation at every moment of the present. Retrospective anthropomorphisation, which lends immanence and holism to narrative, is rejected, so that purposive, unironised agency can be stressed.

The modernist crisis in the novel implies a reenactment of the dilemma that produced the *Bildungsroman*. The conflict at its centre, its 'repressed unconscious' – reconciliation of the nonextension of mind (the human) with the extension of matter (the nonhuman) – is replayed in modernist fiction through narrative: finding a space for the 'inhuman' (antinarrative) within the ostensibly 'human' (narrative).

One of the chief means of dealing with this crisis was mobilising the performative potential of narrative. J. L. Austin coined the term 'performative' in 1955, to designate those utterances that indicated the performing of an action, rather than reported on a preexisting state of affairs.[44] More recent theoretical work, however, has used 'performative' in contrast to 'expressive'. In the work of Judith Butler gender is not an inert category with fixed attributes, but a contingent *doing*, a 'stylized repetition of acts'.[45] Gender attributes are not expressive – they do not express a stable identity preceding the act of performance and enduring through time – but performative, as they depend on reiteration for their existence and are, therefore, potentially fluid and variable. 'Performative', she writes, 'suggests a dramatic and contingent construction of meaning'.[46] Performativity might therefore be seen as a correlative of contingency, a way for language to express nonfoundational states of being.

Performativity can also complicate the distinction between cultural discourse and cultural practice. J. Hillis Miller writes:

All parables, finally, are essentially performative . . . Parables do not merely name the 'something' they point to by indirection or merely give the reader knowledge of it. They use words to try to make something happen in relation to the 'other' that resonates in the work. They want to get the reader from here to there. They want to make the reader cross over into the 'something' and dwell there. But the site to which parable would take the reader is something always other than itself, hence that experience of perpetual dissatisfaction . . . Nevertheless, this tropological, parabolic, performative dimension enables writing and reading to enter history and be effective there, for better or for worse.[47]

The impetus 'to make the reader cross over into the "something" and dwell there' is, I would suggest, essential to experiencing the modernist breakdown of narrative. It is a blow against instrumentality, in the latter's function within the language of proposition and exposition.

The modernist novel liberates narrative's latent performative power by introducing formal irregularities. An analogy might be made with Heidegger's example of the tool. When it functions perfectly we scarcely notice it, as it has become an extension of our bodies. Only when it breaks down does it become an issue for us: 'When its unusability is thus discovered, equipment becomes conspicuous.'[48] Similarly with narrative: formally coherent narrative draws little attention to itself, may even appear transparent, pellucid, natural. Break the form down, however, and it perturbs, by conveying more to the reader than just the content of a story-structure. As Heidegger notes: 'Anything which is un-ready-to-hand [i.e., unusable equipment] in this way is disturbing to us.'[49]

Brokendown narrative is insidiously disquieting in ways that troubling story-content cannot match.

The radical formalism of the modernist novel makes literature perform in anomalous ways. Feeling bewilderment, perplexity, alienation and frustration from a narrative, as a result of overturned convention, undermines the author-reader 'contract' of nineteenth-century fiction. Believing in a 'reliable' narrator and suspending disbelief in technical artifice was considered a fair exchange for various epistemological certainties about the field of representation. The modernist novel removes these certainties, but offers something else: a promise that the narrative will *do* something to the reader, impart something of what it means to be a perplexed city-dweller inhabiting a turbulent cultural matrix. Modernist narrative suggests that literature can pass beyond the limits of what is representable.

In later chapters we will see how different narrative forms convey counterhumanist ideas in ways that are performative. Conrad uses repetition of narrative patterns, stories of loss and defeat mechanically repeating themselves, to strike at humanist overconfidence in man's capacity for betterment. At the other extreme, Lawrence deploys narrative disjunction – stark, unexpected breaks between events – to convey his alter-ego's yearning for posthumanist transcendence; as if the story itself were straining to break free of the causal-linear straitjacket of narrative logic. Further variation is at work in the freefloating, endlessly mutable consciousness at the heart of Woolf's writing, where the human exceeds itself and forms provisional ties with the nonhuman (animal and plant life); this finds a formal correlation in the crisscrossing network of storylines, where narrative strands converge, diverge and radiate in gridlike patterns. Lastly, Beckett offers ample demonstration of how human fallibility and impotence extend, determinedly, to all productions of the mind – including (and especially) the production of stories.

Behind all these examples is the human-narrative link, which could be seen in some ways as a negative one. If narrative keeps us human, then thinking the inhuman means thinking outside narrative strictures. Narrative masks contingency; if the human is really contingent, as I have suggested, it is necessary to see beyond the potent effects of narrative production. A key question then arises: why not *total* abandonment of narrative form? I suggest that anthropological self-importance is more effectively undermined by being taken apart from within. Modernist narrative writing is clearly haunted by the question of the human; but its scepticism is neither so strident nor so encompassing as to permit the overt critique of a later generation of writers, producing a new kind of cultural criticism in postwar France. The strategy rather is to strike at the human where it is most vulnerable, most prone to damage – in the forms and ways of understanding that are exclusive to narrative.

### THE PHILOSOPHICAL DISCOURSE OF MODERNISM

Since a philosophical reading of modernism is at the heart of this argument, a note of circumspection needs to be sounded. What follows does not aspire to be a masternarrative about the inhuman essence of modernism, nor does it claim to be any kind of totalising discourse. The anthropometric tradition, I should stress, is an *imaginary* genealogy, assembled to address some specific questions about modernism. These might be summarised as follows. What are the ways in which the modernist novel imagines the human? How do these ways relate to the radical formal innovations traditionally associated with literary modernism? And what connections do both (the 'modernist' human and narrative breakdown) have with European philosophical discourse? Extrapolating from these enquiries, what significance does modernism's counterhumanist critique have for theoretical antihumanism in the postwar era? These questions belong broadly under the rubric 'philosophy of literature'. The larger question encompassing them, then, is why a *philosophical* reading of modernism?

Literary modernism, I would argue, is the point at which philosophical concerns come into their own. Philosophical anxieties are in a sense *formative* of modernism, whether precipitated by political disenchantment, technological change or spiritual penury. To date, though, critical recognition of this tendency has been somewhat onesided. Though philosophical readings of novelists are legion, literary readings of philosophers are less common.[50] I propose to put the two discourses in dialogue with each other, to address those questions posed above – questions that do not appear to have been investigated from other critical quarters. In seeking to establish links between narrative form and reflections on the in/human, I am assuming that philosophical analysis can illuminate those links in a useful manner. As Edward Said has observed:

The philosopher or historian belongs in his work to a common mode of conceiving experience of which another version is the novel. I refer, of course, to such common themes as succession, sequence, derivation, portrayal, and alternation, to say nothing of authority itself. Here we may remark the similarities between thought that produces philosophical works, for instance, and thought that produces novels.[51]

Three further points must be made on the question of methodology. Firstly, it is a commonplace to note that literary modernism has given rise to a plurality of discourses. The present study is not intended as a comprehensive survey of all the modes of modernism and the various ways of reading them. Though the focus is on modernist novelists, it skirts both North American and purely English-based modernism. Pursuing either of these would involve different philosophical correlates; pragmatism, say, and logical positivism. Instead, the path I follow uses European philosophical and theoretical resources – namely, the nineteenth-century German tradition, with its strong literary ties and certified influence on twentieth-century French thought. This is reflected in the four novelists under discussion: Conrad as a Polish national, Lawrence as a Germanophile (and married to the German-born Frieda, neé von Richthofen), Woolf providing a close literary counterpart to Bergsonian philosophy, and Beckett manifesting a dual, Irish-French identity.

Recent studies have delved deeper into the bedrock of modernist history and charted the social, political and conceptual underlay.[52] Other works have examined the role played by narrative in history, philosophy, ideology and psychoanalysis.[53] Bringing the two areas together, the present study focuses on the dynamic encounters of ideas and narrative forms in the period leading up to and continuing through the modernist transformation. This is not to downgrade those other, equally pertinent determinants mentioned above, nor to suggest that a philosophical reading of modernism is in some way superior. It is with the latter, quite simply, that my interests lie, and where I believe there is sufficient potential to shed new light on the relationship between the disruptions enacted by the modernist novel, and contemporary understandings of what it means to be human.

Secondly, what I have defined as the anthropometric era, with its fraught renegotiations of the human and the inhuman, invokes immediate reference to one sphere in particular: the discourses of race. Culminating in the *Shoah*, the idea of the 'inhuman' has been used to advance the ideologies of racial discrimination. Despite the unarguable ethical import of this association, it does not play a part in the argument I construct. Far from being irrelevant, it is far *too* relevant, and demands another, quite different study from the present one; a study in which, perhaps, narrative would not feature so prominently. Yet having acknowledged this, the role of narrative in the discourses of race has been explored within the past decade or so with great perspicacity by Edward Said in *Culture and Imperialism* (1994), and by the various contributors to Homi Bhabha's *Nation and Narration* (1990) anthology. Race and the history of humanist discourse – in a period intersecting in part with the anthropometric era – is also the subject of Tzvetan Todorov's persuasive genealogy in *On Human Diversity* (1991).

Thirdly, it should be made clear that the periodisation I have layed out is not the only one possible. I have selected it because of what it reveals of the human-narrative problematic. Though the modernism that is the object of study nowadays is considerably different from what it was even twenty years ago, its (contemporary) lack of popular appeal remains an immovable fact of literary history. This should not imply, however, that the anthropometric turn holds only in the rarefied domain of modernist innovation. A possible alternative route through the territory I have mapped out might be made via the popular, early twentieth-century 'novel of ideas', as exemplified by H. G. Wells and Aldous Huxley.[54] Both writers were concerned with relations between human and nonhuman forms of life (i.e., animals and machines), and both wrote *Bildungsromans*.[55] Additionally, the utopian and dystopian novels for which they are best known – *The War of the Worlds, A Modern Utopia, Brave New World, Island* – anticipate the apocalyptic tenor of certain antihumanist polemics.[56] I must stress, then, that the anthropometric tradition is not a predetermined, unilinear path through literary modernism and into cultural theory. The periodisation I have determined is as prone to contingency as the various concepts and ways of thinking it brings together.

## TOWARDS THEORY

Part of the purpose in constructing an anthropometric genealogy is to show the emergence of the conditions of possibility for postwar antihumanism, i.e., as a consequence of the human–narrative problematic of the preceding hundred years. The philosophical lineage of this discourse has been worked through many times, often in great detail, but its literary ancestry is less cogent.[57] In philosophical terms, this has meant that the 'human' is no longer intimately bound up with 'humanism'; in literary terms, it is manifested as a loss of narrativity. The chapters that follow will bear out these two assertions.

Present-day antihumanism, it seems evident, is based on a theoretical framework at least thirty years old. The most significant outgrowth since the watershed of 1968 is 'technological posthumanism', or what could be seen as reinscriptions at the coalface of the human. The result, the technologically transformed human body, marks an intervention at the level of biology to parallel those intrepid discursive infringements of an earlier generation. Such an intervention, however, is not the focus of the writers and thinkers discussed herein; their concern is not with reinventing new forms of *anthropos*, be it 'animal man', cyborg or superhuman. For anthropometric writers new forms of life do not have to be created, as they are in a sense already extant, hidden from view by the metaphysical sheath of humanism.

It is not the human, then, that is under scrutiny, but the 'human': the process that produces the name, and everything that has been done in that name. Antihumanism is an engagement with the being that has come to masquerade as 'human'. It aspires to locate the human within the 'human', the emergent entity after it is shorn of the metaphysical and axiological assumptions accreting around the name, the *a priori* category, the self-legislating entity that is the 'human'.

Humanism possesses a certain unwavering confidence, which licenses it to enact schemas of mastery. Anthropocentric domination of the natural world is perhaps the most prominent modern-day example of this. The source of this humanist self-confidence is a belief in *instrumentality*, the conviction that anything produced by human industry must perforce be subject to human command.[58] One of the most fundamental challenges of theoretical antihumanism, then, is to show that this is not the case. It might be termed the Frankenstein syndrome: humankind's inability to master its own creations. The chief of these in postwar cultural theory is language, although similar processes can be seen in history, money and technology, discussed in Chapter 2. Human agency is an essential prerequisite, as none of these things occurs in nature. But to create something is not necessarily to control it, particularly not through individual action; theoretical antihumanism upholds this, in its recognition that an instrumental relationship to culture and its discontents is not on offer. In terms of what follows, this might be extrapolated as a challenge to the belief that, because human beings make narratives, the latter are always human-shaped, hence concordant with the terms and conditions of their making. I suggest that this is not the case.

Just as the modernist novel takes drastic liberties with narrative logic, much recent cultural theory has developed 'postnarrative' methods of treating history, philosophy, sociology and so forth. John Rajchman offers a pithy summary of the genesis of this 'modernist criticism': 'Criticism can no longer remain a secondary language which accredits and interprets individual works in the primary language. It, too, must take the modernist turn and invent a new style, neither critical nor literary, but "para-literary."[59] The 'para-literary' characterises the extravagant stylistic practices of theoretical antihumanism. The point it makes – that writing our contemporary discourse of the inhuman is a kind of 'modernist' writing – will be examined more fully in the Conclusion.

Theory grants us a glimpse of the pure arbitrariness and potential variability that lie behind the social codes governing our lives, behind our habitual modes of thought and compulsive ways of being. The modernist transformation and theoretical antihumanism both recognise one important factor: the human's unwitting propensity to give rise to the inhuman. Thus it does not reveal contradiction at the heart of human understanding, so much as a hidden shadow, an inhuman other propping up human identity. It discloses not unintelligibility but irony.

Of all contemporary theorists, it is Paul Ricoeur who has come closest to exploring the concerns of this project, in his three-volume *Time and Narrative*. He sees the relationship between these eponymous terms as the solution to a quandary: how to speak of temporality in the direct discourse of phenomenology? The answer is, through the *indirect discourse* of narration. He sums up the intractable difficulties involved as follows: 'the most exemplary attempts to express the lived experience of time in its immediacy result in the multiplication of aporias, as the instrument of analysis becomes ever more precise'.[60] In other words, time as a human phenomenon, as lived experience, cannot be subjected to sustained analysis without losing something essential to it, without it becoming, unavoidably, something else.

Ricoeur's problematic is important here, for two reasons. Firstly, it echoes a similar aporia, outlined above, that underlies our knowledge of the human: the more we know about it, the more it slides from our grasp. Secondly, each of the four literary modernists under discussion attempts to deal with 'lived experience' in various ways. Conrad assays it with a sense of defeat, as if genuine human experience is forever unattainable; he is anxious but resigned. Lawrence, by contrast, treats it with remorseless frenzy, as if what has hitherto been seen as 'lived experience' is but a halflife at best, a faint shadow of man's true experiential potential. Woolf, more serene than either Conrad or Lawrence, is nonetheless aware of the dangers to mental stability that the turbulence of unmediated experience presents. Beckett's explorations of inner experience are hysterical, compulsive, futile, resigned, serene; almost anything, in short, but liberating.

These examples anticipate Ricoeur's solution to his dilemma, for where the 'direct discourse' of phenomenology cannot go, the 'indirect discourse' of narration can move with ease. Thus narrative deals with the above-mentioned aporias as 'so many knots to be untied'; it is a 'guardian of time, insofar as there can be no thought about time without narrated time'.[61]

Ricoeur also echoes the conundrum precipitating the birth of the *Bildungsroman*: the inability of philosophical discourse to resolve the Cartesian coordinates of *res cogitans* and *res extensa*, prompting the turn to a narrative of inner growth through time.[62] And just as the *Bildungsroman* contains philosophical tension because of the nature of its 'founding', Ricoeur is reluctant to ascribe too much to narrative's power of resolution, its ability to mediate experience without transforming it into something else. He is circumspect in his awareness of the 'limits of narrativity'.[63]

A brief summary, now, of the position arrived at earlier. Narrative is originally enlisted to demonstrate the shape of subjectivity, in the humanising form that is the *Bildungsroman*. But there are complications. The *Bildungsroman*, the most anthropocentric genre of fictional narrative, has its philosophical unconscious, its recessive genes. Its teleology, in addition, is illusory, ironic.

These complications create a deadlock. Narrative cannot be abandoned by humanism, because its countenance is *anthropos*-shaped. At the same time, narrative is a constant challenge to antihumanism, a rebuff to attempts at 'purifying' narrative of *anthropos*, and ridding the latter of its temporal condition. Because narrative is *language* arranged meaningfully over time, it possesses the ability to divest consciousness of linearity and causality, to neutralise the urge to turn raw sensation into perception. And because narrative is also language arranged meaningfully over *time*, it reaches into the heart of human epistemology. Our cognitive apparatus is inescapably temporal; once we begin to think in self-consciously temporal terms, we have already allowed in the possibility of narrative.

We have now come full circle. For C. M. Wieland narrative was a solution, a way of demonstrating the growth and integral nature of subjectivity without having to confront Cartesian dualism. But 150 years after Wieland narrative is a pivotal problem, hindering demonstrations of the dispersion of subjectivity, in the fictional worlds of the modernist novelist. For the rest of this work the shape of the above argument is paradigmatic. The modernist novel quickens the conflict that inheres in narrative. It is riven by the compulsion to explore the modalities of the inhuman, to affirm the notion of crisis; and by the need to stay within the boundaries of narrative discourse, however tenuous, for the aesthetic control permitted therein. By problematising narrative, the modernist novel brings to the fore narrative's various struggles – with time and language, subjectivity and desire, voice and machine. It can be explored, therefore, for signs of the struggle between the human and the inhuman. Literary modernism, in trying to break free of narrative, is also seeking release from the grip of the humanistic discourse of Victorian liberalism – a release that it finds in the various categories of the inhuman. The categories nominated earlier – the animal, the mechanical and the transcendent – are thematised, respectively, in the next three chapters of the discussion.

# *Narrating the animal, amputating the soul*

To study Metaphysics, as they have always been studied appears to me to be like puzzling at astronomy without mechanics. – Experience shows that the problem of the mind cannot be solved by attacking the citadel itself. – the mind is function of body.

Charles Darwin[1]

But the awakened, the enlightened man says: I am body entirely, and nothing beside; and soul is only a word for something in the body.

Friedrich Nietzsche[2]

> For life is always expressing itself in us and through us, even in our
> most seemingly ethereal statements . . . One must accept the reality
> of our total immanence to nature, to this biosphere, revolt against
> which can only be pathological, thus provisional, and destined to
> fail.
>
> Luc Ferry[3]

Revolt against the biosphere may be a futile gesture, but its influence
on the mind can be mitigated, and the sense of human helplessness
tempered, through the implementation of an internal order. The dominant Western mode of ordering, which held strong until the eighteenth
century, was derived from Aristotle's comments in his biological works.
These writings yielded a schema of animal and plant life, a linear series of increasing perfection with man at the head. This table, the *scala
naturae*, later dubbed the 'great chain of being', established the hierarchy
of species.[4] After man came (other) mammals, then cetaceans, reptiles
and birds, all the way down to sponges, the lowest of animal forms.

As well as being hierarchical Aristotelian nature is rigidly dualist, based
on a strict division of masters and slaves, rulers and ruled. The source of
this dualism is existence itself: '[I]t originates in the constitution of the
universe; even in things which have no life there is a ruling principle, as
in a musical mode.' And so it falls to man, the most perfect of beings,
to incarnate this division. Because it is natural and expedient that the
soul rules the body, the mental and rational rules the passionate, it is
only just and fitting that the male ('by nature superior')[5] has dominion
over the female. In similar fashion, humankind *tout entier* rules the animal
kingdom. Nature, in short, 'has made all animals for the sake of man'.[6]

There are three orders of 'soul': the vegetative, the animal and the
rational. Living and nonliving entities are separated by being with soul
or without soul. In Aristotle's theory of reproduction it is soul that gives
*form*. The embryo is produced from both material and nonmaterial parts;
from passive, unformed female substance; and from male soul, or *psyche*.
It is the latter that provides the principle of life, the essential generative
agency: 'The female then only provides the material, the male the soul,
the form, the principle, that which makes life.'[7] This is the source of
the gender specificity that opposes masculine 'form-giving' to feminine
'formlessness', an opposition implicit in theories of *Bildung*.

Matter is thus no more than potentiality, whereas form is actuality. In
living things soul bestows form. By making soul a universal substance,
unevenly spread through all of creation, Aristotle's rectilinear scale is
made coherent. Mankind in general, and males in particular, rule over

the rest of animal life because in them soul is rational, stable and well-behaved (unlike in women and slaves who, as reproducers and labourers respectively, manifest more body than soul). Yet despite this apparent coherence, the *scala* has ambiguous implications, as Keith Thomas has observed. On the one hand, it establishes man in a position of relative superiority, below the angels but well above the beasts. On the other hand, though, the chain has no breaks, suggesting that 'each species moved into the next so that the line dividing men from animals was highly indistinct'.[8] This ambiguity has bestowed on Western thought a particularly knotty problem, an unavoidable impedance for any subsequent naturalistic discourse.

The essence of the problem is that human beings are both a part of nature, and apart from nature. *Homo sapiens* is on the one hand a species among other species, and on the other a breed apart. Biology forces us to belong; consciousness keeps us separate. The sense of 'belongingness' comes from naturalism, biocentrism and ecological radicalism. Its converse, the sense of separateness, has been passed down first through Western theology then through philosophical humanism. Any attempt at mapping the human-animal relationship, it would seem, is forced to comply with this intractable dualism. Such an attempt must begin with a statement either to the effect that 'we are an animal species, but . . .' ; or that 'we are rational and moral beings, but . . .' . The terms, that is to say, seem inevitably reducible to either continuity (immanence, belonging, animalism) or discontinuity (transcendence, separation, humanism).

Steve Baker has considered the animal as a way of circumventing the pressure to make meaning (one of the self-appointed duties of humanistic man, as we saw previously). He urges, in *The Postmodern Animal*, a concerted resistance to 'hierarchy-thinking', by recognising the animal's otherness: '[It is an attempt] to think outside familiar human experience of the world, and to find a way of characterizing a non-human experience in non-hierarchical terms.'[9] This process might be seen as running in parallel with attempts to bypass narrative logic through 'the unmeaning of animals'.[10] These philosophical and literary undertakings have attempted to 'animalise' the human, as a reaction to the opposite tendency, the humanisation (i.e., anthropomorphisation) of the animal and of nature generally. In the discussion that follows, such attempts are considered in the light of narrative and how it, along with the animal, is implicated in schemas of fact and value.

Put simply, animals have been convoked to exemplify denarrativised man. In such circumstances they are considered not just as nontranscending creatures, but as creatures unburdened by the *promise* of transcendence, and the temporal awareness that allows the narrated self to come into being. Whether animals do or do not possess 'animal narratives' for negotiating their relationship with themselves and their world is beside the point. (Would such narratives persist across animal species? Might not aquatic creatures have entirely different experiences of themselves than airborne creatures?) At any rate, the animal is used to imagine a being devoid of the repressions and strictures of narrative logic. To 'animalise' the human, therefore, is to denarrativise it, and to envisage it as fact rather than as value. The purpose of this chapter is to show the attempts in which the animal has been narrated in relation to the human.

I begin with the proposition that advances in natural science through-out the nineteenth century led to the need to rethink the animal-human relation. And a significant part of the process of this rethinking involved narrative production. According to Thomas Mann: 'The nineteenth century has been called the century of history, and in truth it first produced and developed the sense of history, of which earlier cultures (considered as cultures, as artistically coherent systems of life) knew little or nothing.'[11] I suggest that the century of history was also, to a large extent, the century of narrative. History, with a capital 'H', served the imperialist, scientific and industrialist projects. It gave European nations a sense of self-importance and a teleology, providing them with ways to unite tradition and destiny.

It was within this frame of reference that it became imperative, in the first place, to define the difference between animal and human; and then to do so in a form that was irreducible, that bore the incontrovertible stamp of temporal difference, of historical advancement. This was the work left to the master evolutionary narrative, animal-into-human. Hayden White has remarked that modern discussions of history and fiction begin with 'a notion of reality in which "the true" is identified with "the real" only insofar as it can be shown to possess the character of narrativity'.[12] From the nineteenth-century purview, therefore, human beings and human activity came to be conceived in terms of narrative and unfolding, rather than as givens. They were seen as taking place in time, rather than as possessing fixed, atemporal coordinates. Thus the great chain of being, that highly spatialised paradigm of animal-human relation was, in the light of the above, translated into a temporalised paradigm, which is to say, a narrative. And in the process the indistinctness noted above was also translated. The consequence of this – and the crux of the argument that follows – is that there was a breach between the overwhelming desire and demand for narrative, and the inability of evolutionist theory to provide such a coherent, all-inclusive story-structure. Which is to say that, the movement of animal-into-human finally defies narration, it resists incorporation into narrative's conventional purposiveness. This chapter reflects on the various discourses registering the interplay between the human and the natural (or animal).

I MAPPING THE ANIMAL

*Discontinuity: Marx and Wilde*

> Landscapes are culture before they are nature; constructs of the imagination projected on to wood and water and rock...But it should also be acknowledged that once a certain idea of landscape, a myth, a vision, establishes itself in an actual place, it has a peculiar way of muddling categories, of making metaphors more real than their referents; of becoming, in fact, part of the scenery.
>
> Simon Schama[13]

This muddling of categories characterises the slippage that accompanies, perhaps necessarily, all our propositions about culture and nature. It is so pervasive as to infiltrate almost any thinking about the human and the natural. One form of it can be identified in Marx's *Economic and Philosophic Manuscripts of 1844*. He acknowledges the intimacy of the human-natural bond in seemingly unequivocal terms: 'Man *lives* from nature, i.e. nature is his *body*, and he must maintain a continuing dialogue with it if he is not to die. To say that man's physical and mental life is linked to nature simply means that nature is linked to itself, for man is a part of nature.'[14] The unavoidable fact of man's ongoing debt to, and reliance upon, nature means that it is man's inorganic body. But the tenor of the analysis changes when nature's function in the human world is unveiled. 'The practical creation of an objective world, the fashioning of organic nature, is proof that man is a conscious species-being' (328–9). Far from being an intimate human companion, nature serves merely to register man's humanness, or distance from nature, at the cost of marginalising his 'naturalness'. So nature mediates man's labouring propensities, by providing a site for his self-realisation as a conscious species-being, i.e., as a cultural being.

The fragile intimacy of the human-natural bond – and how easily it can be sundered – becomes apparent when a particular scenario is

envisaged. When the worker is separated from the objects of his production, and labour is reinscribed as *alienated* labour, man's relation to
nature alters accordingly: 'The relationship of the worker to the *product
of labour* as an alien object that has power over him . . . is at the same
time the relationship to the sensuous external world, to natural objects,
as an alien world confronting him in hostile opposition' (327). So man's
relation to nature is dependent on the quality of the labour he is performing. Labour is the one true measure, defining the value not only
of the human, but of the bond that forms between the human and the
natural.

Among these lucubrations on labour and man is a passage indicating
a further refinement of the link between the human and the natural:
'Just as plants, animals, stones, air, light, etc., theoretically form a part of
human consciousness, partly as objects of science and partly as objects
of art . . . so too in practice they form a part of human life and human activity' (327–8). How do objects of science and art come to inhabit part of
a subject, human consciousness? The link between the two lies in man's
aesthetic temper. The development of aesthetic sensitivity takes place
along with the development of aesthetic artefacts. Artistic receptivity
parallels artistic production, and nature is implicated in the process, becoming humanised by having value bestowed on its raw, inert materials.[15]
Humanised nature, therefore, renders it capable of absorption by human
consciousness, to become 'a part of human life and human activity'.

A similar attitude, although with a decidedly different agenda, lies
behind 'The Decay of Lying', Oscar Wilde's nonprogrammatic account
of the relationship between art, life and nature. It is necessary first to note
the combative aspect of Wilde's foray. He is defending 'lying' (i.e., artistic
imagination) because, as the title indicates, it is in abeyance. It has ceded
its former, pre-Victorian authority to facts, which 'are not merely finding
a footing-place in history, but . . . are usurping the domain of Fancy, and
have invaded the kingdom of Romance'.[16] The realm of facts, the natural,
must be kept in its place, for it is only in the mind that nature truly comes
to life: 'Things are because we see them, and what we see, and how we
see it, depends on the Arts that have influenced us. To look at a thing is
very different from seeing a thing. One does not see anything until one
sees its beauty. Then, and only then, does it come into existence' (54).

Thus there is a point where Wilde's thought converges with Marx's: in
a more specific type of anthropocentrism, centred solely on man's cultural
being. The cultural self is the epicentre of both views of human life, and
nature is made to fit within it, to serve their different agendas. Where

Marx sees nature as a measure of cultural being, Wilde strives to keep it at bay. Both are attempting, in different ways, to negotiate the fact–value divide through the rhetoric of aesthetic appropriation. For Marx the aesthetic is a means to an end, a contributor to the communist project of emancipation through labour. For Wilde the aesthetic is an end in itself, and the cultural self is a human manifestation of the art that he holds dear, nothing more. Both Wilde and Marx are attempting to transmute base fact into precious value through the medium of nature. Yet Wilde's exorbitant claims for the aesthetic secrete a certain unavoidable irony. For all his commitment to the nonutilitarian, noninstrumental uses of art, he effectively turns the aesthetic itself into a pseudo-commodity, fetishising its role in human existence and the powerful, determinative force it exerts upon the mind.

A similarly troubling ambiguity bedevils Wilde's later essay, 'The Soul of Man Under Socialism', where he reflects on individualism and its relationship to social being. Wilde sees socialism as a desirable goal because its cardinal principle – the abolition of private property – will bring about individualism. Though private ownership seems to sustain individualism, its duties far outweigh any pleasures it might confer: 'It involves endless claims upon one, endless attention to business, endless bother.'[17] The kind of individualism Wilde endorses acts as a relay between fact and value, nature and culture. On the one hand, art – 'the most intense mode of Individualism that the world has known' (34) – is potentially humanising and redemptive: 'Art is Individualism, and Individualism is a disturbing and disintegrating force. Therein lies its immense value. For what it seeks to disturb is monotony of type, slavery of custom, tyranny of habit, and the reduction of man to the level of a machine' (36). Properly individualised, human beings are protected from the mindless, impersonal drudgery that Marx saw as the chief cause of alienated labour. The anthropocentric urge of both thinkers, therefore, is best served through the implementation of socialism/individualism.

But as well as underwriting cultural value, individualism is itself underwritten by the deterministic processes of natural fact:

[Individualism] is the point to which all development tends. It is the differentiation to which all organisms grow. It is the perfection that is inherent in every mode of life, and towards which every mode of life quickens . . . To ask whether Individualism is practical is like asking whether Evolution is practical. Evolution is the law of life, and there is no evolution except towards individualism. Where this tendency is not expressed, it is a case of artificially arrested growth, or of disease, or of death. (49)

This is not so much a 'muddling' of the categories of nature and culture as an uneasy conjoining of the two. To say that evolution confers individualism and individualism supports cultural endeavour is to 'naturalise' culture, to make inevitable (and, perhaps, necessary) culture's emergence from the irregularities and contingency of willed effort.

Kate Soper writes of Marx: 'In humanizing nature we also naturalize ourselves in the sense that by creating the objective world of our existence we also will determine the nature of even our most immediately sensory responses to it.'[18] But if Marx suggests a dialectical interchange between man and nature, he has nonetheless contributed to the anthropocentric desire for dominion over nature. Wilde, in a sense, makes explicit this potential in Marx through his (Wilde's) extravagant edicts of cultural priority. As one commentator has remarked, 'we could not go back to nature even if we wanted to, because to think or speak of nature is to be already in the world of art'.[19]

In attempting to bridge fact and value, Wilde and Marx also acknowledge the same problem, the indeterminacy of the human-natural relationship. Wilde admits this to be a problem in a couple of anthropomorphic feints: 'Nature has good intentions, of course, but, as Aristotle once said, she cannot carry them out' (*DL* 35). The implication is that man, as an intention-producing being that *is* equipped to carry them out, is in some sense superior to nature, which is intentionless. 'Nature is so indifferent, so unappreciative' (36), laments Wilde. Yet this, too, begs an important question: why should this separation of the human and the natural be deplored? Could alienation be conceived as a good, rather than a bane? Why should nature's impersonality, indifference and irreducible otherness pose a problem? John O'Neill submits an alternative proposition:

The appeal here is to the value wilderness has in virtue of its not bearing the imprint of human activity. Wilderness, empty mountains, the stars at night, the complex behavior of non-human living things . . . We value the non-human world because we do not want to see in everything the mirroring of human powers or possibilities for human activity.[20]

Yet this still perpetuates the separation of human and natural by assigning it a valency. Where Wilde scolds nature for not possessing human powers, O'Neill praises it for the same reason. Human–nature separation is either negative, i.e., alienating, as it is for the Wildean aesthete whose sense of self is defined by the plastic and artificial ('out of doors one becomes abstract and impersonal'), and for the Marxian labourer whose self-realisation is dependent on being able to transform the natural. Or it is positive, through the meditative, spiritually regenerative capacities granted by the absence of human activity or 'imprint'. But is this valuing of the nonhuman for its own sake *really* for its own sake? Charles Taylor has suggested otherwise:

> The reflection which moves us is that thought, feeling, moral aspirations, all the intellectual and spiritual heights of human achievement, emerge out of the depths of a vast physical universe which is itself, over most of its measureless extent, lifeless, utterly insensitive to our purposes, pursuing its path by inexorable necessity. The awe is awakened partly by the tremendous power of this world which overshadows us – we sense our utter fragility as thinking reeds, in Pascal's phrase; but we also feel it before the extraordinary fact that out of this vast blind silence, thought, vision, speech can evolve.[21]

This is, perhaps, the hidden assumption behind the experience of nature's 'wonder'. In not wanting to see 'the mirroring of human powers or possibilities', the wonder of the fact–value divide seems all the more awe-inspiring. The axiological shift occurs in the move from 'fact' to 'otherness'; fact gives rise to value when fact is inscribed as otherness. Alterity is freighted with axiological weight. It seems then that a human–nonhuman differential will always find ways to tilt the scales in favour of the former, i.e., some value will inevitably be extracted from it. This process is the inevitable convergence of anthropocentrism with value. Muddling categories, that is to say, comes down finally in favour of the human, remaking otherness in the likeness of *anthropos*.

There is, however, an alternative understanding, as we will see in the next section: the animal as mediating between the human and its others, rather than merely being anthropomorphically assimilated. By interposing itself between the human and the natural, animal sentience creates an undecidability in the human-animal relationship. Mapping value on to the human and fact on to the natural then no longer pertains; the rigid division of human–value and nature–fact is destabilised by the presence of the animal.

### The measure of the human

The continuity–discontinuity knot is summed up in Raymond Tallis's maxim that 'man is an animal with an irreducible distance from animality'.[22] Which is to say that, the human is the *transcended* animal, the animal that has overcome its animality, in the polysemous sense of *Aufhebung*: retained, negated and surpassed. Our animal heritage is still present, but tempered by the cultural order that defies impersonal, indifferent natural selection. Yet it could also be argued that animals mediate between the human and the natural realms – between the culture-oriented subject world and the insensate object world, precariously placed between pure instinct and a rudimentary form of consciousness.

If the existence of animal proto-consciousness is notoriously difficult to prove, sentience can be established beyond any doubt and is, from the point of view of the human, the most difficult animal quality to apprehend. From Descartes to behaviourism the 'animal machine' – a purely instinctive, reactive creature – has been a consoling concept. Machines cannot feel, so we need not feel for them. Conversely, a nonhuman sentience is a powerful challenge. It prompts us to see animals as in some way trapped, as having evolved beyond insensate plant matter yet denied the full consciousness and reflexivity – whatever burdens these might carry – of *homo sapiens*. The temptation then is to anthropomorphise the animal as something tragic, as engaged in a blind struggle that it does not even know exists. Behind this anthropomorphisation, of course, is the shadow of our own struggle as 'between worlds' beings, as occupants of the twin realms of matter and spirit. Our fallible, nature-grounded and present-based bodies tender a constant reproach to our mercurial, overtemporalised minds: also present-based, but bounded by the recursiveness of memory and desire.

All this suggests that anthropomorphisation need not *necessarily* entail domestication of the unknown other, the forcible transformation of its difference into sameness. Anthropomorphic practices can just as easily mediate between these two opposites and find a space where self-understanding can recognise difference *and* sameness, without the former being consumed by the latter. This juxtaposition does, however, present further complications, as we are about to see.

The humanist axiom that 'man is the measure of all things' provides an enduring example of the significance of scale for human self-cognisance. Scale can easily be coopted for ideological purposes: it can provide justification for a virulent anthropocentrism, where human affairs dominate and enslave the natural order. But political cooptation aside, it is clear that scale has a hold on our cognitive and sensory apparatus in our everyday transactions with the world. The great chain of being was a means of establishing scale in a teeming biological network, whose diversity and apparent disorder remained a permanent threat. (As Darwin remarked, 'If man had not been his own classifier, he would never have thought of founding a separate order for his own reception.')[23] We transcribe nature in terms of ourselves, and to this end animals help to confer scale. Natural formations can be imposing, forbidding, disquieting. The presence of natural beings in such spaces, however, demonstrating habitability, restores a sense of proportion. A vast tract of wilderness seems less alien, less threatening, less *other* if it can be seen to support an ecosystem. The presence of live beings, existing in balance with a harsh climate, brings such a wilderness closer to human experience, closer to something resembling human scale. If nature can sustain animal life, it can more readily be incorporated within human dimensions.

Animals also provide scale for another form of disquiet, the threat of disease. The intermediary roles they play here, however, are more ambiguous than those described above. Animal surrogacy in scientific research points to an uncertainty in the human–animal configuration. Military use of dogs and monkeys was common in the early days of the space programme, and scientific experimentation has thrived from the use of animals as 'tools of research'.[24] In these latter situations animals mediate the brute contingency and indifference of disease – nature at its most insidiously threatening – by acting as biological markers, filters for control and containment. On the one hand, such surrogacy is predicated on the fact that, in order to be of use to human research, the gap between animal being and human being is minimal. On the other hand, it is human volition rather than animal compliance that makes such situations possible, thereby simultaneously distancing human life and behaviour from its animal counterpart.

A similar indeterminacy is evident in Kant's *Lectures on Ethics*. He declares vivisection to be cruel yet praiseworthy, for its ends are justified and 'animals must be regarded as man's instruments'. Wanton cruelty, however, such as using animals for sport, is not to be countenanced. Animals serve the socially useful purpose of providing practice for human beings to treat each other civilly. In this sense, animals mediate intersubjectively. 'Our duties towards animals, then, are indirect duties towards mankind.'[25] Again, sameness and difference coexist: animals are at once similar enough to humans to provide the occasion for moral rehearsal, and different enough not to warrant 'direct duties' themselves.[26]

These instances betoken an aporetic relation between humans and animals, unravelling the argument about continuity versus discontinuity. The ontological link implied by animal suitability for yielding accurate predictions about human physiology, or for serving as moral 'stand-ins', is severed by the fact that such surrogacy can be performed at all, a denial of ethical and agential equivalence between human being and animal being. The aporia here is the tension between foreclosure and entailment, signifying a linkless link between humans and animals. In addition, we should not lose sight of the fact that this form of animal mediation is, for the most part, illusory. Tim Radford writes: 'There has been an error of scale. Because we occupy five or six feet of vertical space, we imagine it to be a norm for life. But 99 per cent of all living things are less than 3 mm long.'[27] The illusion that is human scale makes our world habitable and stories about our world and ourselves meaningful.

The task of renegotiating the culture–nature divide and human–animal dis/continuity, though inevitably serving the interests of the cultural order (evidenced in the examples of Marx and Wilde) nevertheless is both urgent and necessary, as Mary Midgley has stressed. She declares nature and culture to be unopposed to each other; we are essentially culture-building animals, and 'what we build into our culture has to satisfy our natural pattern of motives'.[28] The remainder of this chapter examines how the human-animal relationship has been extended in such cohabitative ways, by Darwin and Nietzsche.

## Darwin to Nietzsche: down the shaft of being

Earlier in this chapter we saw how Wilde made explicit what was hinted at by Marx, how the extreme conclusions drawn by the former came to possess (unexpected) affiliations with the latter. A similar relation binds Nietzsche to Darwin. By 'reanimalising' the human, Darwin implicitly took narrative out of nature – which is to say that, after Darwin certain processes no longer fitted so comfortably inside the narrative formations that had formerly given them meaning. Similarly, albeit from the other side, Nietzsche's doctrines of 'becoming what one is' and eternal recurrence disable the narrative process, providing impetus for his demand 'to translate man back into nature'.[29]

Darwin's place within the anthropometric tradition, from the mid-Victorian era onwards, is axiomatic. In terms of the 'animal human', Darwinism is the pressure point, a defining moment in the discursive lifespan of the human as a rational animal. The definition survives Darwinism intact, but the stress shifts irrevocably from the first part of the term to the second. Indeed, as will be shown, Darwin did not make a complete break with the figure of 'metaphysical man' sustained by theological and humanist discourses. This (theoretical) ambiguity is matched by an historical ambiguity: the deferred publication of the thesis on the origin of man, and its eventual appearance some twenty years later. The sway of the Church, therefore, was powerful, but not all-powerful; scientific rationality could hold its own against dogma.[30]

Moore and Desmond point to two crucial factors in Darwin's 'breaking cover' after twenty years of silence and secrecy: the support he received from the so-called 'young guard' – which included Huxley, the physicist John Tyndall, surgeon and botanist Joseph Hooker, and William Carpenter the physiologist – all advocates of natural selection; and a letter Darwin received from Alfred Russel Wallace in 1858, apparently preempting Darwin's evolutionary theory.[31] The solution to the dilemma created by the latter – a joint Darwin–Wallace paper, delivered to the Geological Society on 1 July 1858 – led inexorably to *The Origin of Species* itself, the following year.[32] By this time the grip of the Church was weakening. Such a figure as the Reverend Charles Kingsley, a Christian Socialist, could express praise for *The Origin*. In any case, Darwin's supporters were fearless in the face of Anglican autocracy: 'But generally the young guard had no time for priests; their strategy called for confrontation, for edging out the men with dual callings [i.e., science and theology].'[33]

Nietzsche's influence on the anthropometric tradition has been more intermittent, more dispersive, and more various than Darwin's. Sidestepping the Darwinian influence (yet not extricating himself from it entirely, as we shall see) Nietzsche made the antimetaphysical break more determinedly. His most notable anthropometric achievement was not to annul the animal–human difference, but to mark it more clearly than ever, yet do so without reliance on metaphysical surety. In 'Schopenhauer as Educator' he writes:

But how can we find ourselves again? How can the human being get to know himself? He is a thing dark and veiled; and if the hare has seven skins, the human being can shed seven times seventy skins and still not be able to say: 'This is really you, this is no longer outer shell.' Besides, it is an agonizing, dangerous undertaking to dig down into yourself in this way, to force your way by the shortest route down the shaft of your own being.[34]

This 'agonizing, dangerous undertaking' is definitive of the 'human without the "human" ': to explore the human with greater acuity than anyone has previously dared, without the safety net of metaphysical pieties. Such criteria are inextricable from conceptions of value. The human without the 'human' in one sense refers to the nonmetaphysical human after it has been divested of value. (Or, as it is adumbrated in this chapter, the denarrativised, reanimalised human.) Yet even as Nietzschean man is stripped of inherent value, he nevertheless retains, in greater abundance than ever before, the ability to confer value – on himself, on his surroundings, on his fellow creatures. Nietzsche differs considerably from the Marx/Wilde disposition, however. If mankind thinks it has been discovering values (bestowed from above, by God; or from below, by nature), Nietzsche urges that we drop this pretence and realise that what we have always done, and must still do, is create values. Which is to say that, value is not so much possessed as *performed*. I will return to this point in Part III, when the differences with Marx and Wilde become more paramount.

## II DARWIN'S INTERMITTENT CHRONICLES

### *Narrating the animal*

Origin of man now proved. – Metaphysics must flourish. – He who understands baboon would do more toward metaphysics than Locke.

Charles Darwin[35]

This cryptic remark was made in an obscure notebook entry dated August 1838. How are we to take it, more than 160 years later – as irony, as endorsement or simply as regret? In what sense *must* metaphysics flourish? To examine this comment in light of the human-narrative dyad, I am not endeavouring to reconstruct the historical circumstances that surround it. The aim rather is to build an interpretative strategy based on more recent understanding of metaphysics, and the role it plays in the production of narrative meaning.

What are the affinities between evolution and narrative? In the broadest sense, both are preoccupied with time and change. In *Darwin's Plots*, the most thorough recent study of this collocation, Gillian Beer notes: 'Evolutionary theory is first a form of imaginative history. . . it is closer to narrative than to drama.'[36] Mary Midgley, however, is more equivocal about the affinities. On the one hand, she remarks that to evolve:

suggests typically the opening of a scroll or a bud, bringing into action what was only potential within them. This means both that certain definite potentialities were present from the start, greatly limiting what could emerge, and that these, rather than many other changes that may have been possible, were in some sense the right or suitable candidates.

Alternatively, she notes, evolution may simply mean a registration of changes taking place over time.[37] The former account tends towards narrativisation, with its causal linkages and mutual implication, the latter towards the linear itemisation associated with the chronicle. From these two accounts two separate pathways become evident.

Firstly, there is the path of progress and purpose, presupposing if not a designer then at least some kind of design, a pattern of changes that can be made to mean. It is the path, in short, of one thing *out of* another. The second version abjures inherent meaning. It shows evolutionary change as pure contingency, based on mechanism – the mechanism of natural selection. Blind chance replaces meaning, in a series of (natural) law-abiding accidents, without necessity or automatic signification. It is, determinedly, one thing *after* another.

The two types might be mapped as follows. Evolution as a narratable process invokes Lamarckian precepts. This involves orthogenesis, or the innate tendency of organisms to evolve – climbing, in the course of their development, the 'ladder' of species that Lamarck contrived to replace the *scala naturae*. Lamarck's theory of evolution then is an essentialist one, derived from the belief that every organism possesses intrinsic adaptive features. Evolution as nonnarratable contingency, on the other hand, is Darwinian. 'Strictly speaking,' writes Ernst Mayr, 'Darwinian evolution is discontinuous because a new start is made in every generation when a new set of individuals is produced . . . Such evolution is not necessarily progressive; it is an opportunistic response to the moment; hence it is unpredictable.'[38] The Lamarckian and Darwinian types can be mapped as, respectively, transformational evolution (orderly change over time, moving towards perfect adaptation), and variational evolution (random change at the level of both genetic recombination and selection).[39]

Beer remarks that it is Lamarck's account of evolutionary process, with its emphasis on intentionality and teleology, that has become the standard one, in the popular understanding. In this account the source of creativity is not an omnipotent designer or interventionist deity, but the enabling agency of acquired characteristics; through this physical adaptations (which can be wilfully and intentionally acquired) are passed on to inheritors.[40] Darwinian evolution, by contrast, is all 'machine' and no 'voice'. It is pure impersonality, pure mechanism – the mechanism of natural selection – devoid of individual will and intention. Without the anthropomorphic cognates of memory and teleology, there cannot be mutual implication of temporal changes. This is the sense in which Darwin took narrative out of nature.

Human evolution is divisible into two stages, the animal stage and the distinctively human, 'psycho-social' stage. It is the bridge between the two, linking biological history (a history of instinct) with cultural history (a history of conscience) that Darwin explores in *The Descent of Man*: 'Ultimately our moral sense or conscience becomes a highly complex sentiment – originating in the social instincts, largely guided by the approbation of our fellow-men, ruled by reason, self-interest, and in later times by deep religious feelings, and confirmed by instruction and habit' (203). Darwin outlines four stages of development: social instinct gives rise to sympathetic affiliation; mental development engenders enhanced memory, and hence awareness of unfulfilled desire; language acquisition enables cooperative community; and habit strengthens social instinct, sympathy, communal obedience, etc. Darwin's conclusion concerns more than just 'man': 'The following proposition seems to me in a high degree probable – namely, that any animal whatever, endowed with well-marked social instincts, the parental and filial affections being here included, would inevitably acquire a moral sense or conscience, as soon as its intellectual power has become as well, or nearly as well, developed as in man' (149–50).

But although he deems moral awareness 'natural', in the sense of developing from socio-biological interaction, Darwin does not say that it is *necessary*. He reinjects contingency into the process by relativising the moral sense: 'In the same manner as various animals have some sense of beauty, though they admire widely different objects, so they might have a sense of right and wrong, though led by it to follow widely different lines of conduct' (151). His conclusion is unequivocal: 'the difference in mind between man and the higher animals, great as it is, certainly is one of degree and not of kind' (193).

To describe this kind of genealogy, rectilinear descriptions (*scala naturae*, or Lamarck's 'ladder image', which allowed limited horizontal latitude on each 'rung') are plainly inadequate. Instead, Darwin sought to show how the natural order was constructed not with miraculous regularity and perfection, but in the form of an irregularly branching system. The monogenist 'tree model' was thus contrived to replace the great chain of being. H. E. Gruber writes:

The tree model saved Darwin the trouble of looking for the 'missing link' between man and the other primates. If his theory was true, these extant animals represented distinct branchings from a common progenitor, so that the search for living intermediate forms would be misguided. Continuity could be found only by looking backward in evolutionary time to that long-past branching point.[41]

But like the great chain of being, the tree model is a spatialised representation, hence able to convey an implicit coherency that Darwinian natural selection as a temporal process – a catalogue of discontinuity, unpredictability and randomness – cannot. Time, change and chance cannot be transformed into time, change and *necessity*, as they must be for adequate narrativisation.

### The missing link: 'metaphysical man'

*Homo sapiens* has been narrativised as a movement from animal origin to human realisation, or from potentiality to actuality. Animals, on the other hand, lack transcendence, the power to escape the constraints of their primitive state; from the humanist standpoint there is no significant teleology, no metanarrative explaining animal evolution as a meaningful story-structure. But can (human) transcendence, registered in terms of mind, soul or spirit, be plotted in an event-series? Is the genesis of 'metaphysical man', describing his endowment with *anima*, a narratable possibility? Raymond Tallis suggests not: 'My account of the difference between man and animals leaves the relationship between them deeply puzzling and the transition from the one to the other almost inexplicable.'[42] The emergence of metaphysical man presages an origin. The animal-into-human narrative charts the preoriginary, and its supersession by the originary. The animal-into-human narrative has a beginning and an end, but no middle. Or rather, no transitory stage charting the animal premise as it metamorphoses into human culmination.

Similarly, Mary Midgley has described Descartes's division of the world into *res cogitans* (rational human subjects) and *res extensa* (lifeless objects, including animals) as 'bad metaphysics': 'The position cannot in any case be reconciled with evolution. For if it were true, there would have to have been a quite advanced point in human evolution when parents who were merely unconscious objects had a child which was a fully conscious subject. And that situation makes no sense.'[43] She notes that the greatest resistance to animal-human continuity 'now comes not from traditional religion, but from those who do amputate the soul'.[44] In fact, metaphysical humanism has appropriated much of the vocabulary of traditional religious discourse, even where it professes support for evolution.[45]

The gap in the Darwinian narrative reveals the gap between metaphysics and narration, an indicator that metaphysics (i.e., the 'origin of man') cannot be narrated. It is the aporia alluded to above, where the human is both continuous with the animal and discontinuous. The animal-into-human narrative outlined above is not really possible because in order to point to a beyond – to *transcend* – it must encompass an origin, and this is impossible. It is predicated on metaphysical man, a being whose origin can never be reconstructed, and hence never narrated.[46]

The next part of the discussion will examine more closely the coupling of metaphysics and narrative, in relation to Hegelian philosophical narrative. But first let us briefly recapitulate the central argument of this section. The process of animal-become-human is recountable in two versions, comprising two different evolutionary takes. The first version, the Darwinian, is a purely natural process, guided by natural selection. Human beings are continuous with animals, although the process linking them is contingent i.e., discontinuous, antiprogressive and unpredictable and hence defiant of all the criteria for narrativisation. The second version, which I will call the 'metaphysical', separates humans from animals as a matter of kind, rather than degree. At some point in the animal-into-human process there is a leap from instinct into conscience, from reaction into reflexivity, and from 'presentism' into narrative. This transcendent leap cannot be accounted for in metaphysical terms, only in physical: it betokens an origin at some point, a nonnarratable cleft between continuities (animal development and psycho-social human development). Both versions, then, are unnarratable for different reasons. We identified above various ways in which animals mediate between the human and the natural. These intermediary roles illuminated an undecidability in the human–animal relationship, a node of contingency stripping both categories of being of their discrete particularities and meanings. Attempts to narrativise the relationship founder as one category, the animal, refuses to conjoin with its human counterpart. So it would seem that the affinities between evolution and narrative detailed at the outset are disproven by the specific narrative of the origin of man.

## Excursus: *Hegel's Bildungsroman of Spirit*

As Darwin excised narrative from nature, Nietzsche removed it from philosophy. And he did this in tandem with the 'reanimalisation' of the human, hence involving a renegotiation of Darwinian precepts. The context for Nietzschean reanimalisation has been partly provided above, in the discussion of Darwin. For the related movement towards denarrativisation, it is necessary to examine Nietzsche's philosophical antecedents. From these we can better grasp the true nature and scope of his reaction.

Modern philosophical narrative begins, like modern philosophy itself, with René Descartes. His account of how he came to formulate the *cogito* is unrepentantly autobiographical: a dissatisfaction with what the senses register, the subsequent turn to an encompassing scepticism, and the final rediscovery of certainty. '[I]t is a conspicuously narrated story,' writes Jonathan Rée. 'Unlike Descartes' earlier literary experiments, it is not merely decorated with a few narrative ornaments. It is narrated through and through. One critic has even described it as the first real novel.'[47]

Descartes's tale comprises a remote part of the tradition against which Nietzsche is reacting. A more direct adversary comes from his own century: 'Anti-Hegelianism runs through Nietzsche's work as its cutting edge,'[48] declares Gilles Deleuze. However, it is not Nietzsche's rejection of the Hegelian dialectic that is examined here, but his implicit renunciation of that central nineteenth-century metanarrative, *The Phenomenology of Spirit*. It amounts to a repudiation of the most sustained and extraordinary example of philosophical narrative.

In a not untypical letter to Frederick Engels, in June 1862, Marx regales him with an account of his fiscal strife and his family's indigence, a litany of morbid details about 'our filthy situation'. Not surprisingly, this gives him pause to reflect on Malthus. He mentions the separation of plants and animals from human beings in Malthusian theory, and Darwin's traversal of this separation:

It is remarkable how Darwin recognises among beasts and plants his English society with its divisions of labour, competition, opening-up of new markets, 'inventions', and the Malthusian 'struggle for existence'. It is Hobbes's *bellum omnium contra omnes*, and one is reminded of Hegel's *Phenomenology*, where civil society is described as a 'spiritual animal kingdom', while in Darwin the animal kingdom figures as civil society.[49]

Jeff Wallace endorses this view of Darwin, stating that 'the theory of natural selection is consistently and explicitly cast as a theory of political economy in nature'.[50] (Wallace also recognises that natural selection was 'an *anti*-evolution theory', since it describes not so much evolution, development and progress as contingency and discontinuity.[51])

Judged by Marx's comments, Darwin and Hegel are both guilty of culture-nature interchange, freely exchanging metaphors from each to describe their different evolutionary systems. In this the two thinkers are complementary opposites, as they are in other ways, too. Neal Gillespie points out that creationism involved seeing the world as divine activity. '[The creationist's] epistemology was closely geared to a metaphysics, and in metaphysics he tended to be an "idealist".' Ideal-ism, writes Gillespie, means an 'emphasis on mind, purpose, and design in nature'.[52] Hegel's system is notable for being idealist, totalising and necessity-driven. Like Darwin, Hegel is accounting for how we are now in evolutionary terms ('without Hegel there could have been no Darwin', writes Nietzsche).[53] He charts the evolution of subjectivity, of human con-sciousness, filling in the gap that the animal-into-human narrative cannot fill: where the latter attempts an impossible concatenation of physical and metaphysical, Hegel's 'descent of mind' is purely metaphysical.

*The Phenomenology of Spirit* draws on eighteenth-century *Bildung*, and on the literary forms that have blossomed from it. Indeed, in the intro-duction Hegel describes the work as 'the detailed history of the *education* [*Bildung*] of consciousness itself to the standpoint of Science.'[54] But the *Phenomenology* differs from the *Bildungsroman* in that its educative aspect, its use of *Bildung*, is performative rather than expository. The work has been described as 'the *Bildung* (the education, formation, and cultivation) of its intended readership into coming to terms with what is entailed in their form of life and what kinds of alternatives are available to them'.[55] The way in which this was carried out was not in the manner of philosophical exposition, but in the mode of a literary narrative, demonstrating human-ity's growing awareness as it struggles first towards scientific truth, then to timeless systematic truth. And the narrative mode it uses is one of pro-gressive self-education, reaching towards the attainment of maturity.[56] The narrative line follows the classic pattern of the *Bildungsroman*, as de-scribed by Rée: '[It is] a story of a wayfaring consciousness called Spirit, travelling from what Hegel calls its "natural" state, along a road which, though it passes through all sorts of deceptions and disappointments, leads ultimately to "absolute knowledge".'[57]

The surrogate novelistic apparatus of the *Phenomenology* has been out-lined still further: as a philosophical novel containing a central char-acter, consciousness, which breaks down into such subcharacters as sense-certainty, perception and understanding. This is more than just literary whimsy: the repeatability of these terms from one context to the next confers upon them the continuity of novelistic characters. In addition to these 'substantial characters', there are 'functional charac-ters' (the particular, the universal, the notion or conceptual horizon), and a narrated commentary. And as with Proust's 'Marcel', the nar-rative voice of the *Phenomenology* inhabits two time schemes, one retro-spective and omniscient, the other immediate, in the form of narrated monologue.[58]

These different narrative aspects can be assembled to ascertain the particular conventions of the *Phenomenology*. Rée gathers together the use of free indirect speech; the 'double voice' (the contrast between the linked perspective of the traveller, and the global, bird's-eye view encompassing the entire journey at once); and the narrator's point of view, a foreshadowing of Henry James's narrative style: 'The structure of the *Phenomenology*, in other words, is that of an autobiography. Its hero (like the protagonist of Descartes' *Discourse on Method*) is growing up to become the narrator telling the story. Spirit transforms itself into "us", as the "for consciousness" becomes the "in itself".'[59] The work could also been seen as going beyond the *Bildungsroman* and into *Bildungsbiographie*, in the sense of being a spiritual history.[60]

The 'double voice', temporally bifurcated, highlights an important aspect of narrativity. It turns on the polysemous sense of *Aufhebung*, or *aufheben*.[61] The narrative impetus of the *Phenomenology* describes:

> the dynamic by which *Geist* negates, preserves, and surpasses its succeeding determinations, and discovers ultimately that each of these determinations is a necessary expression of its essence. This dynamic, the perpetual *Aufhebung* of self-consciousness, may be regarded as well as a process of recollection (*Erinnerung*), by which process *Geist* finally remembers and reveals the truth of being. Hegel identifies this truth with absolute knowledge.[62]

What 'absolute knowledge' knows, it knows immanently; which is to say that, it does not know that it knows, until it reaches its destination. Narrative logic dovetails with the meanings of sublation; annulment, preservation and supersession echo the function of mutual implication in a narrative's event-sequence.

Despite allusions made above, there is one incontrovertible reason why Hegel and not Descartes is the narrative philosopher *par excellence*. It is because the *cogito*, although recounted in the form of a narrative, is itself not inherently narrativistic. That is, it is not performable exclusively through narrative discourse, but can be just as efficaciously conveyed through standard philosophical exposition. The *Discourse on Method* may be 'novelistic', as Rée implies, but the narrative form resides in the text as a whole rather than in the *cogito*. The *Phenomenology*, however, is quite different in that it is inherently narrativistic. For consciousness to move from sense-certainty to absolute knowledge, it must draw on similar conventions to those that constitute narrative discourse. There must be mutual implication between stages, one step *out of* another. For Hegel to cast this in the form of an autobiographical novel is, if not quite inevitable, at least highly expedient; *The Phenomenology of Spirit* is as implicated in narrative form as the odyssey of spirit that it describes. And Hegel is as much as offering an answer to a question posed previously: is subjectivity inherently narrative-shaped? To say that the *Phenomenology* affirms this is to underestimate the link. Rather, it is subjectivity's narrativistic nature that makes the *Phenomenology* possible, that allows it to exist in the particular form it does.

The incompatibilities of animal-into-human lay bare narrative for what it is: a metaphysical scaffolding. This can partly explain literary modernism's unease with narrative. A key modernist strategy for resisting narrative's metaphysical gravity is to problematise beginnings and endings; not a 'solution' to the metaphysical so much as a way of decentring it and dispersing its totalising bent. The literary figures examined in the ensuing chapters show the implacable problems of maintaining ties, however slender, with narrative organisation.

The undecidabilities engendered by animal mediation (scientific experimentation and ethical intersubjectivity) suggest a determinate meaning to Darwin's supposition, 'Origin of man now proved. – Metaphysics must flourish': neither irony nor endorsement, but regret. The human and the animal, it now appears, cannot be properly juxtaposed without the intervention of narrative; and such an intervention ensures that this narrativised relation is also, ineluctably, a metaphysical relation. There is much at stake, then, in anthropometric attempts to resist narrative, the most far-reaching nineteenth-century example of which is the subject of the next Part.

### III NIETZSCHE'S TROPOLOGICAL CREATURES

#### *The interesting animal*

> The task of determining Nietzsche's relation to Darwin and
> Darwinism is an immensely important one, but also complicated.
>                                         Keith Ansell Pearson[63]

In certain basic precepts, the relation between Nietzsche and Darwin is straightforward. In *The Will To Power*, for instance, Nietzsche declares that ' "man" as a species does not represent any progress compared with any other animal. The whole animal and vegetable kingdom does not evolve from the lower to the higher – but all at the same time, in utter disorder, over and against each other.'[64] This undermines the possibility of an animal-human narrative as effectively as Darwin did in *The Descent of Man*, though for different, less scientific reasons.

Nietzsche's excision of narrative from philosophy depends on the animal's unruly, unnarratable energies. Anthropometric thought typically involves a loss of scale, as we have seen, but Nietzsche has a kind of scale in his work, a means of taking the measure of existence: life. Needless to say, given his denial of man's 'progress' from the animal, Nietzsche does not privilege human life. Although human beings are organic, carbon-based creatures, as possessors of consciousness ('that most impoverished and error-prone organ') they can readily abjure life for antilife.[65] Slave morality, *ressentiment* and bad conscience – endemic to metaphysical man – are all denials of life. It is 'naturalised man' that Nietzsche posits in his stead. This habitation of the less-than-human, the animalised human freed from the misguiding torments of consciousness, is the quintessential Nietzschean move towards the repossession of life. Since life is the only absolute value, the human is valorised only to the extent that it exists on life's terms. Human being is therefore either an enabling condition for life to flourish, or a disabling impediment causing it to wither on the vine.

Animals appear throughout Nietzsche's work in a number of guises, from the historical prehuman beings in 'Schopenhauer as Educator' to the anthropomorphised parahuman creatures in *Thus Spoke Zarathustra*. But the Nietzschean animal appears most often as a trope, a way of undermining human being as transcendent being. 'Man ... is the sick animal' (*GM* 94), 'man is a reverent animal' (*GS* 286), man 'the most endangered animal' (298), 'It was only as a social animal that man acquired self-consciousness' (299), 'man the bravest of animals and the one most prone to suffer' (*GM* 127), 'man first became an interesting animal on the foundation of this essentially dangerous form of human existence, the priest' (18). For Nietzsche that animals are nonnarrativistic creatures constitutes one of the prime features of their existence that he sees as superior to human life. 'Life', in other words, is debased by narrativisation. Narrative is a hindrance, a wedge preventing the human from truly possessing, or from being properly possessed by, life. Instead, the human must make do with a degraded alternative, made manifest through the slave moralities of Judaism, Christianity, socialism, democracy, philanthropism. So in Nietzsche's work 'humanism' is akin to 'narrativism'; both modes of understanding collude in their corruption of 'life'.

The third of the *Unfashionable Observations*, 'Schopenhauer as Educator', includes a sustained meditation on animal being. '[W]here does the animal cease, where does the human being begin?' asks Nietzsche. I noted above the pseudo-anthropomorphic tendency to regard animal life as tragic, to see it as 'trapped' between insentience and consciousness. Nietzsche alludes to this tendency when he remarks: 'It is truly a harsh punishment to live in the manner of an animal, subject to hunger and desires, and yet without arriving at any insight into the nature of this life.' There is no anthropomorphic move here, but rather a zoomorphic one. The tragedy is ours alone: 'for the greatest part of our lives this is the way it is for all of us: usually we do not transcend animality, we ourselves are those creatures who seem to suffer senselessly'.[66] Nietzsche's tropological use of the animal is elaborated:

To cling so blindly and madly to life, for no higher reward, far from knowing that one is punished or why one is punished in this way, but instead to thirst with the inanity of a horrible desire for precisely this punishment as though it were happiness – that is what it means to be an animal. And if all of nature presses onward toward the human being, then in doing so it makes evident that he is necessary for its salvation from animal existence and that in him, finally, existence holds before itself a mirror in which life no longer appears senseless but appears, rather, in its metaphysical meaningfulness [. . .] The tremendous mobility of human beings on the great earthly desert, their founding of cities and states, their waging of wars, their ceaseless gathering and dispersing, their confused mingling, their imitation of one another, their mutual outwitting and trampling underfoot, their cries in distress and their joyous cheers in victory – all this is a continuation of animality, as if human beings were intended to regress and be cheated out of their metaphysical disposition; indeed, as if nature, having yearned and labored for human beings for so long, now recoiled from them in fear and preferred to return to the unconsciousness of instinct.[67]

Pure animal life – instinctive, reactive, nonconscious and nonreflexive – is an affliction. To that extent, the human 'is necessary for its [own] salvation from animal existence'. But even man's redemptive role is perilous. In him 'life no longer appears senseless but appears, rather, in its metaphysical meaningfulness'. The physical surrenders to the metaphysical. But the battle is not entirely lost. The frenzied farrago of human activity – exploring, populating, founding cities and states, warring – is a continuation of animality, it burns through the superficial covering that is the metaphysical disposition. The animal is thus a way of grounding the human, and of curtailing man's propensity for metaphysical flights of self-admiration. The animal's tropological status is, among other things, a scalemaking device, a reminder that human being is body-based being. The animal also mediates, to an extent, between the human and the world – not just the natural world, but the world that is delivered via values, beliefs and proprieties, the world of culture. The animal trope in this sense is an enabling device for Nietzsche to convey perspectivism.

And perspective ('the basic condition of all life', he declares in *Beyond Good and Evil*),[68] is conferred by physiology. To reanimalise the human is thus to stress the biological basis of perspective. It is a way of saying that the human is but a point of view, a nontranscendent entity beguiled by the transcendent promises that inhere in narrative. This indicates, once again, the latent connection in Nietzsche's thought between animalisation and denarrativisation.

### Antinarrative (I): becoming what one is

How might Nietzsche's attitude to narrative be characterised?[69] We saw above how Descartes's account of the *cogito* was an occasion for narrative, 'perhaps the first novel'. Nietzsche responds to this in *The Gay Science* by staging what amounts to a philosophical takeover, a deliberate attempt at dethronement. His famous phrase, 'how one becomes what one is' – perhaps his most haunting philosophical aphorism[70] – is his challenge to Descartes's celebrated *cogito ergo sum*, a riposte to the key tenet of modern philosophical foundationalism.

The *cogito* establishes a relationship between thought and being based on authority, the authority of cognitive self-discipline. Thus thought (mind) authorises being (body); epistemology indemnifies ontology; and philosophy is a justification for physics and physiology. It is not strictly sequential; as Martin Heidegger has remarked, before one thinks, one still is ('The *sum* is not a consequence of the thinking, but vice versa; it is the ground of thinking, the *fundamentum*').[71] But the thinking self, in charging the existing self with awareness, also gives it meaning and value. This makes the existing proto-self, effectively, into a true self; thought is a vehicle of enablement. Nietzsche removes, first of all, the element of authorisation. One is; one becomes; and one is. It is a sketch of the eternal recurrence, an alternative to *Aufhebung*. Being precedes becoming, and ontology precedes morphology. So Nietzsche historicises the *cogito*, but purges it of 'progress' – the singular progress that transforms proto-self into realised self. 'It was' (being) becomes 'thus I willed it' (becoming); so becoming is an act of will. And this willing, this adoption of 'thus I willed it', which can only ever be a project, rather than a result, is what makes self-creation possible.

The challenge is signposted in *The Gay Science*, in the opening passage of Book IV (223). Musing on the new year, Nietzsche considers first the state he is in now, and then expresses 'his wish and his dearest thought'. The wish is characterised as '*Sum, ergo cogito: cogito, ergo sum*';

the Cartesian breakthrough reduced to a whimsical *pensée*. The dearest thought follows directly after: 'I want to learn more and more to see as beautiful what is necessary in things; then I shall be one of those who make things beautiful. *Amor fati*: let that be my love henceforth!' To 'make things beautiful' is the act of will that says 'yes' to the eternal recurrence ('becoming'), to the aestheticisation of one's past; and 'what is necessary in things' is 'what one is'. Nietzsche's New Year's resolution is a variant of his famous expression. To *see* something as beautiful is to make beauty; the connection is implied in the Greek word *aisthetikos*, or perceptible by the senses. In creating beauty one creates, by default, what is necessary (conversely, one does not discover what is necessary). Beauty and necessity are therefore conceived of as inseparable. And just as seeing is making, so is freedom a part of necessity – the necessity inherent in a deterministic universe. Recognising necessity is thus a first step to making necessity; and, ultimately, to mastering it. Nietzsche's biomorphic aestheticism – or bioaestheticism – makes mastery from determinism. There are two larger issues touched on here: the eternal recurrence that defies sublation, and the mastery concomitant with will to power.

## Antinarrative (II): the rapture of recurrence

There are two axes contained within eternal recurrence, not one as is often assumed. The temporal axis is easily determined: to will eternal recurrence is to will the infinite repeatability of every aspect of one's life, exactly as it is experienced the first time. But the spatial axis arises almost as an afterthought, in a detail appended to the original passage. It appears in *The Gay Science*: ' "This life as you now live it and have lived it, you will have to live once more and innumerable times more . . . even this spider and this moonlight between the trees, and even this moment and I myself" . . .' (273). By including 'this spider and this moonlight', the world beyond the willing self, Nietzsche transports the reader elsewhere: to the world of the Marxian labourer, for whom 'plants, animals, stones, air, light, etc., theoretically form a part of human consciousness'; and to the realm of the Wildean aesthete, who avers that 'it is in the brain that [nature] quickens to life'. Is Nietzsche expounding another version of culture-based anthropocentrism, and giving tacit approval to human dominion over nature? There is a form of mastery at work here, but of a different stripe from the two examples above. I will return to this question later, after the antinarrativistic aspects of eternal recurrence have been ascertained.

'This spider and this moonlight' implies that, just as saying yes to something once means saying it an infinite number of times, in a loop of endless repetition, saying yes to something entails saying it to everything. Eternal recurrence is thus a form of embeddedness, mutual implication on a macroscopic scale, where everything is interdependently related in an elaborate causal network. Narrative, too, involves mutual implication of an event-series. But Nietzsche's macroembeddedness, his dense matrix of interconnection, betokens not narrative but its opposite. For events are embedded in the same loop, they cannot break out of the cycle of repetition. By equating (spatial) embeddedness with eternal recurrence, narrative is dismantled, it is laid bare as something nonmetaphysical and nontranscendent. There cannot be any culmination in the endless loop of recurrence. The eternal return enables us, as human beings, as more-than-animals, to break free of our narrativistic constraints without resorting to a Rousseauesque myth of a 'return to nature'.

In giving to one's life the weight of design that an eternally recurring manifestation of it would warrant, one is compelled to experience each present moment as an intense, nontemporalised immersion. The life that eternal recurrence compels is complete, integrated, holistic – but on a moment-by-moment basis. Its integration comes not from the orderly expanse of a narrative formation, but from an intense, singleminded, self-willed surrender to each moment. It is an aestheticising movement, but stripped of the aesthetic appurtenances of narrative convention and the accompanying temporal interchanges, which point in both directions at once (mutual implication and retrospective immanence). The paradigm for such momentary, antimetaphysical oneness is animal being. Animal possession of the moment is instinctive, a consequence of existing as an ahistorical, narrativeless creature. Human appropriation of this mode of being is not instinctive but willed. It is the will to shed narrative's meta-physical coverings of temporal variation and causality, to give oneself over to immediacy. In this sense, the indeterminacy in how the eternal return is to be interpreted – whether as a poetic, a philosophical or a cosmological doctrine – gives way to its potential as an ideal for living, as a doublesided endorsement of narrative demolition and human ani-malisation. The eternal return is a figuration of the nontranscendence of the animal, an outline of the (fortunate) disability of creatural beings to move beyond the perpetual present.

Hegel's *Phenomenology* is a metaphysic-on-metaphysic narrativisation: it uses the metaphysical scaffolding of narrative to erect a metaphysical monument. Nietzsche strips this back to its basics. Locked into the same loop, individual human life cannot strive for a 'beyond', cannot make the leap from the physical to the metaphysical. Self-transcendence is not a possibility in this endless cycle of repetition. The Nietzschean abandonment of modern philosophical narrative – that mode inaugurated by Descartes and culminating in Hegel – prefigures the many bids at narrative disfigurement attempted in the modernist novel.

I began by describing life as the first principle of Nietzsche's thought. This must now be qualified. What is referred to as 'life' in the early work comes under the rubric of 'power' in the later. The switch comes early in the 1880s, in *The Gay Science*. An attack is mounted on 'Spinozistic dogma', Darwinism, and 'English overpopulation': 'The struggle for existence is only an exception, a temporary restriction of the will to life. The great and small struggle always revolves around superiority, around growth and expansion, around power – in accordance with the will to power which is the will to life' (292). Similarly, he writes in *Zarathustra*: ' "Only where life is, there is also will: not will to life, but – so I teach you – will to power!" '[72] In this new understanding, life does not determine who and what we are, it must itself be controlled and mastered.[73] This reopens Nietzsche's thought to the realms of aestheticism. The aesthetic hero was the artist who rebelled not against society but against life, the figure who could mould, alter and master the given.[74] The Nietzschean ethos is also based on mastery – of life, of oneself, and of the temptation to embrace the institutionalised social weaknesses (i.e., slave moralities) – through human creativity. To see the created as somehow oppositional (and superior) to the given is precisely what aestheticism does, as seen in Wilde's displacement of nature with art. The aestheticist doctrine, insofar as it has an imperative, is to maintain this primary distinction. But does Nietzsche insist on the same separation of created and given?

Nietzsche actually collapses the two terms into will to power, a given that has the creative potential to engender culture as well as nature. Will to power is the nexus of aesthetic creativeness and naturalistic givenness. Acknowledging that we are creative beings is identical to saying that we are will to power. Nietzsche states this explicitly: 'This world is will to power – and nothing besides! And you yourselves are also this will to power – and nothing besides!'[75] We are will to power and will to power is us; we do not possess it as an essential part of ourselves, it possesses us, like a biomorphic imperative. Because we are subordinate to this, the driving force of our being, we must say yes to it. The inescapability and inevitability of will to power indemnifies the yes. The will's expansion, as Alexander Nehamas has pointed out, carries a particular ontogenetic ramification:

[It] is the tendency to produce more and more effects upon the world; it is a tendency in connection with which there is no question of a choice. It is the manipulation of what Nietzsche calls a 'drive' which is common to animate and inanimate objects, and to which the idea of freedom, so often associated with the will, is not naturally suited.[76]

Nietzsche's bioaestheticism and his tropological animals bespeak the imbrication of culture and nature. Marx's comment about Hegel and Darwin (civil society as animal kingdom, and vice versa) is even more applicable to Nietzsche. But it would be grossly inaccurate to describe his intermingling of nature and culture as a muddling of categories, or to speak of a slippage between the two, as if there were unavoidable confusions arising from an intractable dualism. To the contrary, there is not so much an interchange between nature and culture, or even a renegotiation, as an endless series of dialectical reversals. The naturalisation of man is an essential prerequisite for Nietzsche's desired cultural transformation. The will to power's protean ability to engender nature and culture leads to an exchange of metaphors to rival both Hegel's and Darwin's. Nietzsche politicises evolution by demonstrating how adaptation serves the cause of modern democracy (even as it denies the will to power). At the same time, he biologises politics, by showing how will to power demonstrates that 'a system of law conceived as sovereign and universal is "anti" the fundamental "activity" of life'.[77]

Finally, we must consider the question posed at the start of this section, about the extent of Nietzsche's exaltation of cultural being. There is one dialectical interchange in particular that separates Nietzsche definitively from the anthropocentric cast of Marx and Wilde. In *The Gay Science* he writes:

We who think and feel at the same time are those who really continually fashion something that had not been there before: the whole eternally growing world of valuations, colors, accents, perspectives, scales, affirmations, and negations . . . Whatever has value in our world now does not have value in itself, according to its nature – nature is always value-less, but has been given some value at some time, as a present – and it was we who gave and bestowed it. Only we have created the world that concerns man! (241–2)

This is not the declamation of cultural man, seeking self-realisation through labour or art, and acknowledging the natural world only to the extent that his quest might be completed. In this passage Nietzsche advocates nothing less than abolition of the distinction between art and life, which is to be carried out via a hypertrophy of the creative will. This, finally, is the point of irreparable rupture from the aestheticist doctrine.

Wilde and his fellow aesthetes pursued what amounted to an aesthetic theodicy: the creation of an aesthetic world that would be autonomous, entirely separate from the nonaesthetic world. For Nietzsche, conversely, there is no separation; he urges instead to ' "give style" to one's character', in order that we become 'the poets of our life'.[78] It was Nietzsche who saw the world in terms of an aesthetic creation, brought into being by a primal aesthetic power.[79] This is a bioaestheticist move so sweeping as to move beyond the aesthetic and into the ontogenetic. And, in the process, the crucial aestheticist distinction between the created and the given, the aesthetic and the nonaesthetic, is removed.

## CREATURES CONDEMNED TO MEANING

Aristotle dispersed soul (*psyche*, *anima*) unevenly, yet thoroughly, throughout the great chain of being. Generally understood as the 'life principle', Aristotelian soul inaugurated a metaphysics of biology, whose modern scions include Lamarck and Bergson. In broader terms, the ubiquity of soul in Western discourses is matched only by its nebulousness. Subsequent to Aristotle's omnivitalist conception, soul becomes associated with conscience, with rationality, with mind in general. Descartes, for example, refers to the 'rational soul' (*âme raisonnable*) and defines it as 'that part distinct from the body ... [whose] nature is only to think'.[80] The notion of the soul is then readily translatable into the idiom of metaphysical humanism. John Keats, a resolute agnostic, famously wrote of the 'vale of Soul-making',[81] a humanist alternative to the Christian view of the world as a vale of tears. Nietzsche dates the development of the soul from the period when the 'outward discharge' of instinct was inhibited, contemporaneous with the emergence of bad conscience and *ressentiment* (*GM* 61). For Michel Foucault the soul's emergence is comparatively recent, manifesting itself in nineteenth-century subjectivity through the disciplines enforced by panoptical surveillance: 'This disciplinary technique exercised upon the body had a double effect: a "soul" to be known and a subject to be maintained.'[82] In secular times soul – 'only a word for something in the body' – has become a synecdoche for the human person ('poor soul').

As I have argued above, the metaphysical soul is the unassimilable element of the animal-into-human narrative. The only way for this narrative to cohere is by excision of the 'origin of man' that it implies. In other words, narrating the animal (the 'animal' animal and the human animal) means amputating the soul. Once it has gone, it makes untenable the epistemological assurance of such views as the following:

On the other hand, it can be argued that we are indeed unlike our closest animal kin, because we (or some of us) can conceive and seek to discover how the world itself is, really; we are not bound, as others are, to how the world must look to creatures of our particular kind. That marvellous ability, to seek the truth, is that same ability that makes it possible to ask what would be good for all, and not just for our accidental kind.[83]

Questioning the efficacy of collective human intervention in history, John Passmore has concluded: 'It is at least realistic, firmly based in human history, . . . that the unintended consequences of men's actions are more important, for the most part, than the consequences they intend.'[84] This is reflected in Gillian Beer's urge that we discriminate between 'agency' and 'intention'.[85] The distinction is important for my later argument: agential capacity does not guarantee for its possessor that its goals will be attained and its purposes fulfilled; unintended consequences intervene to change the course of intended action.

Beer's distinction is not so apparent (she claims) in Darwin's language, as its anthropocentric tendencies inevitably precipitate an 'intentional' bias (in the form of creationism). Ted Benton has questioned the claim that language is unavoidably anthropocentric;[86] and, indeed, it is difficult to sustain. The theoretical position that I have adopted is that language is, like all human productions (history, money and technology, as we will see in Chapter 2) uncontrollable by human users and in a dialectical relationship with them, conditioning and altering them. In this sense, it has inhuman qualities, despite supervening upon human activity, placing constraints on free will and agency without eradicating them altogether. Foucault compresses this into a pointed apothegm: 'People know what they do, and they frequently know why they do what they do; but what they don't know is what what they do does.'[87]

I mentioned in the Introduction one of the paradoxes of the anthropometric turn: that, coextensive with the human becoming harder to account for, there is a loss of narrativity in certain literary forms; yet at the same time there is also an *explosion* of narrativity, as it infiltrates more and more nonliterary forms. Modernist formal innovation meant great disfigurations could be carried out on narrative form, to maintain local structures – albeit in severely attentuated form – while grand narratives began to perish. Storymaking, consequently, could take place even with drastically reduced elements of production and the minimum requirements for narratability.

Evolutionary narratives based on natural selection show the humanist origins of this (antihumanist) tendency. They demonstrate the lengths it is possible to go to in order to produce narrative from otherwise inauspicious materials. As we saw with humanistic accounts of man's evolution, 'metaphysics must flourish' – including the metaphysics of storytelling, maintaining the myths of metaphysical man that, as it were, keep us human. 'Evolution' thus represents a concerted (and successful) attempt to give the random, blindly produced, nonhuman shape of our species development a human countenance. The concealment of this discrepancy – between the scientific facts of how natural selection actually occurs and the discourse surrounding those facts – attests to the power of narrative to compel assent. In narrativising evolution, doubt, uncertainty and contingency are assimilated by a process wherein their counterhuman qualities can be tamed, rehumanised. In other words, even as narrativity is in abeyance in literary and theoretical quarters, narrative production is a growth industry; and yet it is because of literary and theoretical reflection that, as Linda Hutcheon observes, storytelling has become a *problem* rather than a *given*.[88]

If we are, as Terry Eagleton remarks, 'creature[s] condemned to meaning',[89] then we are creatures condemned to the mechanics of meaning imposed by the scalemaking processes of narrative. And for narrative to have that particular hold over us, our anticipations and projections must inevitably conform to a certain narrativistic preunderstanding hardwired to our mental infrastructure. In the next chapter we will discern in more detail the nature of the intention–outcome discrepancy, and its opening out on to the wider question of the tendency of the human to give rise, despite itself – and in the teeth of its own stern warnings – to the inhuman.

# 2

# Conrad and technology: homo ex machina

The secret of the universe is in the existence of horizontal waves whose varied vibrations are at the bottom of all states of consciousness. If the waves were vertical the universe would be different... Therefore it follows that two universes may exist in the same place and in the same time – and not only two universes but an infinity of different universes – if by universe we mean a set of states of consciousness...

Joseph Conrad[1]

> Through the nineteenth century runs the thread of anxiety that
> man may not be man, that his relation to the world may cease to
> be a human one.
>
> Lionel Trilling[2]

The question of free will is most often posed in terms of human agency.
Are we the sum total of our heredity and surroundings, or is there some
autonomous, inner authority that steers our decisionmaking capability?
I suggest that, for the present anthropometric enquiry, the question of
whether human beings are able to behave in recognisably agential ways
or not is less critical than what actually *becomes* of action once it is performed. Intentions often do not tally with outcomes, and causes become
entangled with consequences.

Keith Tester puts this as an imposing question: 'Why is it that the
social and cultural worlds, which would not exist were it not for the actions of men and women, are experienced as almost concrete monoliths
which stand over and above individuals, shaping everything they (we)
do and think?'[3] A possible reply to this might be to say that between
the human and its efficacy on the world come its others. The relation
between human action and its consequences is not an immediate one,
i.e., human action is mediated by the other-than-human, the aleatory.
There is a certain inevitability of this process since human and inhuman
are fundamentally inseparable. Their interdependence means that the
creation of the human world gives rise to domains of the inhuman, which
in turn implies processes of dehumanisation.[4]

Trilling's remark quoted above is part of a discussion of Marx's
'Money' essay, in the third of the *Manuscripts of 1844*. We have already seen
how estranged labour (in the first of the *Manuscripts*) creates a rift between
producer and produced, a rift leading to human dispossession ('the sensuous external world . . . [becomes] . . . an alien world confronting him
in hostile opposition'.)[5] Honing his analysis of this phenomenon, the
young Marx sees the inhuman determinant intervening between human actions and the effects of those actions in the world as money.
He describes it as 'the *pimp* between need and object, between life and
man's means of life. But *that* which mediates my life also *mediates* the
existence of other men for me. It is for me the *other* person.' The sym-
biosis of human and inhuman is made explicit: 'That which exists for
me through the medium of *money*, that which I can pay for, i.e. which
money can buy, that *am I*, the possessor of the money . . . The properties of money are my, the possessor's, properties and essential powers'
(377).

Money mediates between imagination and life, between wanting and having. Everyone has demands, but without money to realise them they become withered, objectless, unreal, figments of the imagination. So money, interposed between the human and the world, becomes a powerful and inescapable impetus. It is 'the external, universal *means* and *power* – derived not from man as man and not from society as society – to turn *imagination into reality* and *reality into mere imagination*'. It becomes evident that the transformative power of money contributes to a process of dehumanisation: 'What I as a man cannot do, i.e. what all my individual powers cannot do, I can do with the help of money. Money therefore transforms each of these essential powers into something which it is not, into its *opposite*.' And morality is as powerless as perception to resist the gravitational pull of money: 'Thus characterized, money is the universal inversion of *individualities*, which it turns into their opposites and to whose qualities it attaches contradictory qualities [ . . . ] It transforms loyalty into treason, love into hate, hate into love, . . . nonsense into reason and reason into nonsense' (378–9). Money is, in short, as Trilling suggests, 'the inauthentic in human existence',[6] transforming human into inhuman, authentic into inauthentic.

Money exists because of collective human activity; it is an effect of socialisation. If it is the deep-rooted problem that Marx makes it out to be, this is because means and ends have become confused. Or, in the terms cited in the previous chapter, the unintended consequences of money (warping of human perception and moral agency) have proven to be more important than its intended consequences (expediting the circulation of goods through society). The confusion of means and ends, writes Hannah Arendt in *The Human Condition*, is intrinsic to *homo faber*. She defines *homo faber* as man the worker, the maker (particularly of tools), the proponent of a ruthless instrumentality towards the object world.[7] Because productivity and creativity are paramount, *means* are all, rather than *ends*. Everything is regarded as a means in itself, an end is only a temporary respite between means.

Bearing this in mind, Keith Tester (whose *Inhuman Condition* is both a complement and a sequel to Arendt's *The Human Condition*) concludes that the world view of *homo faber* is a thoroughly mechanistic one.[8] Like money, machine technology confuses means and ends. The power of technology as a transformative agent is paramount in the culture of modernity.[9] This power, like that of money, puts into question not just the performance but also the ultimate efficacy of human action, and suggests another paradigm of human enslavement to the inhuman. Money and technology are rejoinders to a quintessential question: can the human mind master what the human mind has made?

In this chapter the other-than-human that is the mechanical in/human comes under close and variegated scrutiny. Put crudely, if the expression 'animal human' asks what has been made of the human by nature, then 'mechanical human' asks what the human has itself made. It is the difference between the human as *consequence* (i.e., of nature) and the human as *agent* (of mechanical artefacts). Machine technology is parahuman, in the sense of its being an accompaniment to human effort. Without machines and tools, socialisation would have been impossible to achieve and maintain. Where the prehuman and the preterhuman, in the guises of nature and God, work to produce man, the parahuman is itself *produced* by man; without human design and effort, there is no machine technology to be built, only inert matter. But the terms 'animal human' and 'mechanical human' cannot remain separate for long. In the first case, animality does not define the human, without remainder (human agency provides the rest); and mechanism does not just issue from human agency, it feeds back into conditions of human possibility (human beings as partly a consequence of mechanism).

As will be shown, dialectical complexity underlies the apparently clearcut separation of agent and consequence. For much of the anthropometric era, the relationship between the human and the mechanical has been framed in terms of producer and product. The primary purpose of this chapter is to register the ways in which this division has been blurred, to elucidate the subtlety and complexity underpinning the operation of technology. The discussion is in three parts: some preliminary remarks about the nature of mechanism; the mechanical inhuman, as it is elaborated in the philosophy of Schopenhauer; and the mechanical human, in the fiction of Conrad.

The Conrad novel most associated with the name of Schopenhauer is *Victory*, whose protagonist Axel Heyst expounds thinly veiled Schopenhauerian maxims. The point of the discussion is not, however, to demonstrate the direct bearing that Schopenhauer's ideas have had on Conradian narrative. Rather, it is to show the *mediating* influence of the mechanical on each writer. This means, first, the ways in which the mechanical in/human pervades their work, and then how this motif orients Schopenhauer and Conrad within the genealogy of anthropometric thought. The novels to be discussed, *Lord Jim* and *Nostromo*, are the best equipped to perform this task.

### Rational animals, affective machines

> The world in which the *vita activa* spends itself consists of things
> produced by human activities; but the things that owe their existence
> exclusively to men nevertheless constantly condition the human
> makers.
>
> Hannah Arendt[10]

We have seen how the animal mediates between the human and the natural. If machines are nature made purposive, occupying a zone between
the worlds of man and nature, is the human therefore partly mechanical, or 'made', in the same sense that it is always partly 'animal'? Our
relationship to animal being is salient and conspicuous, in ways that our
relationship to the world of mechanism is not. The claim that human
beings are machines, therefore, 'needs a determinate interpretation if it
is to mean anything'.[11] To formulate such an interpretation, we must
first examine the nature of the machine and of mechanism.

The concept of the machine presupposes two things: some initial
agency or intervention, for the process to begin, and an absence of agency
while the mechanism performs its functions (persistent human intervention would contaminate the idea of mechanism).[12] Mary Midgley defines mechanism as 'the methodological principle of interpreting things
by regarding them as if they were machines . . . it assumes that we grasp
*completely* the aims for which the thing was designed, and have a right
to expect that *nothing will be present except* the minimum means to those
ends. This is true of machines, not of organisms.'[13] Mechanism in its
'purest' sense is based on repetitive action. Instead of teleology there
are laws based on repeatability and regularity. And since mechanism,
unlike vitalism, does not invoke essences, visibility and palpability are
also applicable. These are all commonsense, nonoccult qualities, based
on the immediacy of direct contact and the instantly graspable process
of cause and effect.

The most enduring consequence of the Mechanistic Age, as it has
been called, was the consolidation of the scientific revolution. In order to be acceptable, writes Roger Hahn, 'any new science had to
reveal the mechanism of its theories to the eye, to be grounded on
verifiable evidence, to adopt an unambiguous vocabulary for the sake
of clarity, to argue cogently (preferably employing a logically reliable
language), and to concern itself with immediate rather than distant
causes, in any case, causes that could be tested'.[14] This process has
been described as the 'mechanization of the world picture'. It is a

narrative which began with scientific methodology, leading through to technological expansion and the widespread industrialisation coterminous with modernity.[15] But what of the human actor within this sweeping narrative?

In a mechanised universe a mechanical man was an appropriate paradigm.[16] This led to a blurring of categories, the human and the mechanical becoming more and more indistinct. A situation where there is only process and 'becoming', without ends or 'being' – a condition of constant and perpetual change – prompts the question of what it means to be human.[17] One conclusion drawn is that to be human means to be at least partly mechanical. Man is thus no longer ( just) a rational animal, whose creatureliness has been sublated, but (also) an affective machine. And so the 'determinate interpretation' demanded above can, in the context of the anthropometric era, be condensed into a superposition of terms, the human as rational animal overlaid with its mechanical counterpart, affective machine.

These terms underwrite, as it were, different aspects of human self-regard. In phylogenetic terms *homo sapiens* is a primate, and the animal an ineradicable part of its natural history. For humankind to sublate its animality, as no other animal is capable of doing, is to confer authority on its anthropocentric relationship with the rest of nature. But the machine does not precede the human; it is produced by, and hence subsequent to, human activity. Affixing the term 'affective machine', then, if it does not denigrate the human as a transcendent being, at the very least stresses its parity with the created world of human endeavour, the parahuman mechanical realm in that undefined space between the human and the natural. This is not an *intended* consequence of the 'instrumentalization of the world and the adoption of a purely instrumental relationship to it',[18] but an *unintended* one.

The process of becoming an affective machine is brought about by human-mechanical convergence. Pure mechanism was identified above with a nonoccult quality, where its workings are visible, palpable and immediately graspable. When mechanism enters the world in the guise of a material artefact, however, it ceases to function in 'a mechanistic way'. The predictability and graspability of its operation give way to unpredictability and ungraspability, in its interaction with human beings and other artefacts. Function, in a word, is translated into agential capacity; to create a mechanism is to create a form of potential agency. Unintended consequences are thus inevitable, and endemic to machine performance.

The dream of technological expansion is inspired by the dream of mastery, presupposing an instrumental relationship between human beings and the products of their ingenuity. The frustration and defeat of this dream leads to the conclusion, at one end of the scale, that the universe operates on a guiding principle of chance, or fate, or chaos, a principle making all human effort ultimately futile. (The Schopenhauerian will provides a powerful example of this in the next Part.) It has been claimed that no technology has ever initiated an action not determined in advance by human volition.[19] Nevertheless, the two-way dispersion of agency endows technology with a kind of semi-autonomy, sufficient to turn intended consequences into unintended consequences. Such a dialectic signifies a 'looping effect' operating between human beings and machine technology. It is a bilateral interchange, permitting interaction in ways both discursive (as machine technology is articulated within and circulated through language) and extradiscursive (the same technology as material object, transforming the practices of everyday living). It convokes, then, a reciprocity: agential capability is spread between producer and produced, between human effort and machine performance. Each is both agent and consequence, connected in a dialectical loop of interactivity.

In the philosophical reflection of Arthur Schopenhauer, human-mechanical convergence takes the form of a metaphysical determination. But as we shall see, the 'givenness' of this determination owes a considerable amount both to the mechanistic thinking outlined above, and to the kind of dialectical exchange described by Marx in his 'Money' essay.

I SCHOPENHAUER'S BAROQUE SYMPHONY

In January 1871 an article appeared in the *Journal of Anthropology* entitled 'Schopenhauer and Darwinism', suggesting various affinities between the two thinkers. Darwin himself read it, and quoted from it approvingly in one of the last chapters of *The Descent of Man*.[20] It seems likely, however, that this late addition to the work was based not on familiarity with the Schopenhauerian system but on the article.[21] The passage quoted by Darwin refers to the primacy of the sexual impulse, as a vital factor in sexual selection. As much as Darwin, and more so than many twentieth-century humanists, Schopenhauer credits animals with considerable 'anthropic' ability. Animals do not possess only instinct and sensibility, but also understanding (which includes knowledge of cause and effect, 'the universal form of understanding')[22] and intellect. Human intellect, in comparison, is but a more advanced version of animal intellect: 'The gulf between a very intelligent animal and a man of very limited capacity is possibly not much greater than that between a blockhead and a genius.'[23] Yet there is a difference in kind between animal being and human being: only the latter has the ability to reason and conceptualise. It is these that give man his capacity for reflection, rendering him into a being capable of narrative ('He far surpasses [animals] in power and in suffering. They live in the present alone; he lives in the same time in the future and the past'; *W1* 36).

In Schopenhauerian philosophy the term rational animal does not suffice to define the human. Reason is not the primary quality of the human animal, but *will*, which constitutes 'the true inner being, the kernel, the radical element in man' (*W2* 517). In human subjectivity the will takes its most powerful form as will to live, the primal urge that makes us fear death and cling tenaciously to life. This urge undermines humanity's claims to separation from the rest of nature.[24] Schopenhauer, it is evident, amputates the soul. Animals and humans are equally soulless, for intellect is 'a mere accident of our being, . . . a function of the brain' (*W2* 201); and the brain is not 'a substance (soul), but a mere condition or state' (278).

Schopenhauer unabashedly fuses physical fact with metaphysical lexicon. Which is to say that, in order to amputate the soul, he must first establish his system on a metaphysical standing. The human embodies the condition of 'metaphysical man' only because it is thoroughly and unconditionally will-driven, and will in itself is metaphysical. But the will can be interpreted in nonmetaphysical ways, as will be shown in the final section of this part. Before exploring this antinomy, I will consider first the related areas of Schopenhauer's humanism, and the 'novelistic' aspects of his opus.

### *Humanism without the human: becoming what one is not*

Schopenhauer's conception of the human is unambiguous: '[T]he "I" is an unknown quantity, in other words it is itself a mystery and a secret. What gives unity and sequence to consciousness . . . is the *will*; it alone is unalterable and absolutely identical, and has brought forth consciousness for its own ends' (*W2* 139–40). That the will is 'unalterable and absolutely identical' is the basis of Schopenhauer's universalist view of history and homogeneous sense of cultural development:

The true history of philosophy should therefore recognize the identical in all events, of ancient as of modern times, of the East as of the West, and should see everywhere the same humanity, in spite of all difference in the special circumstances, in costume and customs. This identical element, persisting under every change, consists in the fundamental qualities of the human heart and head, many bad, few good. (*W2* 444)

This unchangeability is reflected in individual being, in a conception of selfhood which seems incompatible with moral agency. As we are fundamentally creatures of will, our characters must, necessarily, be as innate as our being in the world; there is, it would appear, no agential capacity permitting our actions to be freely chosen rather than determined in advance.

Yet if the human has been decentred by the will, Schopenhauer comes close to recentring it with his analysis of character. Egoism, malice and compassion are the three indelible components, and the third of these distinguishes human beings from animals.[25] Compassion is intrinsic to Schopenhauer's theory of impersonality, which is imbricated in his metaphysics, considered in the next section. Nevertheless, as we shall see in the final section of this part, it is the mechanical *in*human that is closest to the heart of the Schopenhauerian system.

I have defined the anthropometric mode of 'humanism without the human' as ethics without metaphysics. Schopenhauer's ethics are 'practical metaphysics',[26] and are counterposed to the Kantian ethical tradition. For Kant human beings are bonded to duty and responsibility, since they possess an essence of rationality at their cores. It is within the human, therefore, that metaphysics is located. Schopenhauer, by contrast, locates metaphysics in the noumenal will, which takes empirical form in all matter, animate and inanimate; his ethical system is thus based not on the human but on the *in*human. The will is the source of all striving and competition, all warring and bloodshed in short, of all malignancy in the world. The human is an excrescence of the will, and possesses no special metaphysical quality to separate it from the rest of the phenomenal world. Because all matter is a phenomenal manifestation of the noumenal will, either *everything* in the empirical world is metaphysically 'special', which would be incoherent, or *nothing* is. Ethics, therefore, cannot be based on a metaphysical essence that is unique to the human. Ethics without metaphysics thus means, in full, ethics without the metaphysical particularity making the human uniquely different from the rest of existence. It is ultimately of greater import, for the anthropometric tradition, that Schopenhauer amputates the soul than that he constructs an overwhelming metaphysical armoury in which to do it.

Schopenhauer's humanism without the human can be seen most starkly when set against Nietzschean ethics. The latter extols the superiority of the strong individual – the reanimalised, denarrativised transvaluator of values. This figure is on the side of life, or what the Kantian–Schopenhauerian tradition would designate the 'phenomenal world' as opposed to the 'noumenal', but which Nietzsche considered a pointless nominalism. As he declared, in *Human, All Too Human*:

It is true, there might be a metaphysical world; one can hardly dispute the absolute possibility of it . . . but we cannot begin to do anything with it, let alone allow our happiness, salvation and life to depend on the spider webs of such a possibility. For there is nothing at all we could state about the metaphysical world except its differentness, a differentness inaccessible and incomprehensible to us. It would be a thing with negative qualities.

In another blow against the idealist tradition, Nietzsche declares: 'No matter how well proven the existence of such a world might be, it would still hold true that the knowledge of it would be the most inconsequential of all knowledge.'[27]

Further divisions become evident when attempting to extract a coherent ethical programme from Nietzsche's writings, a task as frustrating as it is disquieting. It points towards another of Schopenhauer's character components, i.e., an ethics of egoism. Nietzsche is unambiguous on this point in *Ecce Homo*: 'that which is most profoundly necessary for prosperity' is '*strict* selfishness'; while its opposite, the 'morality of unselfing . . . *denies* the very foundations of life.'[28] Schopenhauerian values, even in the absence of the human, are infinitely more humane. His ethics of compassion valorises saintly behaviour, selflessness, denial, asceticism and austerity – the very things that Nietzsche blamed for the modern malaise, for the Western descent into 'nihilism'. The ethical gap between Schopenhauer and Nietzsche is most clearly apparent in a phrase from the concluding book of the second volume. To attain human bliss, writes Schopenhauer, it is necessary 'for a fundamental change to occur in man himself, and hence for him to be no longer what he is, but rather to become what he is not' (*W2* 492). This is in contradistinction to Nietzsche's dictum that one must become what one is. If what we are is *will*, reasons Schopenhauer, then self-denial is the only ethical path to follow. Unwilling the will is the basis of Schopenhauerian ethics. We shall now see the means whereby this is to be attained.

*Schopenhauer as novelist: a symphonic world-poem*

The very thing that has hindered the *philosophical* appeal of *The World as Will and Representation* over the past half-century – its overpowering metaphysical edifice – may well have sustained its *aesthetic* appeal in the earlier period. The work exudes the dramatic power and structure of a well-made novel. Its cogent, four-part design has been described alternately as a 'world-poem' and a 'symphony in four movements'.[29] The aesthetic shape of these 'movements' – the world as, first, phenomenal representation, and then its noumenal substratum, followed by considerations of aesthetic contemplation as regenerative, and ethics as practical metaphysics – alone goes some way towards justifying the standard claim that 'there have been few philosophers who have equalled Schopenhauer's grasp of literary architecture and pacing, and few whose prose style is so eloquent'.[30] Part metaphysical horror story, part history of cruelty, the work is leavened by a recursive narrative voice. That voice, by turns serene, arrogant, vituperative and compassionate, also allows in some redemptive cadences in the denouement. The book has been considered as a meditation, issuing occasional invitations to the reader 'as it were, to co-meditate on his own experience of embodiment.'[31] Equally, the two-volume work can be seen to unfold like a baroque novel, leading through a labyrinth of corrosive pessimism and relentless gloom to an implacable ethical injunction.

Schopenhauer stressed the interrelatedness of the work: '[A]ll its parts have the most intimate connexion with one another. Not only does each part stand in necessary relation to that which immediately precedes it, . . . but every part of the whole work is related to every other part, and presupposes it' (*W1* 285). It is not just novelistic in its design, then, but narrativistic in its mechanics. Yet paradoxically, the key concept binding it all together, remorselessly reiterated throughout its thousand-odd pages, is defiantly *non*narratable. Though the noumenal will, we will soon see, is represented using phenomenal, mechanistic tropes, it is not containable within any scalemaking device – least of all the temporalised, cause-laden scale that is narrative. Despite this, Schopenhauer's literary influence has exceeded his philosophical influence. Writers have been the most numerous of his creative scions, nearly all of them novelists. In the nineteenth century Tolstoy, Turgenev, Zola, Maupassant and Hardy came under his spell. In the twentieth century Conrad, Proust, Mann, Lawrence, Pirandello, Borges and Beckett also succumbed. This latter group comprises a select rollcall of authors of European modernist (and early postmodernist) fiction.

Mark Wollaeger attributes Schopenhauer's modernist appeal to the 'Janus-faced nature' of his idealism, which looks back to the neoclassical identification of nature with reason, and forward to the modernist understanding of meaning as a purely human construct:

Transposing the literary to the philosophical, we may say that Schopenhauer posits, *avant la lettre*, T. S. Eliot's 'immense panorama of futility and anarchy' as noumenal reality, and he anticipates the modernist quest for systems of order by making the phenomenal world available to the individual consciousness as an ordered whole. The illusory coherence of phenomena thus takes on something like the contingent status of the artistic reordering of reality in high modernism.[32]

Perhaps a large measure of his attractiveness – for the modernist pantheon listed above, in particular – is the collocation of a resistance to narrative, in the theory of the will, and the novelistic structure whereby it is explicated. In similar fashion, literary modernism's desire for discontinuity within continuity was a key strategy for disabling narrative. Schopenhauer's own declamations on the novel anticipate this: 'The task of the novelist is not to narrate great events, but to make interesting those that are trifling. A *novel* will be of a loftier and nobler nature the more of *inner* and the less of *outer* life it portrays.'[33] Clearly intended to privilege will over representation, this remark anticipates modernist attempts to track the movement of consciousness and explicate the mundane.

It is the mechanistic aspect of will (the subject of the next section) that Schopenhauer seeks to countermand, so that the will's serene oneness might be recognised. He does this through impersonality, bringing it vividly to life not only as an aesthetic ideal (which it also becomes in literary modernism) but as an ethical imperative. Impersonality is, in effect, a kind of 'cure' for subjectivity – which, as the chief promoter of chaos and conflict in the world, must be extirpated. Individual being is equated with blindness to the will-laden substratum, hence blindness to the wretched acts that will-bound individuals are driven to do. Distanced from individuation and personality, there is oneness and selflessness, the oneness of will. Recognition of this underlying singularity is what leads to practical reason and ethical agency. The incoherences of these animadversions need not be laboured. Perhaps most obviously, there is an apparent 'split' in the will itself. How can retreat from the plurality of phenomena into the realisation that we are all one, all will, bring quietude, when the will is blind, purposeless, the source of all malignancy?

It suggests that the will itself is divisible, into a calm and a chaotic side, yet Schopenhauer's entire system is predicated on will's oneness.

Resolving such paradoxes is not essential to understanding Schopenhauer's humanism without the human. The essential points are that objectivity is the basis of aesthetic genius and ethical agency, and that it is founded on a denial of personality in favour of impersonality. This can be translated as disinterestedness in art and selflessness in ethics. Schopenhauer's cultural pessimism and endless declamations of the narrativeless will, in tandem with the architecture of the novel, can be seen as exemplifying for the sceptical, suspicious modernist literary sensibility, if not the impossibility of the novel form, then at least the uncertainty of its status as a literary artefact. In short, if Hegel is the most narrativistic of philosophers, Schopenhauer is surely the most novelistic. This has particular pertinence for those writers whose transformations of the novel form enact, in various ways and to differing degrees, the newer understanding of the human inaugurated by Schopenhauer.

### *The mechanical inhuman*

Cues from Schopenhauer's biography point to certain nonmetaphysical aspects in his philosophy of the will. One such cue is his financial independence. Though frugal and meticulous in fiscal matters, his fearful disposition and deep-seated mistrust of others brought on compulsive tendencies: 'His valuables were hidden in the strangest places, he even labelled them with deceptive names to avert the suspicion of thieves . . . He hid bonds among old letters, and gold under his inkstand.'[34] Leaving aside the fact that money is a human creation, its transformative power over perception and morality, and its operation as a machine for making desire, suggest parallels with the noumenal will. Writing a generation before Marx, Schopenhauer hints at the later phenomenon of market capitalism, but in a global, universal (rather than national) context. Considered in this way, the will resembles the free market – capricious, self-regulating and uncontrollable by individuals, whose social being is shaped by it. Some of Schopenhauer's pithiest aphorisms describe the will's virulence in economic terms. Life, he writes, 'is a constant suffering . . . a business that does not cover the cost' (*W2* 239), and 'the world on all sides is bankrupt' (574.) In a similar vein, 'our life is primarily like a payment made to us in nothing but copper coins, for which we must then give a receipt; the coins are the days, and the receipt is death' (574). Human existence, in short, is not a gift but a debt:

The calling in of this debt appears in the shape of the urgent needs, tormenting desires, and endless misery brought about through that existence. As a rule, the whole lifetime is used for paying off that debt, yet in this way only the interest has been cleared off. Repayment of the capital takes place through death. And when was this debt contracted? At the begetting. (*W2* 580)

Such remarks suggest analogies with Marx's 'Money' essay. Identifying human with inhuman, individual with capital, Marx enquires: 'I am *mindless*, but if money is the *true mind* of all things, how can its owner be mindless?' Money, like will, inculcates blind, irrational wanting, an appetite that can only ever be temporarily sated. Money 'ties me to *human* life' and 'links me to nature and to man'. Concluding that it is 'the true *agent of separation* and the true *cementing agent*' (*EPM* 377), Marx invokes the dialectic of competition and cooperation, which is also a driving force in Conrad's *Nostromo*, discussed in the next Part.

Schopenhauer's contingent personal traits converge with the intellectual background out of which he emerges. Inside the tradition of evolutionary thought, Schopenhauer has been seen as a vitalist, hence at odds with the mechanical biology of Darwin and the so-called mechanistic cosmogony of Herbert Spencer.[35] On closer examination, however, the coordinates of Schopenhauer's thought reveal a different orientation, the desire to become a sort of metaphysical Newton, pressing further into the noumenon to explore and elucidate what Kant was unable (or unwilling) to embrace. Which is to say that, if Cartesian philosophy and Newtonian physics engendered a mechanical model of the physical universe, Schopenhauer conceived of *meta*physical reality as mechanistic.

The mechanisation of the world picture, we saw earlier, grew out of the scientific revolution and its consolidation in technological development. The success of Newtonian mechanics meant that this world picture infiltrated Enlightenment thought and its understanding of the workings of human society. Schopenhauer, writing first in the 1810s and then in the 1840s, inherited from this mindset one particularly revealing trope. Proving that 'this world's non-existence is just as possible as its existence', he writes of 'the balance wheel which maintains in the watch of metaphysics that never runs down' (*W2* 171). The world, too, can be described in the same manner: '[T]he course of the world is like that of a clock after it has been put together and wound up; hence, from this undeniable point of view, it is a mere machine, whose purpose we do not see' (319). The will to live also complies with this conceit: 'Therefore I have said that those puppets are not pulled from outside, but that each of them bears in itself the clockwork from which its movements result.' This 'clockwork' that is the will to live manifests itself 'as an untiring mechanism, as an irrational impulse, which does not have its sufficient ground or reason in the external world' (358).

Seeking ways to describe the will as *will*, Schopenhauer can only describe it as *representation* – as mercantilism, and as 'untiring mechanism', in the form of watches and clocks. There is an underlying significance to timepieces, those paragons of precision. William Paley, writing at the turn of the nineteenth century, singled out the watch as an example of 'contrivance', of a human design that could not be produced by nature. When a watch is wound up, it 'establishes to the observer two conclusions: one; that thought, contrivance, and design, have been employed in the forming, proportioning, and arranging of its parts; . . . the other; that force or power, distinct from mechanism, is, at this present time, acting upon it'.[36] The watch establishes not just design but a designer, or operator. It is a metonymy of human presence, an emblem of human ingenuity, compact and commodious. To possess a watch is to have a summit of scientific engineering in one's pocket, a portable symbol of anthropocentric achievement. More notably, it is to have at one's disposal an instrument for humanising and personalising time.[37]

Schopenhauer both evacuates time (since the will is atemporal) and strips the machine of its humanist associations of anthroponomical accomplishment. Experiencing the sublime, through aesthetic contemplation, becalms the will. Beneath our phenomenal, individualised existence, all is seen as undifferentiated. This is the basis of Schopenhauer's ethical entreaty, as we have seen, and the starting point for impersonality. But does the will *itself* possess sublimity? Kant states that it is 'in its chaos that nature most arouses our ideas of the sublime, or in its wildest and most ruleless disarray and devastation'.[38] The Schopenhauerian will is as wild and ruleless a force of nature as could be imagined. In which case, Schopenhauer's mechanistic tropes seem singularly inappropriate. In consolidating the will's specifications, Schopenhauer is striving to represent the inhuman sublime, and the nearest he can get is to show it incarnated as 'untiring mechanism'.

Yet the watch-clock motif *is* sublime, in that it evokes a differential. The world, or the individual's life, is 'the momentary intermezzo of an ephemeral existence' (*W2* 466), just 'an ephemeral life-dream' (467). Like all phenomena, it is temporary and provisional, teetering on the edge of the abyss. Watches and clocks, of course, are a part of this, too. They run down and need rewinding, and, eventually, they wear out. Translating this into noumenal terms yields a 'sublime mechanism', something that never runs down, that maintains and reproduces itself, and defies phenomenal laws of decay and entropy: 'Every time a man is begotten and born the clock of human life is wound up anew, to repeat once more its same old tune that has already been played innumerable times, movement by movement and measure by measure, with insignificant variations' (*W1* 322).

Schopenhauer's mechanistic will is thus an image of sublime horror. The will's sublimity is depicted first with a recognisable trope (phenomenal mechanism), and then a transgression of it (an eternity machine). By transplanting the watch motif – symbol of anthropocentrism – into the noumenal, Schopenhauer decentres *homo sapiens* more thoroughly and damagingly, transforming human glory into inhuman horror. As a model of the mechanical inhuman, the Schopenhauerian will is unsurpassable: sublime, scaleless and alien in its otherness, and terrifying in its infinite, immeasureable oneness.

To the extent that Schopenhauer does not imbue the human with any particular essence that might demarcate it from the rest of nature (thereby separating the term 'rational animal' from its axiological force, its self-licensing anthropocentrism), is the rival term 'affective machine' any more applicable? Human beings are programmed at birth with different amounts of malice, egoism and compassion. Life, whose significance is ethical, can be inhabited by man only to the extent that he adopts the third of these traits, and the one least common. And yet, what is Schopenhauerian impersonality but a summons to become more machinelike? There is no alternative, since selfhood has been dissociated from the sense of the free will that is the only effective countermeasure in a mechanical universe. To the contrary, selfhood, as a phenomenal deposit of the noumenal will, is already determined, already mechanised. But the solution – selflessness or impersonality – has unavoidable associations with mechanistic process.

Machines are self-regulating, predictable and most of all *impersonal* constructs. Schopenhauer's ethics of compassion is thus counsel for the human to become a subvariant of an affective machine, a 'compassionate machine'. In the light of Trilling's epigraph, then, man's relation to the world *must* cease to be a human one, since the human is symptomatic of the problem: it is an empty space, a will-shaped hole in the cosmos, filled with blind and unconscious wanting. The sole ethical route is to conjoin man's potential for compassion with his mechanised condition, to become what one is not, i.e., a compassionate machine. Only thus can the sway of the mechanical inhuman operating as the noumenal will be countermanded.

## II CONRAD'S ACCIDENTAL TRAGEDIES

> Conrad was able to see his narratives as the place in which the motivated, the occasional, the methodical, and the rational are brought together with the aleatory, the unpredictable, the inexplicable. On the one hand, there are conditions presented by which a story's telling becomes necessary; on the other hand, the essential story itself seems opposite to the conditions of its telling.
>
> Edward Said[39]

We have seen how literary modernism makes progressively more extreme attempts to disrupt narrative mechanics and break free of the categories, to release voice from its formal constraints. Mark Wollaeger points out that in Conrad's novels 'explicit discourse *on* skepticism is subsumed by an encompassing discourse *of* skepticism . . . far from constituting a particular conceptual arena, skepticism is engaged in a sustained interrogation of the very categories that permit rational discussion to begin'.[40] Conrad's discourse of scepticism emerges through the combination of generic extremes. On the one hand, his works use the machinelike structures of nineteenth-century adventure fiction, which, as a genre, is deeply implicated in the imperial cause, and hence must not allow the narrative's voice to distract from the tempo of its rhythmic thrust, its resolute haste towards a heroically satisfying denouement. On the other hand, there is the meditative timbre of existential introspection, which is often bleakly misanthropic rather than heroic, and digressive where the generic adventure elements are 'progressive', in both senses of the term: steering the narrative to confident completion, while exuding a faith in the noble powers of Victorian ideology and machine technology.[41]

Conrad was no naive apologist for British expansionism. Equivocation is apparent in his fiction, in its resistance to the traditional assumptions of the adventure genre, which demanded a kind of trade-off. Andrea White remarks: 'Choosing to write from within the fiction that had traditionally celebrated an unqualified kind of heroism, Conrad achieved a critical irony but also announced his own regret that the dream of pure, disinterested adventure was no longer possible.'[42] It is my contention that the anthropometric difficulties bequeathed by Schopenhauerian philosophy and Darwinian naturalism were decisive factors in disrupting Conrad's dream of pure adventure. Conrad had almost certainly read the travelogues of Wallace and Darwin, and at such a time that he cannot but have been aware of the basic theory supporting these texts.[43] And John Galsworthy, in his 1924 memoir, recalls: 'Schopenhauer used to give [Conrad] satisfaction twenty years and more ago.'[44] (Aside from this, as Yves Hervouet contends, Conrad 'must have absorbed many of [Schopenhauer's] ideas via Maupassant and Anatole France, who were both strongly influenced by Schopenhauer'.)[45]

Though both were 'connoisseurs of futility',[46] Conrad did not, unlike Schopenhauer, see human nature as changeless and atemporal. Egoism and malevolence abound, as Schopenhauer reported, but Conrad never granted them the same universal, ineluctable status. Human character, he believed, was changeable, not stamped indelibly from birth. Conrad's ethics were more Kantian than Schopenhauerian, 'based on the principles of responsibility, duty, and solidarity – not on compassion, against which he lashed out in *The Nigger*'.[47] In contrast to Schopenhauer's cosmic will, the mechanical inhuman in Conradian texts takes various forms: the knitting machine of the famous letter; its fictional counterpart in *Lord Jim*, Stein's Kosmos machine (contemporaneous with the letter); and the more dialectical example, in *Nostromo*, of the mechanical aura exuded by the San Tomé mine.

> There is – let us say – a machine. It evolved itself (I am severely scientific) out of chaos of scraps of iron and behold! – it knits . . . And the most withering thought is that the infamous thing has made itself; made itself without thought, without conscience, without foresight, without eyes, without heart. It is a tragic accident – and it has happened. You can't interfere with it . . . It knits us in and it knits us out. It has knitted time space, pain, death, corruption, despair and all the illusions – and nothing matters.
>
> Joseph Conrad[48]

This letter of 1897 is perhaps Conrad's most direct comment on the mechanical in/human. Written while he was beginning work on *Lord Jim*, it makes explicit what is suggested in various instances in *The World as Will and Representation*: that the primal force of existence, the cosmic will, is a variant of the mechanistic model of the universe that predominated during the eighteenth century.

The frame-knitting machine dates back to the Elizabethans. The simple technique it employs – a combination of movable hooks and fixed hooks, the former passing in and out of the latter to form stitches – is fundamental to all types of knitting machines.[49] The prototype was therefore 300 years old by the time Conrad wrote his famous letter. The other noteworthy aspect of this machine is its ambiguous conflation of the domestic and the industrial. On the one hand, the Elizabethan proto-type helped establish the machine-knitting industry, which still thrives today in many parts of the world.[50] On the other, the practice of knit-ting in Conrad's day (as often still today) could be regarded as homely and feminine. This antinomical combination evokes the Schopenhauer-ian will, a ridiculous counterpart, as it were, to Schopenhauer's sublime mechanism. Yet Conrad's alignment of domestic comfort with industrial-scale impersonality is effective. Like Schopenhauer, he depersonalises more thoroughly by evoking, then withholding, and finally undermining, the possibility of anthropocentric security, of human self-satisfaction. If the watch is a symbol of anthroponomic achievement, a mechanical marvel for organising human existence, the knitting machine is an im-plicit riposte. It takes instrumental creativity out of human hands and mechanises it completely. Conrad takes this a step further: human cre-ativity, become mechanical, is then made to produce the producer. The possibility of a human–technological dialectic thus begins to take shape.

It should be remembered that the knitting-machine conceit is ex-pounded in a letter, rather than an essay or a work of fiction. Aware of Conrad's propensity for self-dramatisation, Allan Hunter opines that Conrad 'seized upon a readily available cliché' and that he 'is actually using it ironically': 'By the time Conrad writes of the knitting machine he is involved in far more complex discussions of man's nature than these easy visions of despair. He had begun to explore evolutionary thought in order to understand the mechanism, rather than lament its workings.'[51] George Levine, conversely, sees the letter as genuinely melancholic, and not unrelated to the oeuvre: '[T]he question of the materialist reading of nature, the determinist insistence on scientific law and cause and effect, are starting points for the imagination.'[52] Edward Said, too, in his study of Conrad's fiction, devotes a chapter to 'Character and the Knitting Machine', characterising the latter as 'a weird mixture of grotesque hu-mor and piteous self-commentary.'[53]

As an aetiological conceit to account for the mechanical in/human, the knitting machine is desolating, yet nebulous. It assumes, on the one hand, a gap between the human and the mechanical that cannot be crossed. And yet, at the same time, it insists that there is no gap; ma-chine, matter made purposive, has given birth to mind. We are not just influenced or quickened by technology, suggests Conrad's image, we are in some sense produced by it. If the image is a little risible, as Hunter sug-gests, it also lends credence to Levine's impression that it is a first draft, so to speak, of later Conradian explorations. Existence as a 'tragic accident', the torments of consciousness, and the paralysing effects of 'futility' can be quarried from the letter and placed alongside later efforts.

Conradian resonances can be detected in Mark Seltzer's *Bodies and Machines*, an exploration of the human-mechanical interface in what he calls 'machine culture'. This refers to the technological complex on to which those discourses of coordination and control – realist and naturalist texts – serve to map the human body. Considering the period from the mid-nineteenth through to the early twentieth century, Seltzer identifies a 'biomechanics of personation', citing as literary evidence Eliot's *Daniel Deronda* and Wharton's *The House of Mirth*.[54] Automatistic behaviour claims the central characters of both novels and, crucially, their capitulation is made apparent through scenes involving reckless gambling. Reiterating Marx's alignment of money with compulsive behaviour, a similar phenomenon is at the heart of Conrad's *Nostromo*, as we shall see, where characters become 'mechanised' through the insidious power of the San Tomé mine.

Crucial to the mapping of the body on to machine culture is the realist tendency towards 'compulsory and compulsive visibility', the first step towards making everything 'visible, legible, and governable'.[55] Though *Lord Jim* (like *Nostromo*) is neither purely realist nor naturalist, it recognises the importance of visibility, through the interplay of light and darkness, and the philosophical ramifications of this trope. Seltzer's perorations on machine culture depart from the two novels, however, in his contention that the realist text is driven by the urge to exteriorise what is conventionally interior – or what amounts to an extreme form of surveillance, a way of 'turning the body inside-out for inspection'.[56] Conrad's obsessed characters, conversely, become automata by a fervent *interiorisation* of external reality. Their subjectivity is hollowed out, and the chaos of inner division and conflict filled with the remorseless logic of monomania. Just as Conrad's novels appropriate elements from adventure fiction and align them with philosophical reflection, they both validate the workings of machine culture and go beyond it, demonstrating the interactive nature of human-mechanical convergence that has come to characterise twentieth-century technology.

## Lord Jim: *disturbing the kosmos*

Conrad's seafaring narratives evoke the dialectic of alienation and wonder, discussed in Chapter 1. These tales, as Frederick Karl has noted, convey the primal experience of Conrad's years at sea, 'when man's disproportion in terms of waves, sky, and horizon becomes apparent':

For all those years, Conrad had lived within a different scale of reference from that associated with land and urban values. Man was miniaturized when measured against the elements or the scale of the ship — whether crawling on spars, wrestling with huge sails, or being tossed about by wind and waves. He could only achieve size and scale by blending with other men; in the mass, on board ship, a man could gain a more harmonious relationship with nature, although the basic disproportion remained.[57]

In *Lord Jim* the 'basic disproportion' between the human and the natural is implied through meditation on light and its properties. In a sardonic aside Marlow brings the natural splendour of light back to the level of the human, to foreground the latter's venality: 'There were very few places in the Archipelago [Stein] had not seen in the original dusk of their being, before light (and even electric light) had been carried into them for the sake of better morality and – and – well – the greater profit too.'[58] Light is thus equated with the morality and progress found in adventure fiction; with the 'enlightening' influence of Western imperialism, of thinly disguised financial interest. Human-produced light, or enlightenment, is no more reassuring than its natural counterpart.

But if natural light is oppressive, its absence is no more comforting. Marlow situates Jim early on as follows: 'at his back was the dark night with the clear stars, whose distant glitter disposed in retreating planes lured the eye into the depths of a greater darkness' (137). During a bout of letter-writing, Marlow pauses to observe that the 'massive shadows, cast all one way from the straight flame of the candle seemed possessed of gloomy consciousness' (169). Not long after this there is a crisis:

An abrupt heavy rumble made me lift my head. The noise seemed to roll away, and suddenly a searching and violent glare fell on the blind face of the night . . . At the moment of greatest brilliance the darkness leapt back with a culminating crash, and he vanished before my dazzled eyes as utterly as though he had been blown to atoms. (173)

Light and dark conspire to unsettle the human, alternating between alienation and wonder.

The two possibilities reappear in a philosophical discussion based on the machine motif. Stein, the naturalist, declaims to Marlow:

'Marvellous!' he repeated, looking up at me. 'Look! The beauty – but that is nothing – look at the accuracy, the harmony. And so fragile! And so strong!

And so exact! This is Nature – the balance of colossal forces. Every star is so – and every blade of grass stands *so* – and the mighty Kosmos in perfect equilibrium produces – this. This wonder; this masterpiece of Nature – the great artist.' (195)

Accuracy, harmony, balance, equilibrium: this celebration of precision and order is the language of the *philosophes*, derived from Newtonian physics and translated into neoclassical aesthetics. Alienation is refigured into wonder: the knitting machine, that 'most withering thought', which means that 'nothing matters', becomes for Stein's entrepreneurial mind the 'marvellous' Kosmos machine. But accommodating the human in this paragon of order is no easy task. 'Man is amazing,' declares Stein, 'but he is not a masterpiece':

'Sometimes it seems to me that man has come where he is not wanted, where there is no place for him; for if not, why should he want all the place? Why should he run about here and there making a great noise about himself, talking about the stars, disturbing the blades of grass?' (195)

Stein's view of nature as a precise mechanism precludes the presence of the human; man's imperfections render him unfit to find a place among the products of the marvellous. For Stein the Kosmos machine is the given, the centre of perfection, and man can only be an intruder – or a kind of excrescence. 'Blades of grass' are markers of difference, their pristine perfection contrasted with man's frail imperfection.

What the Kosmos machine occasions in discursive, philosophical terms, the work's action presents performatively, as a narrative configuration: a powerful sense of human dislocation, conveyed through formal ordering rather than exposition. The central action organising (or fracturing) the narrative is Jim's jump from the sinking *Patna*. The mysteries surrounding this act defy easy analysis; cowardice, instinct or confusion, they refuse to stay fixed, shading over into that existentialist trope par excellence, the *acte gratuit*.[59] *Lord Jim*'s narrative techniques are manifold: 'the use of a highly individualised frame narrator, chronological dislocations, impressionistic devices, ironic juxtapositions, thematic oppositions, and delayed decoding, to name but the most obvious'.[60] As a consequence of these virtuoso techniques, Jim is located both at the edges of the novel and at its centre, a spectral background presence and a dominant foreground figure.[61] Delayed decoding is particularly pertinent, demonstrating how the separation of cause and effect in narrativistic succession has philosophical resonances. Even when the causal connection is decoded, the damage, as it were, has already been done; the efficacy of an action still cannot be entirely accounted for. By breaking up narrative totality, the unifying clench of causality and consequence, Conrad stresses the temporal difference that is potentially divisive, perhaps permanently so.

Thus Jim's recurrent jumps (resisted on the training-ship, performed on the *Patna* and in the stockade in Patusan) are echoed in the narrative's 'jumps', its temporal leaps to and fro. And just as Jim's leaping is not fully explicable, not entirely satisfactory in terms of his character as it has been presented, neither is the narrative process encompassing these sudden temporal jumps made entirely coherent. Indeed, Conrad's novels 'are for the most part heavily framed and discontinuous, so much so that many critics have decided that chronology is not recoverable'.[62] There is a gap where meaning escapes, as the *Patna* jump itself confounds meaning by offering a plurality of possibilities. At the centre and the periphery of the shifting story planes, the abrupt narrative displacements, Jim attempts to transform himself, to prove he is not the coward who jumped ship.

This leads to a double bifurcation. Jim's self-image as a Romantic hero, enacting deeds of heroic achievement, is severed from his actual performance on the sinking *Patna*; and with the latter event, 'plot construction has been ripped apart at the seams. As a result, that plot spends the rest of the novel wanting to be re-stitched, and Marlow becomes a kind of narrative seamster, helping to sew the hero back into what is left of the fabric of the story.'[63] But reality's dense unknowability – the intractability of 'facts' – is just as applicable to Jim's own psyche. He is a victim of the gap between intended and unintended consequences of action, failing to recognise (like Stein) the power of contingency in overcoming human intentions; he assimilates the contingent to what is knowable and predictable, and in the process brings the inhuman on to the same level as the human.[64]

Jim's failed self-transformation indicates a gap between his self-understanding and his selfhood – an ontic-ontological gap, one might say, in anticipation of the Heideggerian terms to come. This is why the novel cannot function as a *Bildungsroman*, whose efficacy depends on something *happening* in this gap – the gaining of experience and/or education, knowledge of the world and its ways, or just some place for the self to occupy.[65] *Lord Jim* reveals this gap as something mysterious and unfathomable. In *Nostromo* the same anthroponomical space is also mysterious but is given, as it were, a name: mechanomorphism, the end result of human-mechanical interactivity.

Nostromo: *material interests and mechanomorphism*

> [P]aleotechnic industry rested on the mine . . . From the mine came
> the steam pump and presently the steam engine: ultimately the
> steam locomotive and so, by derivation, the steamboat . . . The rail-
> road likewise came directly from the mine.
>
> Lewis Mumford[66]

Just as mechanism entails replication of process, obsession brings about replication of compulsion. The mechanism of obsession, a self-perpetuating enslavement, propels the narrative of *Nostromo*, one of Conrad's grimmest works. Revenge is the novel's driving force – the transformative power of human into inhuman, one face in a multifaceted display of obsession. And as the narrative unfolds, it moves towards a more interactive presentation of machine technology than the examples given by Marx and Schopenhauer.

The silver mine is the motif connecting the actions of the principal characters and determining their lives. Less central, though still pervasive, is the railway, whose development takes place in tandem with the excavation of the mine. Mine and railway, considered together, point in different directions. They gesture outwards to the wider political theme of American and British economic imperialism (development of the mine is dependent on the American Holroyd's money, just as the railway depends on the financial support of the Briton Sir John); and inwards to the psychological landscape of the three central characters most affected by both developments. The cartography of the latter theme describes a series of metamorphoses, the transformation of man into machine. The narrative conveying this demonstrates an acute understanding of the process of mechanomorphism – a process anticipated above by Marx, in his description of the effects of money as transformative of human into inhuman.

Conrad's principal characters are all obsessed, in one way or another, with the mine and its spoils, the silver bullion. The chief victims are Charles Gould, the owner of the mine; Colonel Sotillo, the politician-dictator; and the Capataz de Cargadores, Nostromo himself. Gould is the first to succumb to the mine's metamorphic power. Even before the smuggling out of the silver that galvanises the rest of Costaguana, we learn that '[Gould's] imagination had been permanently affected by the one great fact of a silver mine'.[67] His fixation on the mine is refracted through the agonised awareness of his wife, who 'watched his abstraction with dread': 'Charles Gould's fits of abstraction depicted the energetic concentration of a will haunted by a fixed idea. A man haunted by a fixed idea is insane. He is dangerous even if that idea is an idea of justice; for may he not bring the heaven down pitilessly upon a loved head?' (322). Gould's enslavement is swift, documented in a couple of brisk strokes: 'The mine had got hold of Charles Gould with a grip as deadly as ever it had laid upon his father' (338); 'The Gould concession could not be resumed. His father had not desired it. The son would never surrender it. He would never surrender it alive' (340). Man-into-machine might therefore be a biological condition, passed down from father to son; Gould does not choose his obsession, he is merely the carrier of a recessive gene. His transformation is complete when he presents his demands for the future of the mine to 'His Excellency', Pedrita Montero: 'That stony fiend of a man who said all these things (which were accessible to His Excellency's intelligence) in a cold-blooded manner which made one shudder' (341).

Sotillo's obsession, in contrast, seems more direct and straightforward, and manifests itself as heat rather than cold: 'The only guiding motive of his life was to get money for the satisfaction of his expensive tastes, which he indulged recklessly, having no self-control. He imagined himself a master of intrigue, but his corruption was as simple as an animal instinct. At times, in solitude, he had his moments of ferocity . . .' (249–50). Once in pursuit of the silver, these 'moments of ferocity' escalate into fits of raving and cursing (402–3). Sotillo is unhampered by the abstract idea of the mine and the weight of precedent (Gould senior) that burdens Gould. But his obsession with the silver is no less fraught, a creature of wild physicality in contrast to Gould's cold, indomitable, 'mechanistic' behaviour.

More complex than both Gould's disquieting genetic heritage and Sotillo's hysterical craving is Nostromo's obsession with the silver. Why does he steal it? The question dominates the last part of the book, and although the refrain 'to grow rich slowly' sounds and resounds, Nostromo's character, unlike Sotillo's, is not reducible to simple greed. In terms of the present reading, what Nostromo seeks is revenge against the San Tomé mine, 'which appeared to him hateful and immense, lording it by its vast wealth over the valour, the toil, the fidelity of the poor, over war and peace, over the labours of the town, the sea, and the campo' (417). Nostromo's attitude to the mine thus echoes Marx's sentiments towards money. He is acutely aware of its autonomous power, its capacity to turn something into its opposite – the dependable, incorruptible Capataz de Cargadores reduced to a common thief.

Gould, Sotillo and Nostromo, then, are all enslaved by the mine – Gould to an abstract idea of what the mine represents, Sotillo and Nostromo to the silver that has been extruded from it. What, then, does the mine represent?:

[The miners] were proud of, and attached to, the mine. It had secured their confidence and belief. They invested it with a protecting and invincible virtue as though it were a fetish made by their own hands, for they were ignorant, and in other respects did not differ appreciably from the rest of mankind which puts infinite trust in its own creations. (336)

The fetishisation of the mine by its 'makers' transforms it into a human construct, an example of nature made purposive, brute matter imbued with a Promethean spark. The serial capitulation of Gould, Sotillo and Nostromo recalls Marx's warning of the powerlessness of morality and perception to resist the spell of money. Nostromo, the 'slave of the San Tomé silver' (445), recognises, helplessly, 'his weary subjection to that dead thing' (446). The mine and the silver together become a kind of mechanism, a deterministic force conquering the wills of three men.

'The treasure was putting forth its latent power', we are told (417); in such moments the mine's hold over the three men comes to resemble the exigencies of the Schopenhauerian will. 'Between one man and another falls the shadow of the San Tomé mine,' writes Irving Howe, 'the symbol of the inhuman in human society.' In its inculcation of greed and avarice, it becomes a machine for manufacturing desire. 'The haze of mystery surrounding the mine, its staggering greatness of potential, tempt all who come within its radius to surrender to its power.'[68] Howe's comments lend credence to the analogy made between the will and market capitalism. He notes that when Emilia Gould experiences a vision of the mine, it is 'a vision of nothing less than capitalism itself'.[69] Conrad's acute phrasing is unequivocal:

She saw the San Tomé mountain hanging over the Campo, over the whole land, feared, hated, wealthy; more soulless than any tyrant, more pitiless and autocratic than the worst Government; ready to crush innumerable lives in the expansion of its greatness . . . she saw clearly the San Tomé mine possessing, consuming, burning up the life of the last of the Costaguana Goulds; mastering the energetic spirit of the son as it had mastered the lamentable weakness of the father. (431)

Fredric Jameson argues that these 'destructive effects of capitalism' cannot be reduced to the actions of morally reprobate businessmen. 'Rather the process is objective, and is impersonally achieved, or at least set in motion, by the penetration of a money economy and the consequent need to reorganize local institutions on a cash basis.'[70] The 'money economy' possesses its own agential momentum, subordinating human intervention to the impersonal, uncontrollable machinations of capital. The dialectical nature of the human–silvermine interaction lies in the fact that silver is a dependent currency. Its properties are not all-determining because its status as wealth is secondary, less stable and imposing than the main currency, gold.[71] Similarly, human capitulation to the silver is also not absolute, as borne out by Gould's threats to detonate the mine.

A different sort of fixation is linked metonymically with the silver. A lighthouse is built near the silver cache, and the Violas come to live there. On the night when Nostromo declares his love to Giselle, her behaviour becomes automatistic: '[Giorgio] shouted her name three times before she even moved her head. Left alone, she had become the helpless prey of astonishment. She walked into the bedroom she shared with Linda like a person profoundly asleep [ . . . ] She walked right across the room without looking at anything, and sat down at once by the open window' (448). Giselle makes explicit the parallel with the earlier obsessions: 'Your love is to me like your treasure to you. It is there, but I can never get enough of it' (450). It is an ironic echo of the mine as mechanism, as a machine for manufacturing desire. Here is its counterpart, a desire directed at Nostromo, the agent of the mine who has been transformed into a moral desperado, who enacts a desire that also – like the dehumanising craving of the will – can never be quelled.

Machine technology magnetises human obsession, and that obsession transforms its agents into compulsive, mechanistic beings. This is the command of the mine and its contents: occult mechanism, autonomous agent, desire machine, matrix of obsession. Conrad's multivalent narrative leaves behind the world of heavy industry under human governance and control, and reaches out towards a more complex understanding of the potency of technology, and of human helplessness in giving rise, despite itself, to the inhuman.

For narrative to function properly, there must be a clearcut distinction between cause and consequence (or 'means' and 'ends', as Keith Tester would say). In the mechanistic worldview the two are freely exchanged, producing an interspersion of the two. Narrative is frustrated under such conditions. Because it is voice and machine, it will always be closely allied to mechanism. But narrative is also reliant on causal links between events and consequences of events, to make temporal order and to give direction; when cause and consequence are enmeshed, therefore, the narrative machine seizes up. Human–technological interactivity, in sum, is predicated on the loss of conditions of narrativity.

*Nostromo* is a complex, polyphonic performance, combining the key concern of Marxian money (the silver's power of purchase) with an equally significant aspect of the Schopenhauerian will (a metaphysical force that mechanises human subjectivity). And just as Schopenhauer noted of the cosmic will, there can be no history or progress in the afterglow of the mine's malign aura. In the process enormous stress is brought to bear on narrative development. Allan Hunter refers to the 'circular and self-thwarting narrative of *Nostromo*', how it 'seems to deny the very idea of progression and history'.[72] The word 'progression' is an apt one, as applicable to the movement of narrative as to the Western myth of historical ascendance. Conrad's scepticism regarding the latter is declared early on in the book: a row of telegraph poles, emblematic of Western technological intervention, scores the horizon 'like a slender, vibrating feeler of that progress waiting outside for a moment of peace to enter and twine itself about the weary heart of the land' (166). There is potential malignancy lurking in the shadows of Western achievement.

Since there is no progression from one event to another, nothing appears to be achieved; Costaguana's future, it is suggested at the end, will be almost identical to its past.[73] Jocelyn Baines sums up *Nostromo* as 'perhaps the most impressive monument to futility ever created'.[74] (Readers of Schopenhauer's *The World as Will* might care to dispute that.) Metaphysical significance has been seen in this antiprogressive narrative shape, with its conception of history as a perpetual cycle where human situations are repeated *ad infinitum*.[75] As narrative history, this looping effect echoes the plot's development. The concern with 'revolution' describes the novel's circular form, as much as it does the details of the plot.[76]

Such repetition is the other side of Nietzschean eternal recurrence: rather than bringing individuals closer to life, *Nostromo*'s narrative cycle serves to alienate them from it. Hence, in Said's bleak phrase, '*Nostromo*'s bias for connecting individuals to history, and history to the cruel designs of life'.[77] Said extrapolates further, mapping the effects of the San Tomé mine back on to the concept of the knitting machine: 'Man is never the author, never the beginning, of what he does, no matter how willfully intended his program may be . . . Authority, [the knitting-machine concept] asserts, permanently resides outside man.'[78] Yet the point of the mine is that it *is* begun by human hands; man is the author of his acts, but not the controller of them. The ambiguous situation that results is the dialectical consequence of human-technological convergence. If authority resides outside man, it just as surely resides outside machine; it is in the convergence of the two that agency (or authority) is produced. The knitting machine is therefore a cruder and less nuanced means of understanding the mechanical in/human than the mine and its issue.

Conrad's model of interactivity is not, of course, without precedent. In Samuel Butler's *Erewhon* the narrator anticipates Arendt's remark above about the *vita activa*, by declaiming that 'it is the machines which act upon man and make him man, as much as man has acted upon and made the machines'.[79] Conrad's achievement, however, is in not presenting this discursively but in staging it in ostensibly narrative form. I say ostensibly because – and this is Conrad's other great achievement – the process of presenting human-mechanical convergence is a defiantly *non*narratable one. He senses the inevitable loss of narrativity that comes with compulsive human–technological interactivity. And in the process the mechanomorphised human agents are brought sharply into focus, implicated in the web of agential dispersion encompassing both them and their parahuman productions.

### FALLING INTO CONSCIOUSNESS

> In every respect Conrad's world and Conrad's fiction are reminders of the total unnaturalness of language, of thought, and, of course, of fiction itself.
>
> George Levine[80]

The knitting machine, the Kosmos machine and the San Tomé mine as surrogate machine all suggest that to be human is to be *homo ex machina*, man as mechanised being. The implicit inseparability of human and inhuman, described at the start of the chapter, becomes explicit in Conrad's mechanised humans in *Nostromo*. Their relationship to the world cannot be a human one, it can only be 'mechanical'. But what does such a relationship augur?

Trilling's epigraph at the beginning of this chapter – noting the nineteenth-century anxiety that man was no longer man, that his relation to the world had ceased to be a human one – can now be seen in relief. Agency, as has been demonstrated, is not only divisible but also replicable. Human beings, therefore, are agential beings in two senses: possessing it intrinsically (though not absolutely), and able to reproduce it extrinsically, in the products of human effort. As Werner Heisenberg noted, 'every tool carries with it the spirit by which it has been created'.[81] But there is a further complication as to *when*, exactly, it has been made extrinsic. Certain works of art, for example, can remain dormant, forgotten, culturally inert for long periods of time, before reappearing as powerful cultural determinants. The causative might of aesthetic artefacts is often unpredictable and inexplicable, not easily (or entirely) accountable in terms of formalist, socio-political or historical conditions. Similarly, when agency is replicated in machine technology the coordinates of human-mechanical connectedness are not easily assigned. Is it as old as consciousness, or as recent as the Newtonian worldview? Indistinctness of cause and consequence makes it impossible to say when, exactly, man ceased to be man (or a rational animal), only that he is now an affective machine, a 'machinate mammal',[82] or (in our time) an 'interactive being who is both transmitter and receiver'.[83]

Hannah Arendt has remarked on modern life philosophy and its greatest exemplars, Marx, Nietzsche and Bergson. All three 'equate Life and Being . . . and life is indeed the only "being" man can possibly be aware of by looking merely into himself'. They differ from their philosophical predecessors in their avowal that 'life appears to be more active and more productive than consciousness, which seems to be still too closely related to contemplation and the old ideal of truth'.[84] In like manner, Conrad writes again of the machine, to Cunninghame Graham, three weeks after the knitting-machine letter. It is 'thinner than air and as evanescent as a flash of lightning. The attitude of cool unconcern is the only reasonable one. Of course reason is hateful – but why? Because it demonstrates (to those who have the courage) that we, living, are out of life, – utterly out of it.' And in a final, withering remark, he laments: 'Life knows us not and we do not know life, – we don't even know our own thoughts.'[85] This is Conrad's 'response' to Trilling's epigraph: man's relation to the world is not a human one, because he *has no* relation to the world, he is 'utterly out of it'.

Conrad elucidates this in a (further) letter to Graham. Egoism, altruism, fidelity to nature, systems of rules : all these are promising, beneficent propositions, 'if we could only get rid of consciousness':

What makes mankind tragic is not that they are the victims of nature, it is that they are conscious of it. To be part of the animal kingdom under the conditions of this earth is very well, – but as soon as you know of your slavery, the pain, the anger, the strife, – the tragedy begins. We can't return to nature, since we can't change our place in it . . . There is no morality, no knowledge and no hope : there is only the consciousness of ourselves which drives us about a world that, whether seen in a convex or a concave mirror, is always but a vain and floating appearance.[86]

A mechanical relation to the world keeps human beings separate from reality. For Conrad, as for Schopenhauer, man is caught in an impossible bind, unable either to rediscover his humanity (for that is mined with tragedy), or to recreate it (since he is barred from the world by consciousness).

Human beings are defeated by their own insufficiency in the face of the inhuman, by the fact that agency is not only divisible, but also replicable. They are *fallen* creatures, plunged into the torments of consciousness (for Conrad, an encumbrance preventing man from becoming fully human) and subjectivity (Schopenhauer's *bête noire*, 'overcome' by impersonality). Two tireless expounders of a 'fallen' humanity, D. H. Lawrence and Martin Heidegger, are the subjects of the next chapter.

# 3

## *The Lawrentian transcendent: after the fall*

[F]rom invertebrates to mammals, from mammals to man, from man to tribesman, from tribesman to me: and on and on, till, in the future, wonderful, distinct individuals, like angels, move about, each one being himself, perfect as a complete melody or a pure colour.

D. H. Lawrence[1]

> After Marx, Nietzsche, Freud, and Heidegger, it is philosophically
> impossible to return to the idea that man is the owner and controller
> of the whole of his actions and ideas. We know how illusory and
> dangerous the negation of the unconscious, in all its various forms,
> can be.
>
> Luc Ferry and Alain Renaut[2]

Despite the seeming inescapability of philosophical antihumanism, in-
ferred from Ferry and Renaut's acknowledgment, there is an equally unavoidable precariousness accompanying that disposition. For adherents
of antihumanism are committed to avoiding both outright misanthropy
(the human as an excrescence of the inhuman) and a simple reversal of
priority that might favour the nonhuman over the human. The human,
that is to say, must be disciplined (for its self-aggrandisement) but not
disparaged. What is left, by way of counterhumanist strategy? Steering
clear of misanthropy and logocentrism means, effectively, translating the
human from value into fact, but without *de*valuing it; and this means,
in turn, neutralising the human propensity to claim an *a priori* value for
itself.

Philosophical antihumanism assays man as the 'owner and controller'
of his actions by challenging the notion of the human as an absolute
ground and standard of measure, as the uncaused causer of its own
foundations. This terminology is not literal. It supervenes because 'subjectivity' has come to mean the 'metaphysics of subjectivity'. Once the
subject is camouflaged by metaphysics it takes on the contours of godliness, regarding itself as transcendent. Thus to divest human subjectivity
of metaphysics is to dispel its aura of 'first cause'. This means giving
weight and purpose to phenomena preceding the human, which make
of it a by-product rather than a cause (phenomena that Ferry and Renaut
hypostasise as the 'unconscious').

The human is inconceivable outside life, the natural world and inherited animality, just as it is unthinkable apart from machine technology.
In the two previous chapters, accordingly, we have seen it defined as
a rational animal and an affective machine. Animal and machine are
linked in another way: it is man's devising and developing of mechanical technology that has made him more-than-animal – that has made
him, in effect, man.[3] Technological prowess, in other words, secures
the humanness of the human, by overcoming its animality. If the term
'rational animal' is, in one sense, a simple statement of fact, in another it
is a coded form of self-exaltation – more rational than animal, one might
say, the former partly cancelling the latter. The idea of transcendence

is therefore inscribed in human self-definition. The human is the over-coming animal, the transcending being, the superseding species.

This understanding of transcendence is the most simple and, it should be added, the most narrativistic: human development over time, bringing civilisation into being, runs in tandem with the human becoming human, with the securing of distance from prehuman animality by means of parahuman technology. If transcendence is embedded in human self-definition, it circulates in determinate self-understanding, in the particular self-narratives that prevail. Conscious that part of its makeup consists in surpassing its naturalistic, animalistic heritage, the human seeks *further* overcoming. From this ensue the traits of godliness granted by the appeal to metaphysics. This discourse was inherited from the theological disposition, albeit with a crucial difference. Just as *subjectum* absorbs into itself objects outside its ambit, any 'beyond' is brought within comprehension, is not allowed to remain extraneous to cognitive knowing. Metaphysics thus inherits from theology, but without the crucial sense of wonder, the sacred (and extrasubjective) apprehension of mystery.

There are other consequences for the human as a transcending species. The expectation that intention will map on to outcome is a form of theological misrecognition. It mistakes human agency for divine agency, discounting contingency, chance, randomness, the aleatory in human affairs. It excludes, effectively, the unstoppable, factical, *non*human. The animal human and the mechanical human have already been explored, but a transcendent human is less easily apprehended. It spreads from the mundane – i.e., a tendency possessed by all rational animals – to the extramundane, via the revolutionary energies of Romanticism. Examples of men mistaking themselves for gods are legion in Romantic literature;[4] the 'great man' theory of history, a catalogue of exceptional individuals, has a kind of belief in the 'human transcendent' withal.[5] The transcendent is, then, less a category than a tendency – a tendency inscribed, we have just seen, in the notion of the human. It is hardly surprising, then, that metaphysical man has assumed the mantle of secular deity; it might almost be said to be a part of his nature. And his narrativisation tendencies, his expectation that intention will map on to consequence, reflect that. Alternately, to state the obverse – that unintended consequences will inevitably outrun intended consequences – is another way of saying that human beings are neither machines nor gods.

To recapitulate the above: the human emerges from nature in a transcending movement. What lifts it out of nature, in a practical sense, is technology. What elevates it in a discursive, which is to say a *philosophical*, sense is humanism – an enabling discourse on which is founded social-isation, civilisation, the moral law. For humanism to have any efficacy, it must be underwritten by a nature-overcoming conceptualisation of what the human is, as a being ontologically separate. Anthropometric thought, conversely, severs the bond between the various kinds of pre-scriptive practices associated with humanism, and the type of being iden-tified as human. It is on the basis of the congenital human-humanism connection that transcendence is grounded. To break this bond is to forgo human claims to discontinuity with nature, with the phenome-nal world, with different forms of the nonhuman in general. And to do so means the gap between the human and its others is no longer an irreducible one.

## The decline of the West

Among the scientific, literary and philosophical figures enlisted up to this point, various degrees of interconnectedness are apparent. Nietzsche wrote in the wake of Darwin and Hegel ('without Hegel there could have been no Darwin'),[6] and in the shadow of Schopenhauer, his educator, who openly reviled Hegelian idealism. And Darwin had belated, but significant, exposure to Schopenhauer's work. Conrad's fictions, simi-larly, are formed from varying amounts of contact with the writings of Schopenhauer, Darwin and Nietzsche. The present chapter, by way of contrast, juxtaposes D. H. Lawrence and Martin Heidegger. Although these two have been affected individually by most of the above, there is no record of any direct influence or interchange between them.

Yet if their affinities are cursory and indirect, they are nonetheless undeniable. George Steiner writes: 'Heidegger's invocation of the tene-brous strengths that man must draw from the veins of the earth, his scarcely veiled belief in the mystery of blood and ethnic destiny, his con-tempt for the mercantile, can be exactly paralleled in the vision of D. H. Lawrence.'[7] The two also have a similar attitude towards instrumentality, as Fiona Becket points out:

Certainly Heidegger rejects the view that language is merely the instrument of thought, a position shared by Lawrence. These thinkers start from the position, then, that human understanding does not occur *only* through deduction [ ... ] To talk of the Heideggerian dimension of Lawrence is simply to underscore the observation: the 'philosopher', since Nietzsche, seems to be reaching, or reaching for, a consciousness of language which the creative writer intuitively possesses.[8]

This observation is pertinent in terms of Heidegger's departures from the formal conventions of philosophical discourse, and Lawrence's ability to reveal certain things that Heidegger, despite his departures, cannot attain.

What takes place in this chapter, then, is an implicit enframing, an 'explicatory parallel' between Lawrence's English modernist aesthetic and Heidegger's German phenomenological disposition. The basis for this parallel is the background in German thought shared by both men. As Anne Fernihough has observed: 'Lawrence cannot be fully understood apart from the specifically *German* philosophical tradition in which he was already immersed before meeting Frieda [Weekley, with whom he eloped to Germany in 1912].'[9] Fernihough describes this tradition as 'the romantic anti-capitalism and anti-technology which was so prevalent in Germany before and after the First World War'.[10] The chief figures, in terms of a Lawrence–Heidegger collocation, are Oswald Spengler and Friedrich Nietzsche. Spengler's notorious *Decline of the West* did not appear until 1918; earlier in the century, however, 'theories approximating very closely to Spengler's were in wide circulation'.[11] And Pierre Bourdieu, as Fernihough notes, has established the importance of Spengler for Heidegger's thought. He writes that Heidegger 'picks up a number of Spengler's themes, but euphemizes them', and sees Spengler as the most prominent ideologue of the 'conservative revolution'.[12] This is a central point of convergence for Lawrence and Heidegger: both maintain the belief in a causal link between rising democracy and Western decadence, the conviction that a 'fall' has taken place.

Coterminous with this political temper is an 'apocalyptic' inclination. Heidegger once commented to Hans-Georg Gadamer that his life's goal was 'to be a new Luther'.[13] His turn to Luther began after the First World War, with his 'phenomenology of religious consciousness'. John van Buren writes: 'He wanted to uncover the original experiences of the personal "selfworld" and "kairological" time in primal Christianity, and then explore the universal significance of these phenomena in a phenomenological ontology.'[14] The apocalyptic temper is evident from Heidegger's reference to the 'violent eruptions' in Christian thought of such figures as Augustine, the medieval mystics, Luther and Kierkegaard.[15] It is not difficult to guess who the inheritor of this tradition might be: 'Following in the footsteps of such protest-ant figures as Luther and Kierkegaard, Heidegger's newly conceived phenomenology of religion became the project of a destruction of the Greek conceptuality underlying traditional theological thought . . .'[16]

In the early 1920s Heidegger attempted to complete what the young Luther had begun, a 'deconstructive commentary on Aristotle and Aristotelian Scholasticism', seeing himself as 'a kind of philosophical Luther of western metaphysics'.[17] Despite Heidegger's estrangement from Catholicism, neo-Scholasticism and (eventually) Christian theology *tout entier*, the structure of his thought appears to have been fixed; that he saw himself as a sort of 'high priest of being' is apparent enough. As Steiner remarks: 'From the outset, Heidegger's manner of questioning and defining, Heidegger's tactics of citation and of hermeneutic elucidation, intimately reflect the Scholastic and neo-Kantian theological techniques in which he had been trained.'[18] It was Heidegger who would reformulate the scripture, he who would become the ontological emissary and write the Bible of being.

Lawrence, of course, has long been regarded as the 'priest of love'.[19] Ian Watt situates him within that tradition of novelists who 'have inherited of Puritanism everything except its religious faith'.[20] Lawrence's puritanical upbringing, overturned by his reading of Schopenhauer (discussed below), informed his exploration of the 'metaphysics of love', the revitalising properties of sexual candour. He saw natural sexual activity as restorative, the remedy for a decadent civilisation. The place where religion and sex could meet on equal terms, as it were, was life. Life in general, and the life-giving activity of procreation, were both sacred. Lawrence, like Conrad, held a suspicion of consciousness; but its abandonment brought Conrad no relief, because 'we, living, are out of life, utterly out of it'. For Lawrence, however, surrendering consciousness was a necessary prerequisite for the full inhabitation of life, which led him to questions of birth, death and rebirth. *The Rainbow* exemplifies the cyclical nature of life, and its successor, *Women in Love*, the implications of rebirth. Both texts have historical substrata: the former registers the shift, in a somewhat compressed manner, from the recursive, timeless cycles of nature through to the advent of industrial modernity; while the latter, conversely, begins in extremis, at the end of Western decline, and strives to move beyond it. The apocalyptic temper accompanying this effort acts as a switchpoint between nonconformist religious conviction and the desire for rebirth.

Nietzsche, a philosopher of life, is often aligned with Lawrence.[21] For the discussion that follows, however, it is Schopenhauer who is the important precursor – principally for his metaphysics of the unconscious, as both empirical individual will and all-pervasive cosmic will. Emile Delavenay credits Schopenhauer with being a formative influence in the process of Lawrence's intellectual emancipation, the figure who 'seems to have done more than anyone else to incite him to doubt'. *The White Peacock*, Lawrence's first, and most self-consciously literary, novel, bears the imprint of this encounter: 'Day after day I told him what the professors had told me: of life, of sex and its origins, of Schopenhauer and William James . . .'[22] The narrator, Cyril, is alluding to the theories of sexuality that inspired Lawrence's interest in Schopenhauer. Delavenay describes 'The Metaphysics of Love' as the piece in Schopenhauer's *Selected Essays* that Lawrence 'most closely studied'.[23] This essay is usually cited to construe Lawrence's engagement with Schopenhauer; indeed, it has been claimed that 'there is no evidence that he ever held in his hands *The World as Will and Idea*'.[24] Yet despite this, Lawrence had considerable, as it were, secondhand contact with Schopenhauer's writing. As noted in the previous chapter, Conrad received the main precepts of Schopenhauer not just through his own reading of the works, but from their assimilation by other Schopenhauerian admirers such as Maupassant and Anatole France. Thomas Hardy played a similar role in Lawrence's reading life. For example, the Schopenhauerian sediment is apparent in this passage from the *Study of Thomas Hardy*:

This is a constant revelation in Hardy's novels: that there exists a great background, vital and vivid, which matters more than the people who move upon it . . . Upon the vast incomprehensible pattern of some primal morality greater than ever the human mind can grasp, is drawn the little, pathetic pattern of man's moral life and struggle, pathetic, almost ridiculous.[25]

Even here, it is made clear that the 'vital and vivid' background of the will is something to be celebrated, rather than quelled. It might be said, then, that Lawrence draws Nietzschean conclusions from Schopenhauer's conception of the will, although without adopting Nietzsche's attitude of incredulity towards metaphysics.

The thematic subject of this chapter, transcendence, is treated variously in both Heidegger and Lawrence. Rather than present a chronological elucidation, I begin with Heidegger, establish some theoretical principles of modern 'fallenness' (i.e., Western decline), and then work back from these to Lawrence. Heidegger conceives of transcendence, in the first place, as the ability to stand outside one's immediate spatio-temporal horizon. It can also be seen as the urge to escape from *das Man*, the narcotising sway of the 'they'. Lawrentian transcendence is predicated on this latter point. The 'they' are made to seem an inevitable manifestation of civilisation in general and modernity in particular. And, as with Heidegger, overcoming this is an imperative in Lawrence's work – through 'mastery' or overcoming of the feminine and, finally, through supervention of the human. With the arrogance and assumptions of humanist transcendence comes deprivation – of a relationship with being (Heidegger), or of a sense of connection to all living things (Lawrence). For both, a human being is a fallen being, suffering terrible losses from the determined march of modernity. They take the human not as the overcoming animal, the transcending species, etc., but as the entity that precisely *needs* transcendence, to leave behind the degrading condition of its present circumstance.

Heidegger executes a striking variation on a phenomenon discussed earlier. Chapter 1 charted the slippage between culture and nature, and the attempts at 'reanimalising' the human by regarding man as a natural, 'facted' being rather than an automatic possessor of value. Heidegger's philosophical discourse – an ontology that does not just precede ethics but, by some lights, wilfully ignores or disregards it – uses terms laden with ethical signification and applies them to ontological criteria. The key example of this tactic is 'care': 'The existential condition for the possibility of "the cares of life" and "devotedness", must be conceived as care, in a sense which is primordial – that is ontological.'[26] In Stephen Mulhall's account, this does not mean 'that Dasein is always caring and concerned, or that failures of sympathy are impossible or to be discouraged; it is rather that, as Being-in-the-world, Dasein must *deal* with that world.'[27] Care, in other words, is an *is* and not an *ought*. Heidegger's project does not attempt to reverse the Kantian assertion that an ought cannot be derived from an is (or an ethics extracted from an ontology), but rather implies that an ought *really is* an is. What has hitherto been regarded as value, and hence as human-created or human-possessed, was really fact, a 'given' existing prior to human intervention. Heidegger labours to make Dasein a fact rather than a value, as did those attempts to reanimalise the human (implicit in Darwin, explicit in Nietzsche). If, then, Heidegger's transference of value and fact leads to confusion, it is a strategic confusion. It enables him to make the move he requires, which is to disable *anthropos*.

Heideggerian thought maintains a constant struggle against humanism. In his critiques of metaphysics, truth and *subjectum*, references to humanist precepts are never far from his concerns. Heidegger's principal strategy, as we are about to see, is to take orthodox humanist modes and tropes, and to bend them into anti- or ahumanist shapes. Hence the description of Heidegger as an 'antihumanist humanist',[28] as a philosophical antihumanist who retells, rather than abandons, the history of humanist thought and the construction of the human that has sustained this narrative.

## I HEIDEGGER'S FUNDAMENTAL BEING

### *Propriating metaphysical man*

The figure of metaphysical man is a residual presence in Heidegger's attempted revivification of the 'question of being'. He marks the shift from the human as rational animal (or its technological shadow, affective machine) to the human as 'I', the subjectivising being. The *cogito* is derided for being the uncaused causer, the godlike entity that is the origin of the subjectivism that (in Heidegger's view) has corrupted modern thought. By virtue of the *cogito*, he writes, 'the 'I' thus becomes the accentuated and essential definition of man'.[29] And in historical terms: 'That period we call modern . . . is defined by the fact that man becomes the center and measure of all beings. Man is the subjectum, that which lies at the bottom of all beings, that is, in modern terms, at the bottom of all objectification and representation.'[30] The concept of subjectivity means that human being is conceived as an entity – an entity possessing internal self-identity, prior to any relationship it has with the world. The notion of the subject promotes the tendency to regard everything as flowing from this originary quality of self-containment.

Metaphysics is responsible for the 'ontological difference', the emphasis on beings as particular entities, rather than on the nature of beings' relation to being itself. It is metaphysical subjectivism that is Heidegger's principal target. Michael Haar outlines its historical regard: 'The History of man is that of an absolute emancipation. From what has man not liberated himself? He has delivered himself from any relation to an Other than himself, to God, to nature, to being. He has become the entire relation, the pure medium, the sole object, the sole study of the unique subject: himself.'[31] As a result of this, the entire Western tradition has become fixated on one question: who am I? Heidegger impugns subjectivism (subject, I, *ego cogitans*) because it occludes something more fundamental and primordial: being and its structure. Being precedes metaphysics, in other words, including the metaphysics of subjectivity. Heidegger seeks a domain of truth lying outside metaphysical constructions, a domain known as the unthought.[32] And in seeking it, he is committed to a relentless decentring of metaphysical man.

In *Being and Time* there is little scope for any kind of overcoming. It makes no sense for subjectivity to be transcended if the subject is a fiction, a misprision of what is really Dasein. Heidegger's objections to the traditional understanding of transcendence are plainly stated: 'But the idea of "transcendence" – that man is something that reaches beyond himself – is rooted in Christian dogmatics, which can hardly be said to have made an ontological problem of man's Being' (*BT* 74). Greek thought and Christian theology converge, in modern anthropology, 'where the *res cogitans*, consciousness, and the interconnectedness of Experience serve as the point of departure for methodical study'. But the 'ontological foundations' that support this type of study 'remain undetermined', and so the question of being is still forgotten (75).

Transcendence of a sort *is*, however, addressed in *Being and Time*. It appears as part of 69, 'The Temporal Problem of the Transcendence of the World'. The basis for this is the abandonment of *adequatio*, or 'adequacy' of perception and object, in favour of the mutual implication of Dasein and world. '[The world] "is", with the "outside-of-itself" of the ecstases, "there". If no Dasein exists, no world is "there" either' (417). Thus the world needs Dasein (or being-there) to have a 'there' at all. Dasein and world are linked through transcendence, through being more than each is in itself. Dasein is more than it is, i.e., transcendent, because it is projecting ahead to possibility, rather than staying fixed in actuality; it transcends, in other words, because of its temporalised condition. And because the world is the clearing where the being of individual entities can be disclosed, this means that it, too, must be intrinsically temporalised. Being-in-the-world and being-towards-death can only take place in the clearing that is the world: 'For Heidegger the world is not the totality of beings, but the horizon in terms of which beings may be comprehended as they are.'[33] So the world must *transcend*, in order to permit the disclosure of temporalised Dasein to occur. There is thus a relationship of complementarity between Dasein's need for world-transcendence, and the world's provision of Dasein-transcendence; the necessarily coincident element is temporality.

Neither case is a transcendence that can be striven for, but merely an intrinsic, involuntary part of Dasein's dealings with the world, a condition of its possibility. A less secure kind of transcendent – striving as willed action, or 'resoluteness', in Heideggerese – is freedom-towards-death, an escape from the given, to countermand the soporific conformity of *das Man*.

### After the Fall: narrating finitude

Part of the difficulty of *Being and Time* is its performative orientation, which – invoking the performative poetics of the modernist novel – is wired into the notoriously dense and recondite 'private language' teeming through its pages. The performative is also transformative, as Heidegger himself indicates: 'Questions are paths toward an answer. If the answer could be given it would consist in a transformation of thinking, not in a propositional statement about a matter at stake.'[34] If our minds are to be reattuned to recognise anew the question of being, it will be from the process of inner attentiveness demanded by exposure to Heidegger's prose.

Produced during the years of high modernism, *Being and Time* shares certain narrative characteristics with its (fictional) anthropometric counterparts. This includes, first and foremost, the problematisation of beginnings and endings. There is, in fact, no ending or conclusion to *Being and Time*, as only two of the six proposed parts were written.[35] Its beginning, on the other hand, manifests not deferral but abundance. We saw how *Lord Jim* effected endless displacements of narrative impetus, an immanent refusal to form a coherent shape. And in *Nostromo* narrative development was repeatedly frustrated; the adventure tale, and its promise of purpose and resolution, were undercut by structures of circularity. *Being and Time*, as narrative philosophy, is similarly uncertain – or rather, there is an *over*certainty of beginning, which resolves into a kind of hesitancy. Joanna Hodge writes that *Being and Time* 'begins not once, but at least twice and possibly three, or even four times':

In his discussions of Hölderlin, Heidegger distinguishes between a starting point, identifiable as the first words of the discussion, and a beginning, *Anfang*, the point from which an ordered exposition becomes possible. This distinction makes possible the claim that *Being and Time* has a single starting point but many beginnings, one for each of the different expositions under way in it. There is the question of being; there is the thought of the forgetting of being; there is the analysis of Dasein; there is the proposed destruction of the history of ontology; there is the alternative history of philosophy projected for the unpublished last three sections.[36]

Hodge points out the, as it were, Heideggerian shape of Heidegger's text. Like the Conrad examples, these multiple beginnings adumbrate a narrative that cannot make any kind of headway beyond its own constantly shifting premises.

Within this paranarrative is a continual censuring of such terms as intuition, commonsense and empathy, and all they take for granted. They
are coverings-up of more primal phenomena, eliding processes of understanding and interpretation that are fundamentally determinative.[37] Intuition is criticised for its self-groundedness, as the reflective ego's purely
spontaneous mode of understanding, separated from 'worldly' objects.
' "Intuition" and "thinking" are both derivatives of understanding, and
already rather remote ones' (*BT* 187). At the root of this is Heidegger's
contention that a human being is neither a rational animal, an affective
machine, nor a subjective agent. She is rather 'care', i.e., Dasein's existential constitution, its 'already-inness' or 'thrownness' into the world.
Care is conditioned by time, in terms of the three temporal ecstases,
where Dasein stands out from and transcends the world.

Just as a mechanomorphism arises from human engagement and involvement with technology en masse, yet takes on its own depersonalising
agency, a similar process ensnares Dasein. The dialectic here is not the
human and the mechanical, but Dasein and *das Man*. The latter is the
inauthentic 'they-self', a figure of blind conformity and acquiescence to
mass opinion. Dasein *falls* into this condition; a condition that is, in fact,
the stance of everyday Dasein. But Heidegger also describes *das Man*
as a 'primordial phenomenon' (an honorific, as we have just seen), that
'belongs to Dasein's positive constitution', hence a necessary part of human being. Heidegger describes this, however, not as dialectic – dismissed
as 'a genuine philosophical embarrassment' (*BT* 47) – but as dissolution.
'This Being-with-another dissolves one's own Dasein completely into the
kind of Being of "the others", in such a way, indeed, that the others, as
distinguishable and explicit, vanish more and more' (164).

Dasein's fall into *das Man* appears to enact the transition from a prelapsarian (ideal) state to a postlapsarian (real) state. Such a distinction is
deeply embedded in our shared mythologies, an organising archetype
of the cultural unconscious. It is manifested as a determining aspect of
our story-structures: pre- never maps on to post- without either deficit
or excess. To this end, it is one of the most powerful and enduring of
Western narratives. Its ur-text, the biblical account of the prelapsarian–
postlapsarian difference, has become a paradigm for secular accounts
of cultural decline. The most recent version of the fall is to place the
blame squarely on the shoulders of 'modernity'. Heidegger has invoked
this conception of difference as historical decadence, particularly in his
animadversions on technology. But the myopic conservatism that sees
the past 200 years as intrinsically inferior to an earlier 'golden age' is

apparently circumvented by Heidegger. He sees mankind's fall in ontological terms, as Dasein's fall, rather than as a result of historical circumstance. Thus it is partly the essence of Dasein to fall. As Heidegger explains it, Dasein:

has not fallen into some entity which it comes across for the first time in the course of its Being, or even one which it has not come upon at all; it has fallen into the *world*, which itself belongs to its Being. Falling is a definite existential characteristic of Dasein itself (*BT* 220).

Thus Heidegger has taken a story-based paradigm – the temporal phenomenon that is the prelapsarian-postlapsarian difference – and removed the contours of its narrativity, turned it from an historical phenomenon into a structural, atemporal one.[38]

A further evocation of narrative arises as a consequence of *das Man*. It constrains (inauthentic) *Dasein* into a narrow band of 'presentness', inhibiting its engagement with other temporal modes. The constraints of presentism engender a kind of amnesia, a wholesale forgetting of our cultural legacy (including, of course, the question of being). Nietzschean authenticity – eternal recurrence, becoming what one is – invokes strategies of reanimalisation and denarrativisation, based on the operations of presentness; each moment's concentration of willed action enables value to be precipitated. Heideggerian authenticity, by contrast, is not so defiantly present-centred. Dasein projects itself towards its future, though in a *non*wilful way. Heidegger specifically abjures the latter: 'Projecting has nothing to do with comporting oneself towards a plan that has been thought out, and in accordance with which Dasein arranges its Being' (*BT* 185). Realising oneself in this way would be tantamount to actualisation and, hence, to inauthenticity. Dasein, on the contrary, has already projected itself, prior to any conscious decision; projection is a part of its self-understanding. 'As projecting, understanding is the kind of Being of Dasein in which it *is* its possibilities as possibilities' (185). Furthermore, because we are always already in a world, our lives are never, strictly speaking, begun. They can only be continued and completed, and it is from this that the (demi-)narrative of one's life is composed. Death provides closure, or finitude. Yet the finitude of death is not construed as termination, but as encapsulation, a provision of means for grasping life as a consequential totality (289–90).

Because it is the fate of *das Man* to fall, fallenness is akin to thrownness; being in the world means falling into the world. Transcending *das Man* means, effectively, transcending thrownness, by replacing it with resoluteness. Since death cannot, in any sense, be experienced, it can only be anticipated. Heidegger terms this 'anticipatory resoluteness', the realisation and acceptance of one's mortality. Anticipatory resoluteness is another modality of truth, like disclosure and openness; resoluteness, however, is the 'most primordial' truth of Dasein (*BT* 343). ('Irresoluteness', by contrast, is when Dasein is 'dispersed', when it lacks 'constancy'; 442.) Self-narrativisation is imperative to transcending thrownness, through the contemplation of finitude. Contemplating finitude, rather than fleeing it, means 'positioning oneself at the end of one's life and grasping it as a totality'.[39] The totality of one's life is grasped through anxiety; only then can Dasein become authentic, can transcendence be made possible and fallenness overcome.

### *Full disclosure: the human without the 'human'*

It is axiomatic of philosophical antihumanism that the human cannot fully occupy, and is in fact alienated from, its own humanity. Heidegger maps humanity on to *subjectum*, and beholds a perfect fit. Yet the human is, for Heidegger, a fact and not a value; for it to be otherwise would be to embrace the precepts of metaphysical rationalism.[40] He conducts deft translations of axiology into ontology, or movements from human-as-value to human-as-fact. Like Nietzsche with the eternal recurrence, though with greater stealth, Heidegger unties the human–value knot, dispossessing the human of its metaphysical and axiological inherences.

The 'fact' that is fundamental to Heideggerian thought is being, and this defies metaphysical analysis. Heidegger then takes value-laden terms and plants them firmly in the factical region of human existence: care, concern, solicitude, conscience and guilt. To take the last of these: the 'phenomenon of guilt', writes Heidegger, 'which is not necessarily related to "having debts" and law-breaking, can be clarified only if we first inquire in principle into Dasein's *Being*-guilty – in other words, if we conceive the idea of "Guilty!" in terms of Dasein's kind of Being'. Guilt, in short, is an *is*: 'The idea of guilt . . . must also be detached from relationship to any law or "ought" such that by failing to comply with it one loads himself with guilt' (*BT* 328). Like its siblings, guilt radiates not just value assumptions, but assumptions drawn from the highest axiological level, the ethical. So in shifting them from value to fact Heidegger is transferring, in the process, the infrastructure of human axiology, a defiantly deethicising reassignation.

Heidegger is splitting humanism from the 'human', to reach the human – that nonmetaphysical, nonapostrophised entity, unencumbered by delusions of value. He defines phenomenology as 'any exhibiting of an entity as it shows itself in itself' (*BT* 59). Thus 'the Being of entities can never be anything such that "behind it" stands something else "which does not appear" ' (60). Unconcealment, disclosure, unveiling are routes to the 'human'-less human. Heidegger drives a wedge into the link (hitherto perceived as impregnable) joining the human and humanism, to forge a different, purer, more primal connection between the human and being, which he calls Dasein. The 'human', by contrast, is the entity produced by the forgetting of being, which culminates in Cartesian subjectivism. The centuries of contamination have burdened the human with layers of illusion. This, more than anything, needs to be unconcealed. But affiliated with it is the removal of agency. Thus the 'human' cannot actively divest itself of its layers of illusion. Rather, the human, the quotationless entity, must self-disclose to reveal 'care'; the latter is to Heidegger as the reanimalised, denarrativised human is to Nietzsche.

*Das Man* has been described as a 'free-floating, impersonal construct'.[41] For Schopenhauer impersonality provided relief from the maledictions of existence. In Heideggerian ontology, by contrast, impersonality means *das Man* and so it is a problem, a source of inauthenticity. *Individuation* thus constitutes the fall, for Schopenhauer, because it sets different subjectivities, with different goals and desires, at warring odds with each other. *Massification*, on the other hand, constitutes Heidegger's fall, as it denies each Dasein the freedom to choose its own destiny. Transcending *das Man*, then, is the journey from inauthentic to authentic, from the 'anybody' self to a genuine, self-owning self. It marks the passage, in effect, from the 'human' to the human.

Narrative is stymied in potential alignments of both animal and human evolution, and human and mechanical interactivity. By contrast, the human-transcendent coupling, at least in Heidegger's account of it, is congenial to narrative. But such an account presupposes not the noble, dignified being of the humanist tradition, but something more akin to a fallen creature beset by original sin, the protagonist of the Christian metanarrative. Transcendence is thus made possible only on the basis of a prior 'antitranscendence', or fall. What Heideggerian man, or authentic Dasein, must transcend is not a particularly auspicious portrayal of *anthropos* to begin with, but the diminished, inauthentic entity in thrall to *das Man*. To transcend this counterfeit condition is not to become godlike, but to become more properly humanlike. It is to attain a condition whereby Dasein can, as it were, fulfil its own Daseinness.

Heidegger's central ploy, as I have indicated, is to reconfigure existing humanist ideas into human-decentring ones. Narrative apparatus is dismantled and reconstructed, without causality to brace it. By regarding certain key moments in German philosophy as anticipating (and then paralleling) literary modernism, it is apparent that the line of development is not strictly teleological. Hegel is the most narrativistic of philosophers, and Schopenhauer the most novelistic. It takes the relentless suspicion of Nietzschean transvaluation to curtail both tendencies, in a series of aphoristic, poetic works and through the defiant antinarratives of eternal recurrence and becoming what one is. Heidegger thus represents the reparation of narrative philosophy, but it is an eccentric recovery. For every delineation of finitude and every appeal to the temporalisation of experience, there is an equally resolute assault on causality and closure. And then there are the formal oddities of *Being and Time* itself, which promises a shape that does not emerge, and begins anew several times over. While not exactly undoing Nietzsche's wholesale frustration of narrative order, Heidegger brings enough of it back in to invite comparisons with the modernist novel. Nietzsche's drastic upheavals thus presage a more gradual paring away of narrative's grander claims to embody human experience, in literary modernism and beyond.

Every version of antihumanism foregrounds some aspect of human 'blindness', some part of self or world that remains opaque and inaccessible to (and therefore beyond mastery of) *anthropos*. As Haar points out, there is a Heideggerian imperative that cannot be fulfilled: 'What is proper to man is to be. Yet being – as that which is entirely other than entities or nonentities, as the very emergence of truth – cannot be possessed or appropriated. Man's proper 'site' escapes him . . . Heidegger reminds man of the *essential* dispossession of himself.'[42] In its yearning to submit to the unknowable, to escape the cognitive overdeterminism of metaphysical rationality, Heidegger's antihumanism turns on a single thought: the unconsummated relationship of the human and its other, being. Haar refers to this as the 'false symmetry' of the relation between man and being. It is a theistic phenomenon because being 'uses' and 'manipulates' man, rather than simply maintaining him: 'In this Heideggerian theme, as in many others, do we not find the transposed taking up again of a religious theme and its current expressions: "we are in the hand of God," or "God has need of man" (*brauchen* means both "to need" and "to use"), or again, "Man proposes, God disposes"?'[43] The ontological difference remains; even Dasein cannot attain fulfilment, it can only provide an 'opening'.

Heidegger's version of antihumanism is unusual in that it evokes a quasi-mediaeval celebration of human blindness, redolent of his formative intellectual encounters with Duns Scotus, Eckhart and German pietism. Looking at it synchronically, literary modernism's problematisation of those limits of narrative surety, beginnings and endings, is part of the same desire to inhabit the unknowable, a way of sheltering from the panoptical glare of the metaphysics of subjectivity. In this vein, Heidegger valorises the 'awesome' for its 'undisclosed abundance', even as he disparages the 'familiar and ordinary'.[44] He presents a choice, finally, between being granted limited, yet exquisite, access to the sacral mysteries of being, and remaining cloistered in the dreary, overlit chamber of metaphysical cognisance, with only the cheerless consolations of instrumental reason. A similarly unorthodox religious temperament is apparent in the writings of D. H. Lawrence.

## II LAWRENCE'S IMPERSONAL SOURCE

There is a particular English modernist sensibility – Wyndham Lewis, T. S. Eliot, T. E. Hulme – which sees as fundamental a separation between the metaphysical and the axiological. All these writers cleave to the ideology of metaphysical man (i.e., his resolute transcendence of animal being) yet do not take the logical next step, which is to charge this construction with inherent value. On the contrary, all of the above are 'fall' thinkers, to a greater or lesser extent. Like Heidegger they regard *anthropos* as having undergone a downturn, though *unlike* Heidegger, for them the role played in this by history is never in doubt (hence the 'metaphysical' appellation). Lewis's 'sex-cult' of the Ancient Greeks, Eliot's 'dissociation of sensibility', and Hulme's anti-Romanticist diatribes all describe historical watersheds. Be it pre-Socratic, early seventeenth century or late eighteenth century, there has been a turn away from self-actualisation and a consequent diminution in human potential.[45] The blame for their devaluation of contemporary humanity is not (as was Heidegger's) laid on man's metaphysical propensities, but on a loss of agential capability, a 'dimming-down' of *subjectum*. In other words, human beings have not fallen because they are too metaphysical, but rather because they are not metaphysical enough; the postlapsarian condition results from a metaphysical shortfall, as it were, rather than a surplus. This phenomenon in English letters, a high-modernist disposition, could best be described as 'metaphysical antihumanism'.

D. H. Lawrence belongs with the English company above, rather than in F. R. Leavis's Great Tradition.[46] Leavis's Lawrence is 'a great artist', 'the great creative genius of our age', and 'one of the greatest English writers of any time'.[47] The Great Tradition is, first and foremost, a great *novelistic* tradition. From Austen to Lawrence, Leavis charts the modern inheritors of Shakespeare's crown. '[F]or in the nineteenth century and later the strength – the poetic and creative strength – of the English language goes into prose fiction.' The Lawrence who belongs to this tradition is only incidentally a writer of stories, poetry, criticism and travelogues. 'His genius', declares Leavis, 'is distinctively that of a novelist, and as such he is as remarkable a technical innovator as there has ever been.' The title of Leavis's critical study – *D. H. Lawrence: Novelist* – wears its polemic on its sleeve. In the setting of the Leavisian tradition of Dickens, Twain and George Eliot (though surely not Henry James or Melville), Lawrence's technical innovations are indeed 'remarkable'. But in the alternative tradition of the morose modernism cited above, the tradition of Lewis and T. S. Eliot, Lawrence's debt to nineteenth-century literary forms is more pronounced.

In the novels about to be discussed – *Sons and Lovers*, *The Rainbow* and *Women in Love* – the contours of the *Bildungsroman*, the transgenerational family saga, and the Austenian novel of courtship and marriage are easily discernible. Implicit in the argument that follows, then, is the contention that these humanistic forms of narrative are insufficient, *pace* Leavis, to 'give us faith in the creative human spirit and its power to ensue fulness of life'.[48] Leavis's title, that is to say, cannot but be eclipsed by the alternative I employ here to shape the argument for the rest of this chapter: 'D. H. Lawrence: Metaphysical Antihumanist'.

> 'Transcendence', in its origins, is a transcendence *of* the feminine.
> Genevieve Lloyd[49]

What the feminine has come to stand for, in terms of Western representations, is the body, the earth, Nature herself. Kate Soper writes: 'Conceived as a feminine principle, nature is equally lover, mother and virago: a source of sensual delight, a nurturing bosom, a site of treacherous and vindictive forces bent on retribution for her human violation.'[50] This (male) identification of woman with nature is rooted in the philosophical tradition, passing from Aristotle and Plato through to Descartes.[51] In this tradition the female body is a zone of unpredictability and uncertainty, a collecting depot for every potential hindrance to reason. Unlike mind, body confuses the boundary between the human and the natural by having, as it were, a stake in each. The Cartesian division of *res cogitans* and *res extensa*, though putatively gender-neutral, acquires gender coordinates: male and female, the rational mind and the irrational, unruly body. Assuming the mantle of reason therefore depends on an overcoming of the feminine.

In addition, the woman-as-nature narrative is consonant with the history of patriarchy. Patriarchal relations define and reinforce women's association with nature, by simultaneously limiting female participation in and access to culture.[52] Being closer to nature, the female represents immanence, imprisoned by her biology. The male, to attain reason, is therefore compelled to transcend the body and biological process. 'Femininity is in this sense both that which it is desirable to transcend and that state of immanent self-oblivion which is sacrificed in the act of transcendence – and both these representations are offensive to women.'[53] Human self-definition based on sublated animality thus implies, additionally and unavoidably, an overcoming of the feminine and a sanctioning of patriarchy.

Lawrence both replicates and refigures this androcentric humanist narrative. As I will argue, transcendence of the feminine is imbricated with a supersession of the human that is the abiding concern in Lawrence's major novels, perhaps their quintessential theme. By common consent *The Rainbow* is held to be Lawrence's most profoundly sensitive work, a sympathetic study of generations of Brangwen women (Lydia, Anna, Ursula), each of whom is more vividly and complexly portrayed than her male partner. Indeed, it might be seen as the most feminised of English modernist novels. I do not dispute this claim, but rather align it with a counterclaim, or claims: I begin by acknowledging the composite nature of earlier *Rainbow–Women in Love* drafts ('The Sisters', 'The Wedding Ring'), and then stress the ways in which *Women in Love* strives to eclipse the earlier work, particularly in its treatment of sexual politics. There is, finally, a *double* transcendence at work in *Women*: the characters' pursuits of posthuman or parahuman states of being; and the text's overcoming of its 'prequel', the various and unceasing efforts it makes to supersede the claims made on behalf of female consciousness in *The Rainbow*. It is in *Women in Love*, the last of the famous mid-period texts, that Lawrence's most sustained skirmish with the questions surrounding the human and its others takes place. The apocalyptic temper of this work provides a key to the agonistic,

metaphysical antihumanism that reappears in different guises throughout the oeuvre.

### Sons and Lovers: *Soul mining*

We saw above how Heidegger's philosophical discourse of human ontology, i.e., Dasein, drew on a vocabulary of anteriority, valorising primordial states of being. Lawrence's literary discourse, by contrast, draws on
interiority. The Lawrentian narrator, typically, is more concerned with
rhapsody than with reportage, with inner states and immanent processes
located deeper than sensation or psychological tumult: heart, heart-of-
hearts, unconscious, being and most of all, soul.[54]

*Sons and Lovers* contains an abundance of such moments, particularly
in the early chapters. When Walter Morel cuts the child William's curls,
'[Gertrude] knew, and Morel knew, that that act had caused something
momentous to take place in her soul'.[55] Gertrude looks at the young
Paul, and something stirs: 'And at that moment she felt, in some far
place of her soul, that she and her husband were guilty' (50). What the
characters themselves are unaware of, the narrator supplies: 'It was about
this time Mrs. Morel was destroying her husband's authority. Until now,
she had felt too much alone to stand away from him. But William was
growing up, and his young soul was his mother's' (48–9). For all the
agonies of confusion and despair that Lawrence's characters undergo,
their struggles and tribulations are so relentlessly articulated as to make
them expert readers of souls.

Michael Steig writes of numerous passages 'in which it is virtually
impossible to tell whether we are reading an omniscient narrator's interpretation of the characters, a direct presentation of Paul's and Miriam's
thoughts, or Paul's attempts to understand her and his own feelings toward her'.[56] The point I am making about Lawrentian rhapsody is that
none of this matters. Whether it emanates from the narrator or the characters, directly or reflexively, the nature of the discourse is to make it
all equally 'reliable'. The knowledge most precious to Lawrence simply
cannot be conveyed in any other way. The soul does not lie; it is inconsequential whether its stirrings are mediated or direct, because in effect
'his characters' knowledge of each other is as direct as an omniscient
narrator's'.[57] In the idiom of metaphysical interiority, mere description
is akin to interpretation. Lawrence is the cartographer of the soul, not amputating it as Schopenhauer, Nietzsche and Heidegger did, but exoner-
ating it. To know, as Lawrence's characters surely know – nonreflectively

and nonprovisionally, which is to say, absolutely – is as it were to theo-
logise, to translate back into deistic terms, Nietzsche's reanimalised,
denarrativised being.

Just as Heidegger reminds man how he has been dispossessed of himself, the cumulative effect of Lawrentian immanence is also of a dispossession. The soul, that emblem of authentic selfhood, of unerring
self-coincidence, comes to resemble an alien landscape. It is so insistently reified that the characters, vaguely apprehending a mysterious
force within, can only detail its murmuring. The combined soul reports
are not assembled into a comprehensive picture; Lawrence does not
provide us with a hermeneutic for his novel. Yet these reports are more
than just an agglomeration of exegetical fragments. They diagnose a
particular condition, the wretchedness of a metaphysically diminished
mankind. In other words, Lawrence, having exonerated the soul, has
also succeeded in dehumanising it.

It is soul discourse, too, that eventually undoes the notion of *Sons and
Lovers* as a *Bildungsroman*. The *Bildungsroman* plots the process of adjust-
ment of the protagonist's growing inner selfhood, as it encounters, responds to, and is partly shaped by external events. 'A novel of "education"
only in the broad sense of the word, *Sons and Lovers* pays little or no
heed to formal instruction but, like other Bildungsromane, lays much
stress on the educative results of emotional experience.'[58] Sexual and
aesthetic *Bildung* dominate Lawrence's quasi-autobiographical tale. One
scene in particular, Paul's anticipation of sexual encounter, appears to
be explicitly soul-forming: 'Often, as he talked to Clara Dawes, came
that thickening and quickening of his blood, that peculiar concentration in the breast, as if something were alive there, a new self or a new
centre of consciousness, warning him that sooner or later he would have
to ask one woman or another' (294). Paul's new centre of consciousness seems a significant marker of inner growth, a clear intimation of
the benefits of *Bildung*. Finally, though, such markers are but secondary
phenomena, effects of something more diverse and heterogeneous. It
is in the souls of the various characters that the real 'action' occurs, a
locus deeper than (and often alien to) subjectivity. And it is the correspondences between what happens at this, as it were, ground-zero level
of experience, and the kindred exigencies of something more forbidding, a transhuman 'metasoul', that define Lawrence's real centre of
interest.

Hardy's Clym, writes Lawrence, 'did not know that the greater part
of every life is underground, like roots in the dark in contact with the

beyond'.[59] Lawrentian soul-consciousness conflates the immanent with the transcendent. Seeking the deepest layers of the self, one's innermost bearing, is a passageway *out of* the self, to the inhuman transcendent. Such an immanent transcendence also characterises Lawrence's view of woman. In physical terms, she is a natural, body-based, life-giving being. Metaphysically, though, she points to the beyond. 'She is the doorway,' remarks Lawrence in 'The Crown', 'she is the gate to the dark eternity of power, the creator's power . . . I resist, yet I am compelled; the woman resists, yet she is compelled. And we are the relative parts dominated by the strange compulsion of the absolute.'[60] The involuntary nature of female power characterises Miriam, in *Sons and Lovers*: 'She brought forth to him his imaginations. She did not understand, any more than a woman understands when she conceives a child in her womb' (241). She does not possess, but is rather possessed by, an inhuman force that she can neither control nor fully understand.

To grasp the nature of this force, we must turn to the Schopenhauerian language pervading the text at key moments. As mentioned above, the German philosopher is self-consciously named in *The White Peacock*. By the time of *Sons and Lovers*, he has become part of the complexion of Lawrentian rapture: '"To be rid of our individuality, which is our will, which is our effort – to live effortless, a kind of conscious sleep – that is very beautiful, I think . . . "' (331–2). And as Paul's affair with Clara runs its course:

They felt small, half afraid, childish and wondering, like Adam and Eve when they lost their innocence and realised the magnificence of the power which drove them out of Paradise and across the great night and the great day of humanity . . . To know their own nothingness, to know the tremendous living flood which carried them always, gave them rest within themselves. (398)[61]

Paul recognises that it was 'as if they had been blind agents of a great force' (399). The inhuman force that is possessing them appears both intrinsic *and* extrinsic, both within the human and beyond it.

Lawrence theorises about this beyond as a *before*, similar to the primordial status accorded being in Heideggerian ontology. In 'The Crown' it is referred to as 'a vast infinite, an origin, a Source. The Beginning, this is the great sphere of darkness, the womb wherein the universe is begotten'.[62] It is a metaphysical rendering of nature, feminised by the womb metaphor.[63] A later piece casts the source as the sea, 'the great protagonist'. It is 'a cosmic element, and the relation between the sea and the human psyche is impersonal and elemental'.[64] This is the crux of Lawrentian metaphysics, a post-Schopenhauerian spirit that maps the recondite relationship between soul and metasoul.

Concomitant with Lawrence's immanent–transcendent is the looping of the more-than-human back on to the less-than-human of the natural world. As a gesture, it carries associations of primitive animism, where animals and nature are imbued with preternatural power and treated as sacred. When nature becomes transcendent, the movement whereby the human has sublated its animality – the enabling power for civilisation, and its correlates of socialisation and mechanisation – betokens not transcendence but its opposite, fallenness. Naming man as the transcending animal, in the humanist metanarrative, gives Lawrence pause for lamentation. It means that man is not at home in either realm, he is neither transcendent enough nor animal enough. As Lawrence writes in 'On Human Destiny': 'Man is a domesticated animal that must think. His thinking makes him a little lower than the angels. And his domestication makes him, at times, a little lower than the monkey.'[65] Lawrence's view of women as both transcendent and natural appears to be a solution. As Dasein is to being, so woman is to the Lawrentian source: a route that leads from human to inhuman, or nonhuman.

In the humanist metanarrative, women are recruited for their otherness, then 'colonised' in order to maintain the sameness of the (male) subject.[66] Likewise with Lawrence, who does not depict women as truly other; they interest him metaphysically to the extent that they provide access to the inhuman. The *real* other is the inhuman beyond itself – the great Being; the tongue of flame; the tremendous living flood; the unreachable, impersonal source. And so physical consummation, the sexual union of man and woman, will always be spiritually deficient. Heidegger's ontological difference between beings and being is anticipated here, in the unconsummated relationship of the human and the source. It is the source, I would contend, that is Lawrence's cardinal interest, the core of his philosophical concern.

Located far below the level of consciousness (Paul Morel's 'new centre of consciousness'), the Lawrentian soul is a kind of inhuman determinant. And as with Schopenhauer's identification of the individual human will with its omnifarious correlate, the cosmic will, Lawrence's soul-source coupling can be seen as an *unconscious*. Far from being the seat of rational selfhood that once defined human transcendence – Descartes's *âme raisonnable* – the Lawrentian soul resembles more its nonmetaphysical Freudian counterpart (whose progenitor is also, to a significant extent, the Schopenhauerian will).[67] As Lawrence writes in *Psychoanalysis and the*

*Unconscious*, the soul cannot be deduced biologically, by attending to genetic transmission. 'There is in the nature of the infant something entirely new, underived, underivable, something which is, and which will forever remain, causeless.'[68] And this causeless causality 'is the same as the old mystery of the divine nature of the soul. Religion was right and science is wrong.' The soul individualises, and remains resistant to scientific law and reason:

> By the unconscious we wish to indicate that essential unique nature of every individual creature, which is, by its very nature, unanalysable, undefinable, inconceivable . . . As a matter of fact, soul would be a better word. By the unconscious we do mean the soul. But the word soul has been vitiated by the idealistic use, until nowadays it means only that which a man conceives himself to be.[69]

Like the Schopenhauerian will, the Lawrentian unconscious is potentially fierce and cruel. But rather than be denied through impersonality, as Schopenhauer implores, it is to be respected (resembling, in this regard, the Heideggerian attitude towards being).[70]

Lawrence's metaphysical antihumanism engenders further incongruities between *Sons and Lovers* and the tradition of the *Bildungsroman*. In the genre the hero's progress is ironised; he never finds what he sets out to find. Yet somehow, through circuitous rather than direct means, self-awareness is accomplished. Unintended consequences of the hero's actions prove to be more important than intended consequences; the mismatch between inner life and outer circumstance eventuates in the attainment of *Bildung*. In *Sons and Lovers* this both is and is not the case. The strife encountered by its characters results from the psyche's opacity. But at the deeper level, where the soul persists, there can be no untruths. Similarly, though social life may produce its chimeras, the mysterious source is a provider of redemption. Soul and source are mutually harmonious, in synch with each other's inhuman authenticity. Only at the human level, in the interplay between psychic individualism and social formation, is there conflict.

Finally, as the closing passages of *Sons and Lovers* indicate, there is no adequate scale for the human. Even without the triad of women vying for his soul, Paul is still daunted by a preterhuman power, by an impersonal and universal force:

> Where was he? – one tiny upright speck of flesh, less than an ear of wheat lost in the field. He could not bear it. On every side the immense dark silence seemed pressing him, so tiny a speck, into extinction, and yet, almost nothing, he could not be extinct. Night, in which everything was lost, went reaching out, beyond

stars and sun. Stars and sun, a few bright grains, went spinning round for terror and holding each other in embrace, there in a darkness that outpassed them all and left them tiny and daunted. So much, and himself, infinitesimal, at the core a nothingness, and yet not nothing. (464)

Is there anything to recuperate from this 'nothingness' that is, nevertheless, 'not nothing'? It is tempting to read this as a withering analysis that raises at least the possibility of redemption, opening up a space for a clearer, undeceived self-attentiveness. Lawrence's humanist defenders have done precisely this, fixing on Paul's final resolve to turn towards the 'faintly humming, glowing town', away from the darkness. But as Louis Fraiberg writes: 'The last paragraph of the book, which has seemed to some an affirmation of the victory for life, and for Paul, can yield this meaning only if the plain tendency of all that has gone before is ignored or if the book is regarded as leading to a sequel in which all will be reversed.'[71] I suggest, as Fraiberg indicates, that the opposite obtains. Indeed, one could read this passage as an incipient apostasy, reaching full flower in the ominous fixations of *Women in Love*.

### Women in Love: *apocalypse now*

These are the two great temptations of the fall of man, the fall from spontaneous, single, pure being, into what we call materialism or automatism or mechanism of the self.

Men clotting together into social masses in order to limit their individual liabilities: this is humanity.

D. H. Lawrence[72]

Although *Sons and Lovers* is inimical to the *Bildungsroman*, *The Rainbow* – originally a continuous narrative with *Women in Love*, entitled first 'The Sisters' then 'The Wedding Ring' – invites a guarded comparison. Peter Middleton identifies the connection between narrative form (generations of family history) and subjectivity:

*The Rainbow* is a narrative of the emergence of articulate modern subjectivity through the historical sequence of different relationships. In that way it is very close to Hegel's *Phenomenology of Spirit*. Lawrence's novel shows the lived consequences of different forms of thought – humanism, behaviourism, different kinds of morality, art and science – on a not quite believably small group of people over several generations.[73]

The *Phenomenology*, we saw in Chapter 1, has been interpreted as an account of the *Bildung* of consciousness. Hegelian *Geist*, a sort of metaconsciousness, mimics the lineaments of the *Bildungsroman*, inasmuch as it proceeds via the same causative force animating the narrativised inner life of the individual. Yet the *Bildungsroman* borrows its mastertrope not from the process of cerebration, but from something more direct and unaffected: the Goethean model of organic growth, which is cumulative, gradual and total.[74] This is closer to *The Rainbow*'s contours, which imitate biological rather than mental causation. Its narrative shape, writes Kate Millett, is based on natality: 'Every event, whether it be falling in love or attaining maturity, is described in terms of fertility, gestation, parturition, and birth. In *The Rainbow*, women appear to give birth by parthenogenesis.'[75] Applied to generations of lives, the nine-month pattern presents an iterable eulogy to pastoral life.[76]

Lawrence is thus compelled to engage with a certain formal conservatism. Narrative development must proceed as leisurely and concertedly as an uncomplicated childbirth, in order properly to sanctify the pastoral existence that is the lifeblood of two of the three generations of Brangwens. It makes all the more glaring, then, the fall from this kind of arcadian idyll into the horror of industrial modernity. In this doleful narrative, modern man has fallen not because he has forgotten the question of being – i.e., because thought in general and philosophy in particular has been diverted from its true path – but because of social expansion and the development of mechanical civilisation. In other words, those things that humanism takes as inherently linked to human betterment merely confirm, for Lawrence, the fall from a state of natural self-fulfilment, from a condition of 'spontaneous, single, pure being'.

Thus *The Rainbow* is notable for 'enacting as well as thematically pondering deep continuity or generational transmission in a culture both settled and changing.'[77] The point of transition between the settled and the changing – or the moment when the fall into modernity is announced – is the scene at Wiggiston, taking place under the shadow of the colliery. The town 'had the strange desolation of a ruin', the colliers passing through 'not like living people, but like spectres'. The participants in this episode – Tom, a second-generation Brangwen, and Winifred Inger, his lover – exemplify the hypocrisy that Lawrence now aligns with humanism. Both of them criticise and condemn the colliery, 'the great machine which has taken us all captives'; but still they rely on it for solace, to meliorate the uncertainty of selfhood, the perplexity of being human. For Tom, the colliery manager, '[his] only happy moments, his only moments of pure freedom were when he was serving the machine. Then, and then only, when the machine caught him up, was he free from the hatred of himself, could he act wholely, without cynicism and unreality.'[78] And although Winifred does not live in Wiggiston, still she:

worshipped the impure abstraction, the mechanisms of matter. There, there, in the machine, in the service of the machine, was she free from the clog and degradation of human feeling. There, in the monstrous mechanism that held all matter, living or dead, in its service, did she achieve her consummation and her perfect unison, her immortality. (398)

Machine technology enables Winifred to transcend the depredations of sentimentality, the demands of emotional complicity. Her idealist outlook contrasts with Tom's materialist mindset. Ursula, a third-generation Brangwen, restores a sense of Lawrentian normativity to the scene: 'If she could she would smash the machine. Her soul's action should be the smashing of the great machine' (398). The mechanical is only useful as a force brought to bear on the human; the immanent-transcendent soul must triumph over the mechanical, and its iniquitous humanist affiliations.

But humanism as such is not part of the main drama in *Women in Love*. Instead, the book stages a contest between the mechanical inhuman, as exemplified by Gerald Crich, and the transcendent posthuman, whose embodiment is Rupert Birkin. The nature of their interaction, as indicated by the book's most infamous chapter, is "gladiatorial". (The dynamic of their relationship undoes, in a single stroke, the novel as a tale of courtship and marriage connoted by the earlier title of 'The Wedding Ring'; Birkin 'courts' Gerald with his offer of brotherly love, the substitute marriage of a *Blutbrüderschaft*.) What is human is exposed to remorseless, invidious critique, and kept to the margins. There, its chief representatives are Will Brangwen and Thomas Crich – old, feeble, and impotent.

The arc of the fall describes *The Rainbow*'s narrative trail, or 'the unraveling of English culture over three generations'.[79] But in *Women in Love* the fall is a fact, not a process. The work takes us through a process of dissolution, beginning in the midst of malaise: race, world and individual spirit are all at the end of their tethers.[80] Composed in 1916, and revised in 1917, the text is pervaded by the nihilism of the First World War. Joyce Carol Oates has described this chiliastic countenance as Lawrence's *Götterdämmerung*: 'Time is running out, history is coming to an end, the Apocalypse is at hand.'[81] It is a twentieth-century revision of the Arnoldian diagnosis, a culture trapped between two worlds, one dying and the other refusing to be born. Lawrence's modernist gesture is to hurry the latter's gestation; what appears to issue naturally from the pages of *The Rainbow* must in its successor be forced, or better, induced. Its apocalyptic tenor suggests proto-Beckettian *Weltschmerz*, a kind of *Endgame*-with-transcendence.

But it is not just the disappearance of parturition metaphors that belies narrative continuity between *The Rainbow* and *Women in Love*. It is also the vagueness of the fall, as it crosses between the two texts. What happens in the former work has always already happened in the latter; the fall is both historical *and* transhistorical, or structural. The Wiggiston colliery is transformed from an agricultural hamlet into a mining community in a mere seven years – still time enough, apparently, to fall. At the other end of the prelapsarian scale, in *Women in Love*, is Birkin's contemplation of an African statuette. He decides that the race the figure represented had, thousands of years ago, become extinct. Speculating on the cause, he posits a version of Eliot's dissociation of sensibility: 'It must have been thousands of years since her race had died mystically: that is, since the relation between the senses and the outspoken mind had broken, leaving the experience all in one sort, mystically sensual.' The postlapsarian condition is made plain, with hints of 'orientalist' language: 'We fall from the connection with life and hope, we lapse from pure integral being, from creation and liberty, and we fall into a long, long African process of purely sensual understanding, knowledge in the mystery of dissolution.'[82]

Soon after this meditation, Birkin encounters fallen humanity, or mechanised man, in the shape of Will Brangwen, Ursula's father. Birkin muses:

> How curious it was that this was a human being! . . . Birkin could see only a strange, inexplicable, almost patternless collection of passions and desires and suppressions and traditions and mechanical ideas, all cast unfused and disunited into this slender, bright-faced man of nearly fifty, who was as unresolved now as he was at twenty, and as uncreated. (255)

The human is defamiliarised into a mechanical, disunited and uncreated being. Self-delusion stalks this creature, a mismatch between soul-consciousness and reality. Birkin, of course, can see the contrariety. And by making him an expert exegete, an authentic reader of souls, Lawrence sanitises Birkin's inclination to misanthropy: 'His dislike of mankind, of the mass of mankind, amounted almost to an illness' (61).[83] Birkin's attraction to Gerald Crich affirms Lawrence's antihumanism. Birkin sees his friend as 'fated, doomed, limited' to a single form of existence, knowledge and activity. And this limitation is a 'clog' (like the 'clog and degradation of human feeling' that threatens Winifred), a type of monomania (207). Lawrence is suggesting, in short, that by becoming mechanised the human has stunted its ontological development.

Mechanised man is also, unavoidably, socialised man. Social being, as Lawrence writes in 'John Galsworthy', is subsequent to the urbanisation of modern life:

It seems to me that when the human being becomes too much divided between his subjective and objective consciousness, at last something splits in him and he becomes a social being [ . . . ] While a man remains a man, before he falls and becomes a social individual, he innocently feels himself altogether within the great continuum of the universe.[84]

Becoming a social individual is a form of slavery; it 'takes the place in our civilization of the slave in the old civilizations'.[85] It is, in effect, another way for man to fall.

As we have seen, the postlapsarian condition seems to have intensified between *The Rainbow* and *Women in Love*. Without the incantatory prose that 'redeemed' the early parts of the former, the latter seems dispirited, riven by internal division. At the level of narrative form, its discontinuities are held together by recurrent linguistic devices and images.[86] John Worthen writes:

Its very structure is a refusal of a simple narrative progression; its clear-cut, often unlinked chapters follow not the sequence of a particular narrative but the progress of particular concerns – like individuality, freedom, love and consciousness. Birkin's confusions are the necessary links in a chain of thoughts, as are Ursula's inconsistencies. The novel is constructed to elicit from its characters the complexities attendant upon their advanced lives; it interweaves theory and experience, idea and counter-idea, knowing and being.[87]

The novel also contains a movement, and a countermovement. The movement is the fall into modernity, as outlined above. Counterposed to it is transcendence, implicit in the novel's structure, in its 'clear-cut, often unlinked chapters'. Thus its narrative form, intermittent and dissolute, is directly opposed to *The Rainbow*'s tidal rhythms, its generative cycles of gestation and birth.

The scenes between Birkin and Crich exemplify this more fractured rhythm. They amount to an attack on the idea of progress. The journeying motif of the railway, a common metaphor for narrative progression, is undercut by the lack of purposiveness that characterises the two men.[88] These scenes prepare the way for 'An Island', the chapter in which Birkin

charms Ursula with a scathing attack on *anthropos*. 'Man is a mistake,'
pronounces Birkin, 'he must go' (128). Aidan Burns has defended this
misanthropic remark with the claim that 'this is not the final word spoken
in the chapter and it is certainly not the final position of the author of
*Women in Love*'.[89] But this is hardly the only example of Birkin's overt
misanthropy, as I have already indicated. There is an earlier scene in the
train, with Gerald: 'Humanity is a dead letter. There will be a new embodiment, in a new way. Let humanity disappear as quickly as possible'
(59). And much later in the Alps, musing on Gerald's apparent suicide:
'The eternal creative mystery could dispose of man, and replace him
with a finer created being: just as the horse has taken the place of the
mastodon. [ . . . ] It was very consoling to Birkin, to think this' (479).

Burns also cites Ursula's demurral as evidence of admonition. She
'provides the kick in the wind', and 'senses the falseness in his attempt to
isolate himself from that humanity of which he is so obviously a part'.[90]
But Ursula herself is not exempt from the same charge, for '[she] herself
knew too well the actuality of humanity, its hideous actuality' (128). Later,
when Birkin is away from Ursula: 'From the bottom of her heart, from
the bottom of her soul, she despised and detested people, adult people
[ . . . ] She had a profound grudge against the human being. That which
the word "human" stood for was despicable and repugnant to her' (244).
And near the end, when she has come to accept Birkin's apocalyptic cast
of mind, she tells her sister Gudrun: 'Love is too human and too little. I
believe in something inhuman, of which love is only a little part. I believe
what we must fulfil comes out of the Unknown to us, and it is something
infinitely more than love. It isn't so merely human' (438). Love is another
form of congestion, another stricture imposed on authentic ontological
possibility.

In a letter written to Edward Garnett during the composition of 'The
Wedding Ring', Lawrence writes of a 'new human phenomenon'. He
contrasts the old-fashioned moral schemes of Tolstoy and Dostoevsky
with 'that which is physic – non-human, in humanity'. What interests
him in a woman is the 'inhuman will', rather than 'what she feels according to the human conception'.[91] But at what point does a new human
phenomenon become an *in*human phenomenon? How much strain can
the human withstand before it becomes its antithesis, its other? A revealing exchange between Birkin and Ursula clarifies the Lawrentian
transcendent. They debate creation versus dissolution, wondering why
'the end of the world [isn't] as good as the beginning': ' "If we are at the
end, we are not the beginning," he said. "Yes we are," she said. "The

beginning comes out of the end." "After it, not out of it. After us, not out of us"'(173). Where Ursula envisages the process of creation as one of sublation, elevating what has gone before into a new synthesis,[92] Birkin considers the creative cycle as pure transcendence, as abandonment rather than reconstitution. In seeking what comes after the human he is positing, therefore, not an antihumanism but a posthumanism. Sublation only compounds this problem, the quintessential human dilemma that it has *not transcended enough*, and therefore demands a further overcoming. Birkin, like Lawrence, regards the human as a transcended animal that it is neither transcendent nor animal enough.

Birkin reiterates his diagnosis – 'After us, not out of us' – a few pages later: 'And he wanted to be with Ursula as free as with himself, single and clear and cool, yet balanced, polarised with her. The merging, the clutching, the mingling of love was become madly abhorrent to him' (200). He seeks an independence that is also a mutual *inter*dependence; later it is described as 'this mutual union in separateness' (264). Why should Birkin find merging so abhorrent? It remains an impasse in his relationship with Ursula:

Fusion, fusion, this horrible fusion of two beings, which every woman and most men insisted on, was it not nauseous and horrible anyhow, whether it was a fusion of the spirit or of the emotional body? . . . Why could they not remain individuals, limited by their own limits? Why this dreadful all-comprehensiveness, this hateful tyranny? Why not leave the other being free, why try to absorb, or melt, or merge. One might abandon oneself utterly to the *moment*, but not to any other being. (309)

Metaphysical fusion, however – in transcendent, posthuman terms – is exquisite, man's final redemption. In a letter to his sister Ada, Lawrence writes: 'When we die, like rain-drops falling back again into the sea, we fall back into the big, shimmering sea of unorganised life which we call God. We are lost as individuals, yet we count in the whole.'[93] Human fusion is mutually corrupting, a merging that aggrandises fallenness; posthuman fusion is a shedding of foul humanity, a transcending movement to rescind the effects of the fall.[94]

It is evident, then, that social reality and metaphysical reality are locked into a zero-sum game; attaining oneness or connectivity in the one must always be at the expense of the other. To fall is not preordained, nor is it necessary. If for Schopenhauer the *principium individuationis* has separated us, made us into individual beings, for Lawrence it is something more mundane (though equally virulent): the encumbrances of modern life and the self-consciousness that begets social consciousness. Man is always already connected to forces greater than himself: 'It is the essential innocence and naïveté of the human being, the sense of being at one with the great universe-continuum of space-time-life, which is vivid in a great man, and a pure nuclear spark in every man who is still free.'[95]

Finally, Lawrence/Birkin's rage against fusion returns us to the original meaning of transcendence. *Women in Love* brings to the surface the nascent agony of sexual difference in *Sons and Lovers*, the dispirited conviction that sexual union is incomplete, that the male–female sexual covenant can never be truly consummated.[96] Overcoming sublation, fusion, or one thing out of another (the principle of narrative causation) implies, in fact, a repudiation of narrative in general, and the particular narrative form of *The Rainbow*, the iterative process of conception and birth. Transcending fusion demands, therefore, a transcendence of the feminine; and 'sublation' and 'transcendence' assume gender roles. Transcendence is masculinised as pure discontinuity, a clean break with precedent. And sublation is feminised, irrevocably bound to the procreative process of parturition, a process exclusive of male participation.[97] Resistance to fusion is symptomatic of the urge to transcend the love of women (which further ironises 'The Wedding Ring', the novel of courtship and marriage). *Women in Love* thus describes the 'shift in Lawrence's thought from the glorification of procreative sexuality toward the transcendence of desire'.[98] And narrative discontinuity, so central to modernist literary form, is gendered by Lawrence. The modernist urge to make it new is taken up by him as the imperative to break with feminine literary form and engage with masculine 'separation'. The heterogeneity of *The Rainbow* and *Women in Love* now appears more pronounced than ever, the gap between them – notwithstanding their common origin – as wide, in terms of narrative formation, as could be imagined.[99]

## ANTHROPOS AGONISTES

> Is 'humanity', as a reality and as an idea, a point of departure – or a point of arrival?
>
> Antonio Gramsci[100]

We have seen how easily adaptable theories of fallenness are for antihumanist thought. Man has fallen either, in Heideggerian terms, because of hypertrophic self-regard (the metaphysical mistake that is subjectivity); or, from the Lawrentian outlook, because of unrelenting self-circmscription (humanism as a clogging of genuine ontological possibility). And although both are regarded as Nietzschean inheritors, there are irreducible eccentricities on both sides, which have helped shape the genealogy of anthropometric thought: Heidegger's discrepant use of narrative philosophy, which parallels the literary-modernist temper; and Lawrence's unapologetic metaphysics, a cleaving to the Schopenhauerian at the expense of the Nietzschean. Heidegger dispossesses metaphysical man by agential reversal, by 'propriating' him to extrahuman sources (language, technology, art). Lawrence, conversely, dispossesses metaphysical man from *within*, by dehumanising the soul.

Lawrence sees the transcendent as truly transcendent, hence beyond human apprehension. And as with Heidegger, this disposition is essentially a religious one. Heideggerian being and the Lawrentian source are both unconsummable by human involvement, and so they identify, implicitly, a split between religion and ethics. Their theistic tendencies are nonethical in terms of application; there are no compelling intersubjective consequences that ensue from thinking the beyond.

For Lawrence the human is an 'interesting animal', in Nietzsche's expression, only to the extent that it is a transcending animal – not, however, in the sense that it has already overcome animality, but rather in that it can look ahead to a future overcoming. So he values the human only insofar as it possesses the potential to triumph over its humanity, where humanity is synonymous with fallenness. Similarly, Lawrence values woman only for her (unconscious) ability to grant access to the transcendent. For vulgar humanists who see transcendence as a form of self-exaltation, humanity is a point of arrival. Lawrence, in contradistinction, regards humanity as a sort of evolutionary aberration whose sole usefulness is as a point of departure. With the arrogance and assumptions of humanist transcendence comes loss – of a relationship with being (Heidegger), or of a sense of connection to all living things (Lawrence). Heidegger and Lawrence begin with a degraded entity: fallen from a relationship with being into the abyss of modernity that is *das Man*; or fallen into the social mechanism that begets self-consciousness and systematised abstraction.

The multitude of similarities between Heidegger and Lawrence – the background in German thought, the religious refigurations, the conviction that mankind is ontologically diminished from a fall into modernity – are finally superseded by a crucial difference. Where Heidegger endorses accession to the nonhuman, Lawrence is locked in a struggle – a struggle with his own malignancy, manifesting itself as impatience with human ways of being. Daniel Allbright notes: 'Through all of Lawrence's work he flirts with the idea of self-expansion, the hope that one can become the universe.'[101] But there is an obverse to this hope, a potential pitfall when self-expansion is frustrated by the decline into industrial civilisation. It yields an irascibility towards fallen humanity, born of disconsolation and defeat. In contrast to Heidegger's 'antihumanist humanism', his serene endorsements of being and the endless compensation it provides for human frailty, Lawrence's is an agonistic antihumanism. He displays perpetual frustration at human frailty and limitation, particularly at the irreconcilable gap of sexual difference.

Hardy's Clym, in *The Return of the Native*, provides Lawrence with an inventory of human shortcomings: 'Impotent to be, he must transform himself, and live in an abstraction, in a generalisation, he must identify himself with the system. He must live as Man or Humanity, or as the Community, or as Society, or as Civilisation.'[102] Clym's predicaments constitute a shortlist of Lawrence's animus, all of a piece and all responsible for the limited halflife that is postlapsarian human existence. Lawrence's position in the anthropometric genealogy is an extreme one, where there is little hope for human self-renewal. In the next two chapters, by contrast, Virginia Woolf and Samuel Beckett invoke a less virulent conception of *anthropos*, opening the way to new, nonanthropocentric possibilities for human being.

# 4

## Woolf's luminance: time out of mind

Movement and change are the essence of our being; rigidity is death; conformity is death: let us say what comes into our heads, repeat ourselves, contradict ourselves, fling out the wildest nonsense, and follow the most fantastic fancies without caring what the world does or thinks or says. For nothing matters except life; and, of course, order.

Virginia Woolf[1]

[T]hese two discoveries – that the life of our sexual instincts cannot be wholly tamed, and that mental processes are in themselves
unconscious and only reach the ego and come under its control
through incomplete and untrustworthy perceptions – these two discoveries amount to a statement that *the ego is not master in its own house.*
Together they represent the third blow to man's self-love, what I may
call the *psychological* one.

Sigmund Freud[2]

According to Freud's narrative of human disillusionment, the first two
body-blows to human pride were the Copernican theory of planetary
motion, and the Darwinian affirmation of animal, rather than divine,
descent. Taken together, heliocentrism, natural selection and the psyche's unconscious may have served to cripple, as Freud declared, *homo
sapiens*'s claim to autonomy and discontinuity with the rest of nature.
But this antihumanist narrative does not follow a strict teleology, as it
overlooks the many and diverse attempts to shore up waning humanist
self-confidence. These efforts go by the names noted in previous chapters:
anthropomorphism, transcendence (of nature), instrumental reason, and
even narrative itself, in its orthodox guises. What they all share, at bottom, is another primary theme: scale. It is the regulatory effects of scale
that bring the extrahuman within the boundaries of cognition, where it
can be assimilated.

In anthropometric terms, the two axes conferring scale are the
geometric and the chronometric. The former, derived from the body,
is made manifest in human-scale architecture and design. The latter,
derived from the lifecycle of *homo sapiens*, betokens one of the grandest
scalemaking endeavours in human history: the quest to make time first
measureable, and then personal. As we saw in Chapter 2, William Paley
decreed an ownerless timepiece to be a metonymy of human presence. In
more general terms, watches and clocks transformed time from a cosmic
phenomenon to a personal one. Individual beings could conduct their ac-
tivities in consonance with a chronometric scale that was human-created,
rather than empirically notated. Technological timekeeping provided a
way of possessing time, of humanising it by individualising it.

Allied to this was Kant's so-called 'Copernican revolution', which
transformed time from a property of the world into a property of the self –
or rather, made time a condition whereby the self could experience the
world. With this understanding, time became an *a priori* intuition, a form
of experience structured by the mind: 'Time is nothing else than the form
of the internal sense, that is, of the intuitions of self and of our internal

state. For time cannot be any determination of outward phenomena. [...] [T]he conception of time ... inheres not in the objects themselves, but solely in the subject (or mind) which intuites them.'[3] For post-Kantian philosophical thinking in the nineteenth century, this meant that time was always already complicit with subjectivity, and hence with human being.

The same was not true, however – or not to the same extent – for the literary organisation of time in this period. In Victorian poetics it is not the personal stopwatch that exemplifies time, but the public clock, and the sound of church bells. Accordingly, the realist novel's mimetic authority, its 'truth to individual experience',[4] in Ian Watt's phrase, was underwritten by the depiction of inner *and* outer worlds – though with the former strictly subordinated to the latter, and always subsequent to it. The stability of individual experience was dependent upon the stability of its world; for the former to compel readerly trust, the latter had to be convincingly concrete, whole and material; in short, it had to be habitable. And accompanying this abundance of mimetic detail, furthering the illusion of realism, was a similarly imposing legibility of time. Through the temporal authorities of Church and State, time was made to seem determined and univocal. It came to assume almost a reified, participatory role in the action, as reliable and unflagging as the omniscient narratorial voice. As a consequence, Victorian narratives of progress and conformity – whether historical or fictive – made time irrevocable, inexorable and monumental. Through the nineteenth century, and the age of expansion (urban, imperial, industrial), time became steadily more impersonal and less human.

### Bergson, Lewis and the rehumanisation of time

The vitalist philosophy of Henri Bergson is at odds with both these versions of temporality – Kantian idealism and literary realism – and with chronometric devices (watches and clocks) in their entirety. For Bergson time is not chronometric but experiential, and any attempt to quantify it – through subdivision or categorisation – has already dehumanised it. Independent of the divided, discrete world of extension, which our superficial selves inhabit, is the realm of *durée*, a zone of pure continuity and heterogeneity, where the *moi fondamental* resides. The true, qualitative experience that is *durée* is not based on a transcendental notion of time, as it is not a presuppositional condition for experience; rather, it *is* that experience, immediate and intuitive, and it provides a pathway to the absolute (which Kant bracketed off as 'noumenal'). Freedom is a fact, declares Bergson in *Time and Free Will*.[5] This is not the freedom whose governance is reason, as Kant asserted ('Reason, with its practical law, determines the will immediately'),[6] but the freedom of intuition, which enables us to experience the flux of life. And it is opposed to the 'facts' that literary realism, in its bid for objectivity, freely adapts – transforming, in the process, a positivist, determinist conception of time into the measured steps of progress, the narrative of inevitable, forthright advancement.

*Durée* has been called 'psychological time', but it might more accurately be termed 'soul time'. As Bergson writes, 'in the simplest [states of consciousness] the whole soul can be reflected'.[7] Events do not take place in a homogeneous medium, measurable by instrumental means; they are coextensive and permeable, stored as memory below the level of consciousness. Measurability means that human beings are unaware of *durée*, because they are caught up in 'spatial' time, or *l'étendu*. To rehumanise time, therefore, is to retemporalise it, to recognise it as that which cannot be recovered, hence cannot be measured.

Bergson's role in the formation of literary modernism has slipped in importance considerably throughout the past half-century. He now means far less to historiographers of modernism than does the post-Kantian German tradition, and the 'masters of suspicion' (Marx, Nietzsche, Freud) who provide the template for French cultural theory.[8] Yet Bergson's influence on T. S. Eliot remains unassailable,[9] and, more obliquely – for there is no evidence of her having read Bergson – Virginia Woolf, the literary subject of this chapter, continues to provide numerous striking parallels and coincidences with Bergsonian thinking.[10]

The measure of Bergson's earlier importance for high modernism is apparent in the attention paid to him by his most outspoken opponent, Wyndham Lewis. Like Bergson, Lewis has receded into the background of literary history, his influence waning since the first half of the twentieth century. Lewis's allegations in *Time and Western Man* – more polemical than philosophical – coalesce into what he calls 'time-philosophy', of which Bergsonism is the main culprit. Lewis's disapprobation is centred on the fact that time-philosophy is relativistic and decentring, curtailing man's sovereignty in the world. He posits the self as 'our only terra firma in a boiling and shifting world', and insists on a rigorous dualism of subject and object, mind and matter.[11] In Berkeley's time, he writes, materialists believed that dead matter was real; now they are obsessed with making it real, 'by pumping it full of "time", until it is a quicksilver beneath his hand'.[12] With remorseless logic Lewis avers that bringing the external world to life demands a concomitant surrendering of the vitality of the internal world, the life of the mind.

To countermand time-philosophy, Lewis propounds a version of objective realism that exalts the physical and the tactile while remaining firmly grounded in the immediate present. Like Nietzsche, Lewis believes that any emphasis on the not-here and the not-now – suggestive advertising, rampant nostalgia, unconscious urges, the rhetoric of Revolution and its accompanying myth of Progress – serves to undermine the here and now. There is an emphasis in Lewis's work on *hardness*, on the concrete. It echoes Pound's declaration that the image must be 'hard' (where the symbol is 'soft'), and translates into a sweeping cultural vision. Lewis describes himself as a '*realist*, in the most sensible acceptance of the word', and argues that since we live in the real world, what can any of us be other than realists? In this world stability is essential, and so is *deadness*, 'for the fullest, most concrete "realism"'.[13]

Lewis's endorsement of objectivity, tactility, stability, the present, the real and concrete, is countered in every instance by the literary poetics of Virginia Woolf. 'On or about December 1910, human character changed': this phrase of Woolf's is justly famous for encapsulating an essential part of her thinking. It indicates her preference for Georgian culture over Edwardian, and for modernist art over its realist forebear (1910 being the year of George V's accession, and of the controversial post-Impressionist exhibition at the Grafton Galleries). It also affirms her belief that such a vast and vague thing as 'human character' exists, and can be ascertained. But most of all, the phrase acknowledges, even endorses, radical change. For Woolf reality is mobile, mind is boundaryless, and memory is as vivid and real as perception.

### Virginia Woolf: timelines and lifelines

In *Men Without Art* (1935) Lewis describes Woolf's writing as a 'fashionable dimness' fixated upon 'the half-lighted places of the mind'.[14] His choice of metaphor is neither accidental nor gratuitous, parodying Woolf's own turn of phrase in perhaps her most quoted critical passage:

Life is not a series of gig lamps systematically arranged; life is a luminous halo, a semi-transparent envelope surrounding us from the beginning of consciousness to the end. Is it not the task of the novelist to convey this varying, this unknown and uncircumscribed spirit, whatever aberration or complexity it may display, with as little mixture of the alien and external as possible?[15]

It is the task of the novelist to purvey this spiritual luminance, as shown by Hardy, Conrad and W. H. Hudson, whom she champions over Wells, Bennett and Galsworthy. The latter are condemned for being 'material-ists', who are 'concerned not with the spirit but with the body' (147). The problem with their work is clear: 'Life escapes; and perhaps without life nothing else is worth while . . . Whether we call it life or spirit, truth or reality, this, the essential thing, has moved off, or on, and refuses to be contained any longer in such ill-fitting vestments as we provide.'[16] Is life like this, she asks, and must novels be like this?

Nothing is so clearcut for Woolf's protagonists, however. Clarissa Dalloway's moments of purity are 'buds on the tree of life, flowers of darkness'[17] (the botanic metaphors are heavy with significance, as we will see in the next section). She stages parties ('offerings'), she thinks, so as to bring people together, to feel their continuous existence. '"That's what I do it for," she said, speaking aloud, to life' (133). These rela-tively untroubled, affirmatory reflections are clouded in the party scene, with the news that Septimus, the distressed war veteran, has committed suicide. The tenor changes, and life is considered as something exter-nal to the self, with its own exorbitant demands that it be *lived*: 'the terror; the overwhelming incapacity, one's parents giving it into one's hands, this life, to be lived to the end, to be walked with serenely; there was in the depths of her heart an awful fear' (202–3). This fear is prompted by the feeling that one is outside life, and must find an entry point to it. For Mrs Ramsay, in *To the Lighthouse*, there is no equiv-ocation: life must be conquered anew, day in, day out, lest it become oppressive. '[A]gain she felt alone in the presence of her old antago-nist, life.'[18] At the end of the dinner party she has arranged, she gives herself a 'little shake' (like a watch) and, 'life being strong enough to bear her on again, she began all this business' (*TL* 91–2). Both women's struggles with life are also struggles with death. Clarissa is touched and haunted by Septimus's demise, seeing it as somehow implicated in her own continuance. And Mrs Ramsay speculates about immor-tality, about her 'afterlife' in the generations succeeding her. When she dies, in the strange, impersonal second part, 'Time Passes', these thoughts become paramount, steering the narrative to its conclusion. For both women, death is immanent in life and an inherent part of their being.

The different understandings of time considered so far all lay claim to a more intimate and exacting relationship with human being. Yet each, inevitably, has been censured for doing just the opposite. Time was personalised by chronometric technology, and made a property of the self by Kantian idealism. But still Bergson sought to 'rehumanise' it, by developing a deeper, truer understanding of the time in which people actually live and have experiences. And again, Lewis declared that Bergsonian *durée* had disastrous consequences for selfhood, by scattering it recklessly across temporal fault planes. Does Virginia Woolf seek to (re)humanise time in her novels, as Bergson attempted in his philosophical reflection?

Of all literary forms, the novel is most closely associated with time, through the preeminence it grants to narrative. If plot, as we saw in the Introduction, is 'an organization that humanizes time by giving it form',[19] then all novels are unwittingly complicit in the rehumanisation of time. This leads us back to Ian Watt's remark alluded to above, that the novel form contains the implicit premise, or convention, that 'the novel is a full and authentic report of human experience'.[20] The two preceding chapters have shown how Conrad and Lawrence strove to depict not human experience but human expropriation, by focusing on the dispossessive forces of machine technology and metaphysical transcendence. Woolf, by contrast, restores human experience to the forefront of novelistic practice. Her manner of doing so, however, widens the notion of experience to such an extent that it finally breaks with Watt's dictum. Her unrelenting demonstrations of instability, lack of fixity, and metamorphic change entail the dissolution of many of the traditional distinctions between human and nonhuman (animal and plant) existence. Human self-definition is thus confiscated as assuredly as it is in Conrad's and Lawrence's narratives, although for very different reasons.

The remainder of this chapter explores Woolf's position through her two high-modernist opuses of the 1920s, *Mrs Dalloway* and *To the Lighthouse*. The accompanying argument suggests that her concern is less to humanise time than to show human performance in negotiating time's vicissitudes. In these novels the conventional boundaries between the human and the natural are very liberally policed. The narrative poetics they deploy – that is, the particularities of their *telling* – suggest that it is stories that maintain those boundaries in the first place. If narrative is human, for Woolf, it is also a restriction of an individual's humanity, a singleminded severing of ties with the nonhuman world. The difficulty to be assayed is how the novel form, of all things, can be exploited to keep faith with these precepts. The philosophical attitude that emerges denotes a signal reworking of humanist tenets, and their reinscription as a mutable, variegated form of ahumanism.

> I mean to eliminate all waste, deadness, superfluity: to give the moment whole; whatever it includes. Say that the moment is a combination of thought; sensation; the voice of the sea.
>
> Virginia Woolf[21]

The idea of 'connection' was put on the modernist agenda by E. M. Forster, through his protagonist Margaret Schlegel, in *Howards End* (1910): 'Only connect! That was the whole of her sermon. Only connect the prose and the passion, and both will be exalted, and human love will be seen at its height.'[22] 'Only connect' has become an all-purpose plea for communicative action, but in the context of Margaret's 'sermon', her subsequent remark is no less significant: 'Live in fragments no longer.'[23] Woolf, by contrast, is more sanguine and accepting of life's fundamental incongruities and disharmony. In 'Mr Bennett and Mrs Brown' she writes: 'We must reconcile ourselves to a season of failures and fragments' – a statement that so incensed Lewis that he made it the epigraph to his jeremiad.[24] Woolf's position is further complicated in *Mrs Dalloway*, which is both a repudiation of Forster's plea, and an ironic elegy for it.

Although Woolf's novels do much to support a Bergsonian experience of time, that support is always ambivalent. Her writing articulates not one but two interpretations of experience, as both flux and fragmentation. Life consists of flowing streams of sensation, yet it is also centred in the singular, heterogeneous moment. These two renderings – of vertiginous, wavelike fluidity and atomised, isolated particularity – are especially noteworthy in *Mrs Dalloway*. Despite appearances to the contrary, though, they are not oppositions, bound in a relationship of meaningful tension. Nor can they be properly understood as an economy of dialectical exchange. They operate, rather, along an axis, as covariant properties of experience. Like wave-particle dualism, the two modalities do not cancel each other out but exist in tandem, coextensive of each other. The chief consequence of this variability is to render meaning radically unstable. As we shall see, it is either elusive and ungraspable, or it is all too evident, to the point of oppression. 'Connections' between human beings thus cannot be other than ironic, given this mobility of meaning, this oscillation between extremes.

### *Translations: human, nature, technology*

In contrast to Conrad's seafaring stories and Lawrence's mining-town tales, Woolf's *Mrs Dalloway* exemplifies one particularly significant aspect of the high-modernist undertaking. The novel's urban temper, scenes taking place in various inner-city London locales, determines in advance the sort of experience its characters will undergo. Laura Marcus writes: 'In the literature of the city, the city itself becomes a text to be read and interpreted. Woolf emphasizes the graphic and textual elements of the city as well as its visual and cinematic qualities.'[25] When it comes to deciphering those elements, however, there are invariably complications, confusions, equivocations. *Mrs Dalloway*'s opening set-piece scene, for example, has an aeroplane writing letters in the sky. One by one, onlookers attempt to make sense of these letters, to no avail; the message, or product, that is being announced remains mysterious and unknowable. On the other side of interpretability are the vivid, acutely nuanced glimpses into the world's nature – or what he takes for it – gleaned by Septimus Warren Smith.

Instability as an attribute of character, as a psychological marker, is embodied in the mentally disoriented Septimus. He is the nervecentre of the novel, a hypersensitised conductor of impressions, receiving the faintest, most subtle of them as unambiguous messages of hope, despair or damnation. As an exemplar of what ails, or strengthens, all of Woolf's characters in the novel, Septimus is an alarming portrayal of human sensory potential gone awry, with all the cognitive filters removed. In one sense, he might almost be a Lawrentian parody. If all the walls between characters were down and sensation unimpeded, we would not be made privy to multifarious soul-readings, or become one with the extrahuman source, but instead be condemned to a condition of overstimulated neurasthenia. Septimus gives frightening credence to Woolf's attempt to 'record the atoms as they fall upon the mind',[26] by being permanently crushed beneath an avalanche of sensation. His final, desperate decision – a suicidal leap from a window – does not merely denote a physical means of escape, but also points to a wider concern.

When Conrad's Jim jumps from the deck of the sinking *Patna*, he provides a centre for the novel's temporal anomalies – a centre composed of negative space, hollowed out by the accrual of surrounding events. If it satisfies some narrative needs, such as accounting for Jim's traumatised condition, it complicates others, by defying full elucidation. Septimus's leap also functions as a key structuring device, its aftermath confirming the rapport he had with Clarissa. But it is a culminating event rather than (as in the case of Jim) an initiating one, and it brings into focus a central anthropometric theme. For Septimus's leap is also a *fall*, a physical enactment of the sort of being he has become since the war.

'Once you fall, Septimus repeated to himself, human nature is on you' (107). Unlike the Lawrentian alter-ego Birkin (and his soulmate Ursula), he does not look down on a fallen mankind, a species incapable of can-celling its debts to civilisation and transcending its condition; on the con-trary, he looks *up* to it. Septimus is the fallen, towered over by the anony-mous mass of humanity indifferent to his terrible plight. He discovers in Shakespeare, Dante and Aeschylus 'the message hidden in the beauty of words. The secret signal which one generation passes, under disguise, to the next is loathing, hatred, despair' (97). Such reflections accord with Birkin's attitude to the mass of humanity. Both men are expert haters of 'human nature', born of peering beneath the superficies of experience into people's souls. (Septimus feels that 'human nature had condemned him to death'; 99.) What separates them is that Septimus's hatred is not the snarling howl of rage emitted by Birkin, but a numbed, anomic emptiness: 'For the truth is (let her ignore it) that human beings have neither kindness, nor faith, nor charity beyond what serves to increase the pleasure of the moment. They hunt in packs. Their packs scour the desert and vanish screaming into the wilderness. They desert the fallen. They are plastered over with grimaces' (98). Septimus's misanthropy is directed inwards as well as outwards, encompassing self-hatred. This further separates him from Birkin's stolid, self-assured detachment from the unthinking, unfeeling masses. Yet Septimus and Birkin are united in another, more important way: they both show antipathy towards instru-mental technology.

The novel's most trenchant critique of technology is directed at the medical establishment. Holmes and Bradshaw are not, in the world of the text, strictly doctors; they are also technocrats, attempting to make individual experience conform to their theories of human be-haviour. 'Communication is health; communication is happiness' (102), mutters Septimus. But he is condemned to a state of miscommunication – in the most egregious instance, through Dr Holmes's stunning indiffer-ence to, and ignorance of, Septimus's condition. His facile prescriptions – increased calorie intake, new hobbies – are occasions for self-indulgence (his own weight loss and interests) rather than sympathetic diagnosis. William Bradshaw, with his 'understanding of the human soul' (104), seems initially to be more responsive. Unlike Dr Holmes, he sees the gravity of Septimus's condition: 'It was a case of complete breakdown – complete physical and nervous breakdown, with every symptom in an advanced stage, he ascertained in two or three minutes' (104–5). Yet Bradshaw's superior understanding does not elicit any greater compassion. 'We all have our moments of depression,' he intones glibly (107). Bradshaw demonstrates the tyrannical side of moderation – or, as he calls it, 'proportion': 'Worshipping proportion, Sir William . . . made it impossible for the unfit to propagate their views until they, too, shared his sense of proportion' (109). Even more so than the novel's (minor) political personages, it is the establishment figure of Sir William Bradshaw who comes to represent state interference in personal 'soul time'.

The civilisation that has failed Septimus, in its secret tyranny of 'proportion', is lauded by Peter, when he hears the ambulance carrying Septimus's dead body: 'One of the triumphs of civilisation, Peter Walsh thought . . . the efficiency, the organisation, the communal spirit of London' (165). There is an implied relationship between technology (civilisation) and its discontents (the insensitive treatment administered to Septimus). The technological artefact that is the ambulance – a mobile part of medical and automotive technology – is made to seem an ominous indicator of human sovereignty, making plain the inability of technological civilisation to interact positively or benignly with the human ingenuity that has spawned it.

It conjoins with that other, earlier technological 'accomplishment', the technology of war. Besides Septimus, the other significant war victim is Doris Kilman, Elizabeth Dalloway's tutor. As well as losing a brother in the trenches, she has been made a pariah for her pro-Germanic views. Like Bradshaw's professional fervour, Miss Kilman's religious impetuosity – her craving for 'conversion', which determines her behaviour towards Elizabeth – has instilled in her the urge to tyrannise. When she confronts Clarissa, 'there arose in her an overmastering desire to overcome her; to unmask her. If she could have felled her it would have eased her. But it was not the body; it was the soul and its mockery that she wished to subdue; make feel her mastery' (137). This parallels Bradshaw and his 'understanding of the human soul'. Both he and Kilman represent outside interference, by State and Church, respectively, in the sacrosanct chamber of human interiority.

It is Septimus, however, who has sacrificed most to the technology of war. Five years on he is broken and shellshocked, with no protection from the punishing effluvium of experience. His terrible state bespeaks a precariousness of individual identity, confusing where the self ends and the world begins. Such precariousness is signposted by one of Woolf's most vivid and insistent tropes: waves, in all their multiform guises, produced by heat, sound, sea, hand and hair. Waves are human-produced, used by the body as gesture, to convey meaning ('with a wave of the hand, the traffic ceases'; 114); natural and technological, in the form of heat and light; and ineffable, perceived only intuitively: 'So on a summer's day waves collect, overbalance, and fall; collect and fall' (43).

Just as waves fluctuate, so is the Woolfian self dispersed diachronically, by the mutability of memory, and scattered synchronically, in its involvements with the world. Woolf's conception of human being breaks ranks in other directions, too. It conforms to neither the intractable mechanomorphism of Conrad, nor the aspirant deomorphism of Lawrence. It is, rather, human–animal divisions that are uneasily maintained. In accordance with Nietzsche's dictum of translating man back into nature, zoomorphic figures recur with great frequency. At the most literal end there is the agitated, overwrought Septimus, the most responsive to these figures, who finds it 'horrible, terrible, to see a dog become a man!' (74) More figuratively, Peter Walsh compares Elizabeth to 'a long-legged colt, handsome, dumb' (168), and Lady Bradshaw is described as 'balancing like a sea-lion at the edge of its tank' (200). It is ornithological allusions, however, that occasion the most frequent superimpositions of animal being on to human ontology.

Birds provide a way of establishing a connection between Clarissa and Septimus, through physiognomy (she has 'a ridiculous little face, beaked like a bird's' (11), while he is 'pale-faced, beak-nosed'; 15). Clarissa displays a special interest in bird metaphors, Septimus in birds themselves. She remembers Sally as 'all light, glowing, like some bird or airball that has flown in' (38); tells a story of a housemaid, comparing her to a cockatoo (64); and imagines Miss Parry dying 'like some bird in a frost gripping her perch' (178). Undergoing his visionary seizures, Septimus twice hears the 'voices of birds' (75, 103). The text also features sundry references to sparrows (26), swallows (76), seagulls (103), birds of paradise (184, 186) and birdcages (66).

Birds, of course, have a metonymic relation to trees. Clarissa stares intently at Peter, and then 'her look . . . rose and fluttered away, as a bird touches a branch and rises and flutters away' (47). Out in public, Septimus 'watched [Rezia] snip, shape, as one watches a bird hop, flit in the grass, without daring to move a finger' (98), and feels her mind, sensing that it is 'like a bird, falling from branch to branch, and always alighting' (161). The 'tree' image provides a way of understanding the novel's use of continuity and discontinuity, as Hillis Miller has suggested. It manifests as 'a great enshadowing tree which is personified, a great mother who binds all living things together in the manifold embrace of her leaves and branches'.[27] The image is certainly a pervasive one;

so pervasive, in fact, that it cannot be restricted to a 'mothering presence'. Rezia, for example, feeling the acute injustice that is her life, is 'surrounded by the enormous trees, vast clouds of an indifferent world' (72). Elizabeth is compared to, among other things, poplar trees, which 'made her life a burden to her' (147). And, more ominously, Clarissa's sister Sylvia (as Peter Walsh reflects) was 'killed by a falling tree' (85). Trees are both images of comfort and connection, and agents of separation and disconnection.

In *A Room of One's Own*, Woolf describes the experience of engaging with male writing. After one or two chapters, she writes, she becomes aware of a shadow, a 'straight dark bar', lying across the page. It may be a tree, a woman walking, or the letter 'I'.[28] There is a momentary (con)fusion of human and inhuman: arboreal solidity, feminine figuration and symbolic selfhood all line up together. But an implicit reduction ensues; the three are really two, and the two become one. As Woolf goes on to remark, the phallic 'I' evokes the stolid self-assurances of masculine writing. The tree image, then, is set alongside competing images of gender: feminine movement (walking) and masculine fixity (the over-confident 'I'). Trees, in a sense, are capable of sustaining both modes. They convey solidity, through connection to a vast, immovable body. And they convey flexibility, with branches that bend and sway, and evanescence, by shedding leaves in accordance with seasonal change. Trees are thus conveyers of life and death, personality and impersonality, durability and ephemerality.

The trope also has a historical provenance. As we saw in Chapter 1, natural selection posited a monogenist tree model, an 'irregularly branching system' to replace the vertical hierarchy of the great chain of being.[29] This model accounted not just for irregularity, but also for continuity; intermediate life forms on the tree linked *homo sapiens* to a common progenitor. As will be explained further on, Woolf's narrative procedure attempts a similar kind of synthesis, attempting to transform the potentially haphazard into a particular kind of order.

Woolf's tree metaphor is thus, in part, a means of portraying interhuman relations. But in terms of individual characters, it is not branches but flowers that provide botanomorphic distinction. Flowers appear in all varieties, and Clarissa's disposition towards them is established in the first scene. At Mulberry's the florist's she experiences a voluptuous sensory tremor, in the midst of 'delphiniums, sweet peas, bunches of lilac; and carnations, masses of carnations' (13). She seems to have an almost paranormal connection to flowers, as their scent summons up vivid scenes of rapture. It lingers after she returns home, when she feels the morning 'soft with the glow of rose petals' (33). The florist's scene becomes almost a hermeneutical resource for the rest of the story. Flowers act as determinants for different locales: the flowerbeds in Regent's Park, significant to the aeroplane scene (29–30), the tulips in Hyde Park (86). They are also identifiers of character: there are carnations (Hugh Whitbread), lilies (Elizabeth), red and white roses (Richard Dalloway), and even Clarissa's fanciful, quasi-symbolist coinage, 'flowers of darkness'. Sometimes one character can inspire different varieties, as Sally does: hollyhocks and dahlias, for Clarissa (36), blue hydrangeas, for Peter (79). At other times a flower is attached to more than one character, as with orchids: Septimus's dead comrade, Evans (76), and Clarissa's Aunt Helena (195). It is suggested that part of Clarissa's attraction to Sally is the latter's 'way with flowers' (36). For Clarissa flowers are also a metonymy for sexual longing. What she calls 'the most exquisite moment of her whole life' involved her and Sally passing a stone urn containing flowers: 'Sally stopped; picked a flower; kissed her on the lips. The whole world might have turned upside down! The others disappeared; there she was alone with Sally' (38). For her part, Sally has a gloomier attitude: 'Despairing of human relationships (people were so difficult), she often went into her garden and got from her flowers a peace which men and women never gave her' (211). Yet Sally is oblivious to the rampant botanomorphism making people inseparable from their floral counterparts.

As with birds and trees, flowers have strong affinities with interhuman activity. Traditionally markers of femininity, they inspire many and varied everyday associations: love, affection, gratitude, sympathy, remembrance, aesthetic refinement, congratulation. Flowers provide a multirouted bridge between the human and the natural, exemplifying more strongly than ever human susceptibility to metamorphic power.

### *The hermeneutical effect: resonance and rupture*

Woolf's engagement with the question of 'experience' suggests correspondences with that humanist literary paradigm, the *Bildungsroman*. Traditionally restricted to male development, and the imprinting of intellectual encounter and (hetero)sexual initiation, the growth of subjectivity was held a purely androcentric affair. Yet rather than dismiss the genre for its masculinist bias, some critics have sought to reshape it from within, by demonstrating the existence of its gynocentric 'other', the female *Bildungsroman*.[30] Woolf's writing has often been enlisted in this project, with problematic results. Elizabeth Abel, for example, contends:

'The story of female development in *Mrs Dalloway* . . . is a clandestine story that remains almost untold, that resists direct narration and coherent narrative shape. Both intrinsically disjointed and textually dispersed and disguised, it is the novel's buried story.'[31] Can something that resists narration and coherence, that is disjointed, dispersed and disguised, really qualify as a story about anything, let alone one concerned with 'female development'? The antinomies in Abel's assertion render it unsustainable. Clarissa possesses a 'self' only when she sets her mind to projecting one, to pulling her multiform attributes into a 'meeting-point' (40). With her discrete particles of identity held in place only by sheer effort of will, subjectivity is not characterised by development so much as provisional self-variance. The model of the *Bildungsroman* is problematic because Woolf's interiorisation technique spurns both decline and growth. As Daniel Allbright notes, 'one cannot say that [Woolf's] characters develop, for when they are moving it is with dizzy speed, swirling into the wind and the waves; when they are still they are struck dead still, grounded, sunk'.[32] Their mysterious affiliations with trees and flowers are not 'organic' paradigms, as the *Bildungsroman* describes, but rather show the permeability of that closed system, the human, its vulnerability and susceptibility to the nonhuman. Its porous properties permit neither growth nor decay, only change and self-difference.

The *Bildungsroman* insists not just that narrative is human-shaped, but that subjectivity is narrative-shaped. It maintains, by implication, that the particular process whereby human self-awareness is formed, from the inside out, corresponds at some deep level to the temporal-based orderings of storymaking. *Mrs Dalloway*, conversely, suggests that bestowing narrative shape on inner experience, with all its inchoate wavering and dispersion, betrays its unshaped indeterminacies, its formless fluctuations. Subjectivity, that is to say, cannot be fully identified with the artful sculpting of personal experience that defines the *Bildungsroman*. The latter's purposive concern with growth and shape – the 'conciliatory and conservative nature of the genre'[33] – is incapable of expressing subjectivity on its own extemporaneous terms.

Woolfian subjectivity is marked by being directionless, intuitive and potentially contradictory. It is, in other words, *form-defying*. This quality demands both a relinquishment of 'authority' and a distrust of totality, which indicate that subjectivity cannot be entirely narrative-shaped; there is something 'unruly' about it that resists the ordering process of narrative construction. Woolf charts the rustle of consciousness, its associational inconstancy, rather than the arc of its development from incipient self-formation to fully developed self-awareness. *Mrs Dalloway*, and the prose experiments that follow it, offer acute examples of subjectivity as other than narrative-shaped.

Yet despite this, deep-rooted questions remain concerning the nature of the narrative voice. Preceding chapters have detailed human dispossession by vast, uncontainable extrahuman sources. The template is Schopenhauer's cosmic will, a metaphysical field encompassing all of existence, instantiated empirically by the human will. Conrad parodies this model in the 'knitting-machine' conceit, and treats it more gravely in *Nostromo*, with the San Tomé mine casting a mechanomorphic spell over the narrative's participants. Lawrence's 'source', on the other hand, is closer to the Schopenhauerian blueprint: an impersonal, oceanic, inhuman beyond, taking on human proportions in the soul or unconscious.

*Mrs Dalloway* appears to share little of this metaphysical fervour. There is no point of stability or reference against which human existence can be measured, and no force that is both transcendent and immanent. But there might be said to be a *textual* equivalent to the above examples. J. Hillis Miller writes:

> The narrator is that state of mind which exists outside the characters and of which they can never be directly aware. Though they are not aware of it, it is aware of them. This 'state of mind' surrounds them, encloses them, pervades them, knows them from within. It is present to them all at all the times and places of their lives ... Though the characters are not aware of this narrating presence, they are at every moment possessed and known, in a sense violated, by an invisible mind, a mind more powerful than their own. This mind registers with infinite delicacy their every thought and steals their every secret.[34]

That this narrating presence, a 'universal, impersonal mind',[35] as Miller terms it, possesses, violates and steals every secret from individual minds, suggests a capacity remarkably similar to the metaphysical forces of dispossession outlined above. And, securing for it the same immanent–transcendent status, Miller notes that 'though for the most part the characters do not know it, the universal mind is part of their own minds, or rather their minds are part of it'.[36] He also appeals to the 'cave' metaphor in Woolf's diaries, where she describes 'how I dig out beautiful caves behind my characters; I think that gives exactly what I want; humanity, humour, depth. The idea is that the caves shall connect, and each comes to daylight at the present moment.'[37] That the caves connect, forming one central source, replicates the structure of the Schopenhauerian will.

Seen in this way, the narrative model of voice and machine undergoes significant reconstruction. For Woolf, in effect, *extricates* voice from the machinations of narrative process. The result, as Edward Bishop has noted, is 'a voice that moves effortlessly in and out of the minds of the characters, absorbing the myriad individual voices, a voice that lies like a film over the whole novel, not only uniting it but *becoming* it so that, unlike in *Jacob's Room*, the action of the narrative is inseparable from the action of the voice'.[38] This is not, however, to make the voice more human. As in the botanomorphic and zoomorphic figures described above, it is to demonstrate the shifts of identity between the human and its others. That we fail to perceive these shifts is not because of the *principium individuationist*, as Schopenhauer might insist, but because we do not have the transhuman capacity of the universal mind, the ability to apprehend multiple perspectives. We only have our frail, individual points of view, prone to both the levelling effects of civilised company (Clarissa, who must assemble her 'unreal self' for public display) and the exacerbating effects of trauma (Septimus, the victim of a hypertrophic sensibility).

We saw in Chapter 2 how Conrad's 'delayed decoding' showed events and their meaning to be temporally divided, indicating the recalcitrant nature of reality, its stubborn resistance to human ways of understanding. His characters suffer from a tragic lack of insight, and the nature of human limitation is such that no remedy is available; consciousness and experience are permanently out of alignment with each other. Lawrence's narrative technique, conversely, might be called 'immediate decoding', or unmediated soul-knowing; his characters, unlike Conrad's, suffer from an overabundance of insight. Because all the socially erected barriers between them have been removed, characters can peer into each other's deepest selves, knowing that it is petty, decorous, human ways of being that prevent them from fulfilling their posthuman destiny. Woolf's characters are different again, displaying a curious amalgam of paradox and irony. Paul Ricoeur has referred to this as 'the incessant weighing of souls that the characters practice on one another'.[39] Access between selves is readily available: 'They went in and out of each other's minds without any effort' (69), the universal mind reports of Clarissa and Peter; the two of them 'had this queer power of communicating without words' (65). But this access is incomplete and does not necessarily lead to greater intimacy ('And he couldn't see her; couldn't explain to her; couldn't have it out'; 66). If individuals act at crosspurposes, divided by discontinuities, the larger continuities uniting them are, at best, grasped only liminally and onesidedly (as in the case of Clarissa and Septimus).

Lawrence's soul-readings, abundant and authoritative though they may be, are not accompanied by any hermeneutical guide to their overall function in the novel; the declamatory narrative voice overrules any formal reflexivity. *Mrs Dalloway*, by contrast, contains critical hints for understanding the kinds of textual effects the novel has been generating. The key passage arises from Peter's recollections, his reminiscence of the young Clarissa's attempt 'to explain the feeling they had of dissatisfaction; not knowing people; not being known'. Clarissa had felt herself dispersed, not 'here' but 'everywhere'. With a gesture towards the polysemic wave motif ('she waved her hand'), the universal mind elaborates Clarissa's theory:

> She was all that. So that to know her, or any one, one must seek out the people who completed them; even the places. Odd affinities she had with people she had never spoken to, some woman in the street, some man behind a counter – even trees, or barns. It ended in a transcendental theory which, with her horror of death, allowed her to believe, or say that she believed (for all her scepticism), that since our apparitions, the part of us which appears, are so momentary compared with the other, the unseen part of us, which spreads wide, the unseen might survive, be recovered somehow attached to this or that, or even haunting places, after death. Perhaps – perhaps. (167)

This goes some way to explaining the strange spiritual affiliation of Clarissa and Septimus, and anticipates her resolve to continue living when he has died. It also acknowledges the importance of the 'tree' motif, and gives voice to a final, unassailable declaration of doubt. But the first proposition, that people are 'completed' by other people and by places, seems contrary to the assertion that we 'must reconcile ourselves to a season of failures and fragments'. To understand this antinomy, we must attend to *Mrs Dalloway*'s unconventional narrative ordering.

Contrary to appearance, Woolf does not deny narrative causality, but multiplies it. As she recorded in her diary: 'Waste, deadness, come from the inclusion of things that don't belong to the moment; this appalling narrative business of the realist: getting on from lunch to dinner: it is false, unreal, merely conventional.'[40] Yet the Clarissa–Septimus correlation, intuited by Clarissa when she hears of his suicide, could not be oriented the way it is without narrative. The temporal organisation of the day and the changes taking place therein (Septimus's mistreatment by the medical establishment and subsequent anguish, Clarissa's searching self-analysis prompted by Peter's reappearance) are necessary structuring principles to maintain coherence. What is missing, however, is a causal-linear culminating element – say, a real encounter between the two characters – which might solidify their latent affinities and make their bond seem more than a conceit or affectation.

That Woolf resists such explicitness, yet without making the 'relation-ship' seem any less real, is owing to her antinomical narrative technique. Ricoeur has described this in terms of a 'resonance-effect' and a 'rupture-effect'.[41] Motifs resonate throughout the narrative, but resist insertion into a holistic pattern, the pattern of consecution necessary for narrative formation. In fact, part of the novel's purpose is to show the modali-ties of conjunction and communion that lie outside of, or are at best subordinated to, traditional storytelling practices.[42] Thus the narrative path of the eponymous heroine – a classic love-triangle scenario, involv-ing a 'safe' marriage to one man and a residual emotional attachment to another – is less important than implied associations with Septimus, and her reflections on instability, mortality and impermanence. When, after an interminable delay, the narrative gestures towards a resolution, by bringing Clarissa and Peter together, it concludes immediately. *Mrs Dalloway* thus yields a particle theory of narrative (motif organisation), but not a wave theory (serial-event causality). And as everything textual is made to connect, potentially, with everything else, so with the beings at the centre of these changes. They, too, are always already in the process of becoming *other* – birds, dogs, horses, trees, flowers, wave formations. At the core of the 'multipersonal representation of consciousness' is a movement towards synthesis.[43]

To produce these kinds of textual effects, Woolf is casting in narrative form the suggestive, associative, performative codes normally associated with poetry. Encompassing the characters' apparently diffuse, meander-ing reflections is a heavily patterned prose design, using repetition and arrangement in overdetermined ways. Norman Page writes: 'Beneath the suggestion of a free flow of thoughts and memories, echoing at ran-dom in the mind . . . a strong principle of ordering is at work, resulting in a rhythmic quality which makes such prose closer to free verse than to the fictional prose of (say) H. G. Wells or Arnold Bennett.'[44] But more than just 'rhythmic quality' is lent by Woolf's prose experiments. In 'The Narrow Bridge of Art' (1927) she describes a new narrative form:

It will be written in prose, but in prose which has many of the characteristics of poetry. It will have something of the exaltation of poetry but much of the ordinariness of prose. [ . . . ] In the first place, one may guess that it will differ from the novel as we know it now chiefly in that it will stand further back from life. It will give, as poetry does, the outline rather than the detail.[45]

And the following year, in a diary entry: 'The idea has come to me that what I want now to do is to saturate every atom . . . Why admit anything to literature that is not poetry – by which I mean saturated?'[46] Still later, in 'Phases of Fiction' (1929), she describes 'another poetry more natural to the novel, which rises inevitably out of situation rather than language'. Woolf, as Reuben A. Brower has noted, was clearly 'obsessed by the dream of the pure poem-novel'.[47]

All these remarks are evidenced in the complexly ordered, motif-laden narrative that is *Mrs Dalloway*. Life may not be a 'series of gig lamps', yet beneath the apparent cacophany of experience is a network of studied pattern formation. These fixations on order and patterning suggest a kind of kaleidoscopic arrangement, with individual passages generating wilder and more vivid configurations of motifs. A kaleidoscope, one might say, is not so much a machine as a device for transforming a narrative's 'machine' elements (fixity, repetition, regularity) into 'voice' elements (surprise, chance, irregularity). It is not a purely machinelike mode because the patterns dissolve and disperse as spontaneously as they congeal. Woolf's thoroughgoing transformation of the mechanical aspects of textual construction produces, finally, a kind of *over*coherence, where everything has a potential relationship to everything else. Connections multiply with vertiginous rapidity, hold momentarily, then shift into still further configurations. As text, as object and as performance, *Mrs Dalloway* is a machine for resisting machination.

## II *TO THE LIGHTHOUSE:* LESSONS IN DARKNESS

Though continuing many of the thematic concerns of *Mrs Dalloway*, *To the Lighthouse* is substantially different in other ways, not least in its cast of characters. The former work features a host of literary pretenders. There is Peter Walsh, the ever-aspirant writer ('And if he did retire, that's what he'd do – write books'; 172); Lady Bruton, a compulsive, yet incompetent, letter-writer ('one letter to *The Times*, she used to say to Miss Brush, cost her more than to organise an expedition to South Africa'; 119); Sally, who more than thirty years ago 'wrote reams of poetry' (83); and Septimus, a would-be *poète maudit* ('Was he not like Keats?' wonders his wife; 93). *To the Lighthouse*, by contrast, has genuine philosophical thinkers in Mr Ramsay and Charles Tansley, a diligent artist in Lily Briscoe, and a successful poet in Augustus Carmichael. These characters enable the aesthetic control evident in *Mrs Dalloway*, which guides its effects of resonance and rupture, to be translated into more direct terms in its successor. For

*To the Lighthouse* is about vision: in straightforward optical terms, as seeing; and in creative terms, in the sense of artistic vision and the struggle to bring a work of art into being. Implicated in this is a countertheme, the loss or absence of vision, in the form of darkness, both literal and metaphorical.

The countertheme takes on contrary meanings for Mr and Mrs Ramsay. For Mr Ramsay, the professional philosopher, darkness signifies lack of knowledge. He stands 'on his little ledge facing the dark of human ignorance, how we know nothing' (50). The most egregious indicator of this conviction is the type of character he presents to the world, with all its concealments and subterfuges, 'the refuge of a man afraid to own his own feelings' (51). Mrs Ramsay, by contrast, abjures 'vision' as it is associated with intellect and knowledge; she seeks not knowledge but intimacy, a more immediate, intuitive form of knowing. Darkness provides solace for her: '[I]f there, in that corner, it was bright, here, in this, she felt the need of darkness' (59). A few pages later, in an extended meditation, she elucidates the 'darkness' trope that shapes the rest of the novel. She begins by acknowledging that the kind of intimacy she values can only be recognised, paradoxically, in solitude:

To be silent; to be alone. All the being and the doing, expansive, glittering, vocal, evaporated; and one shrunk, with a sense of solemnity, to being oneself, a wedge-shaped core of darkness, sometimes invisible to others . . . This core of darkness could go anywhere, for no one saw it. They could not stop it, she thought, exulting (69).

This 'core of darkness' is the key to negotiating the instability of an unfixed, changeable, metamorphic self: 'There was freedom, there was peace, there was, most welcome of all, a summoning together, a resting on a platform of stability. Not as oneself did one find rest ever, in her experience (she accomplished here something dexterous with her needles), but as a wedge of darkness' (69–70). Reflecting further, Mrs Ramsay spells out the process of merging demonstrated throughout *Mrs Dalloway*: 'Often she found herself sitting and looking, sitting and looking, with her work in her hands until she became the thing she looked at – that light, for example' (*ibid*). In addition, she recognises the botanomorphic sensibility pervading the earlier work: 'It was odd, she thought, how if one was alone, one leant to things, inanimate things; trees, streams, flowers; felt they expressed one; felt they became one; felt they knew one, in a sense were one; felt an irrational tenderness thus (she looked at that long steady light) as for oneself' (*ibid*).

Just as Clarissa Dalloway's experience at the florist's, early on in the book, provides a key to the manifold translations between human and natural realms, Mrs Ramsay's thoughts on darkness hint at a multitude of human-nonhuman links. The trope of darkness enlarges *Mrs Dalloway*'s exploration of metamorphic instability, and conjoins with it meditations on death, impersonality and artistic creation.

### *Narrative diffusion: rhythm and melody*

The trip to the lighthouse, first implied and then actual, provides a narrative envelope for three principal struggles: Lily Briscoe to realise her painting; Mrs Ramsay with 'life' and its wavering intensity; and Mr Ramsay 'getting beyond Q'. As with the motif of darkness, the Ramsays reveal two very different relationships to narrative. The more staid and traditional is Mr Ramsay. A man 'tyrannical with certitude and tyrannized by uncertainty',[48] his attitude to family matters is at odds with his belief in his own philosophical powers. He reflects on:

that old, that obvious distinction between the two classes of men; on the one hand the steady goers of superhuman strength who, plodding and persevering, repeat the whole alphabet in order, twenty-six letters in all, from start to finish; on the other the gifted, the inspired who, miraculously, lump all the letters together in one flash – the way of genius. (40)

Theorising that thought runs as an alphabet runs, from A to Z, Ramsay recognises that 'He had not genius . . . but he had, or might have had, the power to repeat every letter of the alphabet from A to Z accurately in order' (*ibid*). As Rachel Bowlby has noted, Ramsay 'makes of the moves from A to B to C a logical rather than simply a linear progression . . . [He] takes up the notation of propositional logic, and suggests that each letter attained is an advance upon the previous one, not just a neutral point on a line made up of points of equal value.'[49] In other words, Ramsay envisages the gaining of knowledge – and overcoming of the 'dark of human ignorance' – as a narrative progression. Narrative is a deterrent to darkness. Equally as telling, Ramsay compares the potential longevity of his books with the afterlives of *novels*. And not just any novels, either: those by Balzac and Scott are his measure of success, both authors having mastered the *roman fleuve*, the most extensive form of literary narrative ever devised.

Mrs Ramsay, who welcomes the darkness and recognises it as constitutive of selfhood, reads a story of 'The Fisherman and His Wife' to pacify her son James. Her reading, however, makes the story seem intermittent and almost arbitrary, as she continually interrupts it with her mental wanderings. Amid these wanderings, the tale becomes something quite different: '[F]or the story of the Fisherman and his Wife was like the bass gently accompanying a tune, which now and then ran up unexpectedly into the melody' (63). Diegetic narrative development is reduced to a rhythmic underpinning, beating out a rhythm for the 'melody' of rumination. James's reaction, when the story concludes, is also noteworthy: ' "And that's the end," she said, and she saw in his eyes, as the interest in the story died away in them, something else take its place; something wondering, pale, like the reflection of a light, which at once made him gaze and marvel' (68). What mars James's narrative satisfaction is the light of the lighthouse, signalling his desire to go there in the morning. This particular light is thus contrasted with the light of narrative, the antidote to the darkness and ignorance that Mr Ramsay dreads almost pathologically.

That the trip to the source of this particular light is thwarted by Mr Ramsay takes on further significance when he appears before his wife, after the story's conclusion: 'She had been reading fairy tales to James, she said. No they could not share that; they could not say that' (75). They cannot share it because of their very different relationships to narrative. This difference is apparent not just in James's unconcern about a satisfactory conclusion, but also in daughter Cam's awareness of the inadequacy of stories:

So we took a little boat, she thought, beginning to tell herself a story of adventure about escaping from a sinking ship. But with the sea streaming through her fingers, a spray of seaweed vanishing behind them, she did not want to tell herself seriously a story; it was the sense of adventure and escape that she wanted . . . (204)

And although Cam does construct a narrative of sorts, en route to the lighthouse, she remains as aware of its frivolity, its secondary status to the task of living, as her mother is: 'Would the water last? Would the provisions last? she asked herself, telling herself a story but knowing at the same time what was the truth' (222).

Like Mrs Ramsay, her children reject the patriarchal nature of narrative progression, and the claims to knowledge and human betterment made for it by Mr Ramsay. Narrative, for Mrs Ramsay, is something almost frivolous, a background accompaniment to the foreground of living, and to the 'darkness' that living enjoins. For her husband, however, narrative is implicated with progression, with longevity and with immortality – the kind of cultural authority he covets, but fears himself insufficiently gifted to possess. If his desire is, at bottom, merely narcissistic self-enlargement – wanting to defy ageing and death by joining the Western canon – Woolf counterposes its opposite, self-effacement. It is presented in the guise of impersonality, which, as we are about to see, is endemic to the agonising process of artistic creation.

### *Several folds of blackness: X-rays and impersonality*

In 'Time Passes', *To the Lighthouse*'s extraordinary central part, the instrumental relationship to the object world that is the basis of humanist understanding is reversed. In these sections of the novel, impersonal worlds, both natural and human-created (the remnants of the Ramsays' habitation) endure; it is people who are ephemeral, appearing only parenthetically. Rather than de- or rehumanise time, this part attempts to depict temporal difference without *durée*, without the presence of human beings to register it as experience. It is nonhuman time that passes here, time expunged of mind.

The part's sections unfold as if narrated by a metaphysician, by a mind exploring with great acuity the possibilities of human withdrawal from the world, and how the world of matter, both organic (nature) and inorganic (the house and its contents), might fare. Is Mr Ramsay the unnamed, unacknowledged narrator? Is his ghostly presence what enables the story to continue without pause through this part? The metaphysic-minded narrator is a ruthless, dispassionate reporter, clearly not troubled (unlike Mr Ramsay) by such dispiriting matters as egotism and self-doubt. By (literally) bracketing off human ways of being, Woolf offers a glimpse of how her notion of impersonality might appear on an X-ray, no longer occluded by the surface exposures of character and event.

Human presence has not been effaced entirely, however; the 'darkness' enclosing the ten short passages suggests continuities with Mrs Ramsay's conception of selfhood. As the inhabitants prepare to leave, a 'downpouring of immense darkness' (137) enters the house. In the years that follow, the comings and goings of Mrs McNab, the cleaning woman, barely manage to keep entropy at bay. It reaches a climax of sorts: 'For now had come that moment, that hesitation when dawn trembles and night pauses, when if a feather alight in the scale it will be weighed down. One feather and the house, sinking, falling, would have turned and pitched downwards to the depths of darkness' (151). As with the tree motif in

*Mrs Dalloway* (and that novel's attempts to portray, as it were, both wave and particle), darkness threatens as much as it protects. The house is spared, however: 'But there was a force working; something not highly conscious; something that leered, something that lurched; something not inspired to go about its work with dignified ritual or solemn chanting' (*ibid.*).

This force – semi-conscious, intermittent and inhuman – is what lies behind the narrative voice's penchant for making parallels between the fate of the disintegrating house and the lives (and deaths) of its former inhabitants. The chaos of inclement weather thus echoes the turmoil of warfare: an exploding shell in France, which kills Andrew Ramsay, is prefigured by the 'thud of something falling' in the house (145). The X-ray becomes a double exposure, revealing human traces that cannot be erased, even by complete human withdrawal and the abrasions of time. Just as the human is partly composed of the inhuman (animals, machines, transcendents) so, too, does the reverse apply: nonhuman nature reveals the after-images of human lives, which can never be entirely obliterated. This is not an example of anthropomorphisation, such as we examined in Chapter 1; there is no assimilation, deliberate or otherwise, of nonhuman to human. The part ends when 'curtains of dark [have] wrapped themselves over the house', enveloping its returned inhabitants, who sleep 'with several folds of blackness layed over their eyes' (155). Whether menacing, liberating or protecting, darkness confers no privileges; it swallows living and unliving alike.

Those two markers of human darkness and its associations with narrative, Mr and Mrs Ramsay, also display strikingly different temporal attitudes. Both are future-oriented beings, although they manifest it in dissimilar ways. His concern with the future is an egotistical one, involving anxious speculation about the longevity of his work and the durability of fame. She, on the other hand, projects other lives forward, seeing the moment as generative, as giving birth to future time. It is her form of immortality:

> She felt, with her hand on the nursery door, that community of feeling with other people which emotion gives as if the walls of partition had become so thin that practically (the feeling was one of relief and happiness) it was all one stream, and chairs, tables, maps, were hers, were theirs, it did not matter whose, and Paul and Minta would carry it on when she was dead. (123)

Her conjectures are, indeed, borne out by her death. It is not Paul and Minta who ratify them, however, but Lily Briscoe. Spellbound by

Mrs Ramsay's beauty, she strives to realise her feelings in a painting, to formalise them through the visual codes of line, mass and colour. At the same time, Lily feels acutely the sense of darkness, in both understandings of the term. She is aware of collective ignorance, the lack of knowledge afflicting us all: 'Who knows what we are, what we feel? Who knows even at the moment of intimacy, This is knowledge?' (187) But rather than introduce despair, darkness has a positive role to play, by being the condition of art's possibility. Art comes from darkness, not by emitting light and banishing shadow, but by conveying it in a different form. Congruent with this, artistic practice is akin to entering the unknown, making 'this passage from conception to work as dreadful as any down a dark passage for a child' (23).

*To the Lighthouse* defines the difference between art and life in terms of closeness and merging, on the one hand, and distance and separation, on the other. 'So much depends, thought Lily Briscoe . . . upon distance: whether people are near or far from us; for her feeling for Mr. Ramsay changed as he sailed further and further across the bay' (207). In similar fashion, Lily cannot paint while she feels so acutely the presence of Mrs Ramsay. She recognises it as a choice between creating and feeling, between experiencing the impersonality necessary for artistic creation, and the personalising surrender of emotional attachment. In the gap between art and life come doubt and frustration, casting uncertainty in both directions. Lily reflects: 'Always . . . before she exchanged the fluidity of life for the concentration of painting she had a few moments of nakedness when she seemed like an unborn soul, a soul reft of body, hesitating on some windy pinnacle and exposed without protection to all the blasts of doubt' (174). Successful artistic creation promotes impersonality, but loss of personality is predicated on a surrendering of one's defences, which opens the way to doubt. And it leads to a denuded self, an 'unborn soul'. The endpoint of this withdrawal of personality, we might assume, is a 'wedge-shaped core of darkness'.

Lily also experiences frustration with conventional human limitations, similar to the strictures blighting Lawrence's posthuman pioneers: 'It was a miserable machine, an inefficient machine, she thought, the human apparatus for painting or for feeling; it always broke down at the critical moment; heroically, one must force it on' (209–10). Lily's relationship to painting is akin to Mrs Ramsay's relationship to living. Both are involved in struggle and strife. The act of painting is expressed as 'this formidable ancient enemy of hers – this other thing, this truth, this reality, which suddenly laid hands on her, emerged stark at the back of appearances and commanded her attention' (172–3). Mrs Ramsay expresses her feelings towards life in similar terms, where to live is to contest:

A sort of transaction went on between them, in which she was on one side, and life was on another, and she was always trying to get the better of it, as it was of her; . . . for the most part, oddly enough, she must admit that she felt this thing that she called life terrible, hostile, and quick to pounce on you if you gave it a chance (66).

In retaliation against this, freedom is recast as an impersonal experience, via the anonymous, agential capacity of the 'wedge-shaped core of darkness', conjoining the human world with its inscrutable, nonhuman other. Unlike her ego-bound, fame-besotted husband, Mrs Ramsay sees freedom, impersonality and the conquest of existence as all of a piece: 'Losing personality, one lost the fret, the hurry, the stir; and there rose to her lips always some exclamation of triumph over life when things came together in this peace, this rest, this eternity' (70).

Schopenhauer's advocacy of impersonality was based on what he believed to be the rapacious tendencies of individual consciousness. Only the countersubjective forces of artistic impersonality and ethical selflessness could yield oneness and quietus, in harmony with the metaphysical oneness supporting the phenomenal world. For Woolf individuation is just as illusory, but less nefarious – our botanomorphic and zoomorphic tendencies do not allow us any distance from our nonhuman others. Yet impersonality is, nevertheless, a strenuous cast of mind for Woolf's characters. In terms of interhuman behaviour, self-sacrifice is Mrs Ramsay's route to impersonal freedom. And its cognate, the fierce concentration of aesthetic contemplation or artistic creation, is characterised by Lily. The connection between the two women implies a connection between living and painting, ethics and aesthetics.

Artistic completion dovetails with another form of completion, the enforced finality of death. Clarissa Dalloway described it in these terms: 'Death was an attempt to communicate, people feeling the impossibility of reaching the centre which, mystically, evaded them; closeness drew apart; rapture faded; one was alone. There was an embrace in death' (202). The tension between merging and separation returns to the fore. Death is a means of connecting, though *without* closeness; Clarissa connects with Septimus in this way, and it enables her to carry on living. Death's function in *Mrs Dalloway* is equated with the promotion of artistic activity in *Lighthouse*. Lily connects with and 'completes' Mrs Ramsay, even as the latter enables her to complete her picture. Thus if *Mrs Dalloway* exemplifies the undoing of the *Bildungsroman*, *To the Lighthouse* performs a similar operation on the *Künstlerroman*. The growth in artistic awareness and fulfilment of creative potential endemic to the genre is a highly personalising experience; its efficacy depends on the development of artistic personality. Lily's artistic project is enabled by another's death, and by curbing her own self-expressive tendencies. With this impersonal suspension of selfhood, there is nothing to express and no means of expressing it.

## OUT OF TIME, OUT OF MIND

Woolf's time (or *durée*) is not the time of Church and State, which registers as 'conversion' (Doris Kilman's calling) and 'proportion' (William Bradshaw's motto). The world of *Mrs Dalloway* is a world where synchrony is futile. Big Ben's 'official time', the mocking call of order, attempts to regulate human activity. But its measured, intermittent tones cannot compete with the flux of human interiority; experience has prior claims to temporal engagement. Woolf's 'soul time' of memory and anticipation, the time resistant to clerical and political authority, amounts to a blow struck for individual freedom. But can it be seen as an emissary for the unfettered, self-willed cognitive or transcendental subject of humanist lore? Although *Mrs Dalloway* does give credence to the entity persisting in the matrix of inner experience, the question as to what sort of entity this is, exactly, remains to be answered. Any unification it has, as Clarissa realises, is a public front deliberately willed. Left to its own devices, the soul is self-divided in time and dispersed in space, its claims to unification split in several directions at once.

Taking this entity out of the matrix of inner experience, and seeing what remains, is the boldest move Woolf makes in *To the Lighthouse*. 'Time Passes' peers beyond *durée*, or 'soul time', or any kind of temporal experience, and into nonhuman time. This is a time of disintegration and darkness, a time without luminance. Yet it curiously invalidates what chronometric devices, the critical philosophies of Kant and Bergson, and the literary polemics of Wyndham Lewis have each, in their turn, attempted to do. All these claims to rehumanise time, and counter claims (or accusations) of dehumanisation, are rendered untenable by 'Time Passes'. There is nothing to rehumanise, and nothing to dehumanise: human and nonhuman are inseparable, darkness unites both worlds. Woolf's luminance is intimately involved with its others.

Unlike Lawrence's Birkin, who abhors merging (reflected in Lawrence's carefully episodic narrative design, one thing meticulously after another), Clarissa and Mrs Ramsay accede to it, albeit guardedly and cautiously. Woolf dematerialises the soul, which Lawrence had transformed into a hard kernel of truth, knowledge and authority. Rather than showing the torturous density of the inner life, and the urgent necessity of breaking through it into freedom, she recognises its arbitrariness and contingency. If Lawrence's agonistic posthumanism sees transcendence as struggle – a violent shaking free of the shackles of civilised culture, i.e., modernity – Woolf's metamorphic ahumanism demonstrates that there is nothing to break free from, because individual identity is always already afloat, its inner life both fractured and recombinant. Far from resembling Lawrence's dull, limited creatures (excepting the gifted, sensitive few), human beings in Woolf's world are constantly negotiating a superabundance of sensation, finding order and meaning in inscrutable places, and missing the most obvious understandings. Yet her adumbration of the human, as metamorphic and unstable, seems, finally, to be less important than the sensations it experiences.

Conrad is unflinching in his depictions of loss of moral confidence, but still proffers a kind of morose certainty, a depressed assurance about human being. Lawrence, too, displays certainty, but as agonistic and transcendental rather than empirical like Conrad; a degree of certainty is, for Lawrence, necessarily prior to his posthuman extravagances. Both these variants, the one gloomily downcast and the other wildly euphoric, contrast starkly with Woolf's depictions of doubt. Clarissa's cautious rejoinder to her theory of individual instability ('Perhaps – perhaps') is also Woolf's recognition of the fragility and incompleteness of self and world. From the troubled, defeated creatures of *Mrs Dalloway* to the agonised artist figures in *To the Lighthouse*, her characters must habitually struggle with the provisional, ephemeral conditions that have formed them. Doubt, in these novels, is a function of Woolf's determination to express both flux and moment, wave and particle, in a coherent form. But as textual artefacts, these works are remarkably sure-footed, paragons of precision and organisation. They never lose sight of the possibility of completeness, even if (as Clarissa and Mrs Ramsay believe, or suspect) it means achieving it via impersonal means, through the conjunction of selves, or the union of selves and their (inhuman) others. Radical incompleteness, conversely, is the starting point of Samuel Beckett's literary work. His fraught, late-modernist novels burrow still deeper into the narrative infrastructure, finding dark seams of contingency and doubt at the most basic level. The next chapter explores the remedial possibilities of this undertaking.

# Doubting Beckett: voices descant, stories still

I don't know, perhaps it's a dream, all a dream, that would surprise me, I'll wake, in the silence, and never sleep again, it will be I, or dream, dream again, dream of a silence, a dream silence, full of murmurs, I don't know...

Samuel Beckett[1]

A man lies in bed asleep, assailed by dreams and phantoms. In his feverish, precarious condition images of chaos and tumult unsettle his mind – thunderstorms, violent winds, and an evil, supernatural genius trying to claim his soul. He experiences severe disorientation, until his already waning confidence vanishes completely. Terror seizes him; he is bent double and reeling, unable to regain his posture although the fierce winds have subsided. And as he struggles with these apparitions, these phantoms and demons, he floats in and out of consciousness. Finally the series of dreams comes to an end, and the dreamer awakens. Another man, in another era, alone in the dark. Alone on his back in the dark. A voice comes to him. Only a small part of what is said can be verified. The voice tells of a past. Apart from the voice and the faint sound of his breath there is no sound. None, at least, that he can hear. May not there be another with him in the dark to and of whom the voice is speaking? Is he not perhaps overhearing a communication not intended for him? If he is alone on his back in the dark why does the voice not say so? Why? Perhaps for no other reason than to kindle in his mind this faint uncertainty.

There is, at first glance, an incommensurability in these two accounts. The first is from the life of René Descartes, describing a turbulent night on, or round about, the eve of a great philosophical breakthrough. The second, by contrast, is fictive, from some early moments in Samuel Beckett's novella *Company*.[2] Biographical nonfiction is thus counterposed with psychological fiction. But a number of extenuating details cause these clearcut separations to become blurred as the two sides converge. Descartes's night of dreams, dated by his first biographer Adrien Baillet as 10 November 1619, has become an entrenched part of Cartesian mythology.[3] The most recent account of it, by Stephen Gaukroger, contends that Descartes was in a severe state of nervous exhaustion and excitement, and may even have been undergoing a nervous breakdown.[4] This turbulent condition culminated in the night of dreams. But if this was the price exacted, it was a bargain: Descartes woke from it enlivened, in possession of the wherewithal to put him on the road that led to the *cogito*.

The Cartesian mythos is matched, albeit in different ways, by the Beckettian mythos. Beckett's aversion to publicity and the other trappings of fame, and the fact that recognition failed to alter his early acceptance (or better, active pursuit) of the aesthetics of failure and the politics of penury, all suggest a figure at home in the dark, in communion with the voices of self-doubt. Returning, then, to the earlier dichotomy, the categories of biographical nonfiction and psychological fiction must be tempered with, respectively, intimations of biographical mythology and spiritual autobiography.

Additionally, there is parity of an altogether different stripe in these two accounts. Let us assume that the account of Descartes's night is true, at least in its broadest sense: the torment, the struggle with his demons of scepticism, and the deliverance from turmoil that enabled him, when he awoke, to find certainty. Suppose, now, that the outcome had been different. What might it mean, for Descartes never to have formulated the *cogito*? How might human thought have fared over the next three centuries without this example of cognitive self-grounding? At least one possible answer is not hard to find, as it is presupposed in everything that carries Beckett's imprimatur. He makes manifest, that is to say, a precognitive scepticism – a Descartes without the serene assurance of the *cogito*, transplanted to the mid-twentieth century. Every cleft of consciousness is filled with doubt, with the unremitting possibility of alternative. It is surely no accident that in his 1929 essay on 'Work in Progress', Beckett illustrates the idea that English language is 'abstracted to death' by seizing on one particular example: 'Take the word "doubt": it gives us hardly any sensuous suggestion of hesitancy, of the necessity for choice, of static irresolution ... Mr. Joyce recognises how inadequate "doubt" is to express a state of extreme uncertainty ... '[5]

Scepticism has an intimate relation with traditional humanism. As Peter Faulkner suggests, it is the starting point of humanist enquiry:

The humanist, it has been suggested, will be sceptical about many assumptions which are acceptable to the religious mind, whether in its traditional Christian form or in recent Positivist and Marxist variations. But the scepticism of the humanist, like that of the scientist, is a tool, a method of enquiry. It is not the absolute principle that it becomes for the nihilist; it does not preclude the assertion of value.[6]

But the virtuoso Irish doubter is no absolute sceptic; he propounds 'an art that registers the possibility of a minimal affirmation'.[7] Yet even short of an absolute condition, extreme scepticism is still in some sense a form of the inhuman. If we do not pursue it as remorselessly and as helplessly as a Beckettian monologist, it is because our bodies will not allow us to. The vicissitudes of the flesh shortcircuit the mind's hunger for self-scrutiny that characterises Beckettian man; a hunger that has ramifications in terms of Beckett's conception of the human.

Doubt, then, is the mastertheme that organises the Beckettian topoi. It ravels and unravels the late 1940s fictions, the trilogy of novels produced by the legendary, prodigious 'siege in the room'.[8] Starting with the comedy of uncertainty, it wends its way first through the virtualisation of birth and death, then through the snares and binds of aporia, to alight, finally, at a paradoxical form of apostasy. As Beckett himself said, 'The key word of my work is *perhaps*.'[9] In fact, so thoroughgoing is his sceptical temper that it is self-undoing. Thus if doubt is the Beckettian mastertrope organising the work, its unruliness makes it the undoing of all tropes, master and subordinate, a disruptive force that also *dis*organises the work. Paradox, as will become apparent, is Beckett's stock in trade, as necessary as it is unavoidable.

### I *MOLLOY:* BECKETT'S COMEDY OF UNCERTAINTY

Beckett's 1969 Nobel Prize for literature was won, according to the presentation speech, for a body of work that 'had transmuted the destitution of modern man into his exaltation'.[10] This 'humanist Beckett', the mainstay of Beckett studies, until recently, could be seen as deriving from the need to close ranks in the face of public neglect, or even hostility. Jean-Michel Rabaté indicates the elements comprising that glib caricature, the 'Beckettian age': 'despair, cynicism, minimalism, a suicidal nihilism, the reduction of human endeavours to futile games at the end of which metaphysical clowns wink at the audience while hesitating between logorrhea and silence'.[11] On the other hand, the particular makeup of Beckett's writing would seem to *demand* 'humanist protection': unremitting bleakness, striated with wild, unexpected humour. To face the void so unflinchingly – 'a void', what is more, 'that tantalizingly and painfully refuses to be transformed into a cosmos'[12] – even to adopt an attitude of fierce comedy towards it, makes such humour as there is cathartic, therapeutic and heroic. And from therapeutic heroism it is but a small step to an ethic of redemption. Humour, then, is the chief means whereby the transmutation of destitution (antihumanist pessimism and alienation) into exaltation (humanist heroism) can be identified most clearly.

The social utility of humour is also expressed by Henri Bergson in his book *Laughter*. The comic spirit dreams, he writes, 'but it conjures up in its dreams visions that are at once accepted and understood by the whole of the social group'.[13] He suggests that the incontrovertible humanism of a shared social reality is an essential prerequisite for the complicity of laughter: 'Laughter must answer to certain requirements of life in common. It must have a social signification' (8). And it is edifying, for laughter 'pursues a utilitarian aim of general improvement' (20). Furthermore, it must have a human as well as a social signification, for 'the comic does not exist outside the pale of what is strictly human' (3). Anthropomorphism is crucial to comedy. If an animal or an inanimate object generates laughter, 'it is always because of some resemblance to man, of the stamp he gives it or the use he puts it to' (4).

But these proto-humanist ideas are undercut by a single phrase that points from the human to its other: 'To produce the whole of its effect, then, the comic demands something like a momentary anaesthesia of the heart' (5). Laughter can take place only where there is a disengagement of feeling, an emotional indifference. Aligned with the necessity of anthropomorphism is the deanthropomorphism of the mechanical, which can be seen in a certain 'mechanical elasticity, just where one would expect to find the wide-awake adaptability and the living pliableness of a human being'. As a result, then, the comic is 'accidental: it remains, so to speak, in superficial contact with the person' (10). Bergsonian laughter begins with the human – the social, the utilitarian, the anthropomorphic – and ends with the inhuman, with automatism, emotional anaesthesia and mental torpor, body disengaged from mind. A paradox thus ensues. Humour itself is therapeutic, as a contributor to social bonding, but the conditions of its production are inhuman. It is the inhuman possibilities of humour that are most visible in Beckett's comedy of uncertainty, indeed, that go some way towards begetting loss of certainty.

Theories of laughter have been codified in terms of 'superiority' and 'incongruity'.[14] Charles Baudelaire suggests a variant of the superiority theory in his meditation 'On the Essence of Laughter'. In this essay he revitalises the spirit of lapsarian thought. Counterposed to the socially binding and humanising aspects of humour is the notion of laughter as emblematic of a fall. From the orthodox standpoint, writes Baudelaire:

it is certain that human laughter is intimately connected with the accident of an ancient fall, or a physical and moral degradation . . . In the earthly paradise . . . joy did not reside in laughter. As no sorrow afflicted him, man's countenance was simple and composed, and the laughter that nowadays shakes nations did not distort the features of his face. Neither laughter nor tears can show themselves in the paradise of bliss.[15]

Hence the comic is indicative of damnation and diabolism, a mark of the satanic in man (144–5). The human, the satanic and laughter are all of a piece; their combination leads to the other side of the fall, to transcendence:

Laughter is satanic; it is therefore profoundly human. In man it is the consequence of his idea of his own superiority; and in fact, since laughter is essentially
human it is essentially contradictory, that is to say, it is at one and the same time
a sign of infinite greatness and of infinite wretchedness, infinite wretchedness in
relation to the absolute being, of whom man has an inkling, infinite greatness
in relation to the beasts. It is from the constant clash of these two infinities that
laughter flows. (148)

Laughter is aligned with humanness, and humanness with fallenness.
As with Bergson, and his notion of an inhuman premise (emotional
anaesthesia) having humanising consequences (shared social being),
Baudelaire sees laughter as conjoining antinomies. Because man has
fallen, he partly inhabits the diabolic; but it is man's transcendence, his
superiority over nature, that produces the conditions of possibility for
laughter.

Applied to Beckett's work, this notion of transcendence creates a
quandary: either it has transcendence surreptitiously coded into it, despite appearances to the contrary (i.e., desolation is somehow transfig-
ured into exaltation); or it is performing a transvaluation of the idea
of comedy as a mark of superiority or transcendence. Beckett, as I will
show, pursues the latter – he exploits the undecidability of humour, rather
than (as the critical orthodoxy has done) reformulating it into an affirmatory humanist credo. His work demonstrates 'anaesthesia of the heart'
without a positive, socially beneficial outcome. And it begets a world
without 'infinite greatness', only 'infinite wretchedness', and devoid of
the transcendent model of an 'absolute being'.

### Drifting bones in a dismantled world

In Beckett's work the link between comedy and uncertainty is not a
given, because uncertainty is not a given; it must first, as it were, be
won. Beckett's narrators are compelled to reach out for certainty, before
arriving at uncertainty. It is the pursuit of certainty that actuates the
flights of rigorous logic, the mathematical gymnastics of permutation
and enumeration, and the unstoppable flux of recall. Paul Davies writes:

In Beckett, one of the first steps, often a hilarious one, is a bid for certainty, skir-
mishing and random in manner, often feebly desperate, often bungled. Nevertheless, like a sentence begun, a bid for certainty is a spur to action: it is
something after which, and in relation to which, something must come.[16]

Bergsonian detachment (inhuman premise leading to human result) and
Baudelairean superiority (a composite of the human and the diabolic)

conjoin human and other, to form an unstable composite. The same can be said of Beckett's comedy of uncertainty, which registers as not a momentary but a prolonged 'anaesthesia of the heart'. It takes shape in *Molloy* as denigration of the body.

Molloy himself is 'a vivacious buffoon of benightedness, a spirited clown of decay. But in the most obvious sense, he is only drifting bones and a disordered consciousness in a dismantled world.'[17] His attitude to his body is one of savage indifference, bordering on hostility:

> I had so to speak one leg at my disposal, I was virtually onelegged, and I would have been happier, livelier, amputated at the groin. And if they had removed a few testicles into the bargain I wouldn't have objected. For from such testicles as mine, dangling at mid-thigh to the end of a meagre cord, there was nothing more to be squeezed, not a drop.[18]

His body becomes no more than a prop, a source not of complaint – unusual in such an expert sufferer – but of bitter comical asides. After Lousse's dog dies, Molloy looks on while she digs the hole, consoling himself with the thought: 'In any case it wasn't their fault I couldn't dig, but my leg's' (47). Later on in the shelter, having fled Lousse, he muses: 'My knees are enormous . . . My two legs are as stiff as a life-sentence' (83). And in a Bergsonian near-parallel, he declares: 'it does not beat, my heart, I'd have to refer you to hydraulics for the squelch that old pump makes' (121).

Bodily processes inspire comical digressions as much as body parts; indeed, Molloy's chronic flatulence leads him to calculate his rate of emission ('Extraordinary how mathematics help you to know yourself'; 39). And contemplation of his physical decline brings on an orifice-oriented meditation, forcing him to pronounce the anus the 'true portal of our being' and the mouth 'no more than the kitchen-door' (107–8). This incessant self-absorption is broken by a late episode in the first half that reasserts the comical disregard for the body – another's body, this time, possibly a charcoal-burner, 'but I really don't know'. Resisting an advance of some sort, Molloy snaps into action: 'So I smartly freed a crutch and dealt him a good dint on the skull. That calmed him. The dirty old brute . . . Seeing he had not ceased to breathe I contented myself with giving him a few warm kicks in the ribs with my heels. This is how I went about it . . .' The best part of a page is then spent detailing how a partially crippled old man can overcome his physical disabilities and deal blows to a prostrate body; not in the ribs, as he proposes, but 'something soft', probably the kidney. After performing it on one side of his comatose victim, Molloy applies himself to the other side, voicing acutely the note of emotional anaesthesia: 'I always had a mania for symmetry' (113–4).

Beckett's comedy of uncertainty contains its own tonal instability, as when it crosses over into grim philosophical reflection. Thus the humour of emotional anaesthesia is preliminary to a more bewildering ontological amnesia: 'Yes it sometimes happens and will sometimes happen again that I forget who I am and strut before my eyes, like a stranger' (56); 'Yes, there were times when I forgot not only who I was, but that I was, forgot to be' (65). The latter admission rises forcefully to the surface in an astonishing passage of bodily abandonment:

> And there was another noise, that of my life become the life of this garden as it rode the earth of deeps and wildernesses . . . Then I was no longer that sealed jar to which I owed my being so well preserved, but a wall gave way and I filled with roots and tame stems for example, stakes long since dead and ready for burning, the recess of night and the imminence of dawn, and then the labour of the planet rolling eager into winter, winter would rid it of these contemptible scabs. (65)

Neglect, in this passage, gives way to loss, to a state of complete severance and disembodiment.

In sum, then, Beckett's body-based comedy, revelling in wretchedness, is the first of several transvaluations of humanist orthodoxy. The final loss of bodiliness contains a hint of potential terror. For there is in Beckett's work mind–body discontinuity, but not hierarchy; cerebration cannot compensate for the frailities of the flesh. Molloy's apparent 'superiority' to his body engenders macabre comic possibilities, the suggestion that his body is a gratuitous adjunct to his identity. But the idealist alternative – that consciousness is 'really him', that he is more mind than body – is equally untenable, as we are about to see.

### *The narrating mind: 'Sick with thought and fastened to a dying animal'*

Beckettian comedy is not just a blackly comic affair about bodily disintegration and/or distortion. It also takes the more nuanced form of ironic uncertainty. For Beckett's fiction is founded on the gap between intended and unintended consequences of his narrator's actions. The shortfall between promise and performance provides a source of comedy; as Andrew Gibson has noted, 'Beckett clearly takes great delight in engineering this kind of narrative disparity, and narrative contradictions in general.'[19]

There are prime 'narrative contradictions' in the generic liberties taken by the trilogy. Beckett's narrators are all in retreat: Molloy's search for his mother could be construed as seeking the shelter of the womb; Malone withdraws into memoir/fiction, to what has been characterised as a 'death-bed confession' and 'the broken memoir of a dying man';[20] and the Unnamable's molten outpouring of language suggests he is seeking asylum within the words and narratives he compulsively disgorges. But although in retreat they are also, paradoxically, engaged upon quests.[21] Malone's quest is to finish dying and to conclude his tale, simultaneously. The Unnamable, like everything in the text, has purpose and motility but no objective; 'quest' is stymied by the aporetic bind of the necessary and the impossible: 'I shall have to speak of things of which I cannot speak' (4).

*Molloy* appears to be the most 'genred' of the three, with its topoi of quest, detection and pursuit. But if Molloy's story brings to mind an ordeal novel or a quest-romance, it is a quest that goes astray. This part of the plot 'involves the hero's quest for some form of transparent relations with his mother, a quest that ends, as it were, in failure and transfiguration'.[22] The problem of beginnings that we saw at work in Conrad and Heidegger achieves something of a limit-case here. Molloy attempts to mark his beginning with resoluteness and precision, by deferring to the man who comes every Sunday to collect his written pages:

It was he told me that I'd begun all wrong, that I should have begun differently. He must be right. I began at the beginning, like an old ballocks, can you imagine that? Here's my beginning . . . Here it is. It gave me a lot of trouble. It was the beginning, do you understand? Whereas now it's nearly the end . . . Here's my beginning. It must mean something, or they wouldn't keep it. Here it is. (8)

Molloy's determined invocation ('Here's my beginning'), like the successive beginnings of *Being and Time*, unravels rather than accrues. Certitude does not accumulate, it dissolves into hesitancy. Eric Levy writes:

All of *Molloy* is an attempt to find a beginning, but the seeking is successively diverted on to different tracks by different seekers. Nothing moves successfully in a straight line; neither the personae nor their narration can avoid circular movement, an inevitable return to the point of departure . . . Molloy's search for a beginning has gone on unsuccessfully for so long that a replacement is sent in to make a fresh start. There is, of course, a regress here, a second beginning looking for the first.[23]

This is even more problematic than the circular structure of *Nostromo*, and its play on the word 'revolution'. 'Beginning' is not just suspended, it is actually rolled back, to something less than a start.

There is another literary genre evoked (or demolished) in the trilogy, the *Bildungsroman*. Technically, a *Bildungsroman* is an ironised quest narrative, where the protagonist finds something other than he sets out to find. *Molloy* conforms to this ironised structure – though whether or not Molloy and Moran find anything at all through their searches is open to dispute. Both characters, in fact, appear to end up with significantly fewer resources than they started with. David Hayman writes: 'The quest hero is generally conceived of as going into the darkness to retrieve the light and achieve a meaningful existence. In *Molloy* shabby versions of the shining knight-errant achieve deeper darkness and meaninglessness.'[24] These dubious spoils, where personal growth is stymied, leading to its opposite, are alluded to by Patricia Alden: 'The dream of the harmonious expansion of the self in a society which nurtures it becomes a nightmare of estrangement and loss of self. Those painful experiences which, in earlier novels, might have led to maturation here contribute to disintegration: "Experience *un*teaches."'[25] The examples Alden gives, from Gissing and Hardy, are also suggestive: 'As anti-Bildungsromane, *Born in Exile* and *Jude the Obscure* treat this conception of the individual as a yearned-for ideal which cannot be realized.' Jude ends in a 'chaos of principles – groping in the dark', and Peak comes to experience a 'tormenting metaphysical doubt of his own identity'. Groping in the dark and chronic self-doubt are Beckettian tropes, of course, as we saw at the outset with the Descartes anecdote.

'Experience unteaches,' writes Alden. So, too, does the conventional aspect of *Bildung*, the process of formal education, asserts Beckett in an early poem, 'Gnome':

> Spend the years of learning squandering
> Courage for the years of wandering
> Through a world politely turning
> From the loutishness of learning.[26]

The world of learning is prominent in Beckett's two great progenitors. To move beyond literary modernism, suggests Richard Begam, Beckett had to move beyond Proust and Joyce: 'Thus Beckett's heroes function as parodic versions of Marcel and Stephen: aging invalids who lie in bed, obsessively writing inventories of their past, or vagrant derelicts who wander from place to place, carrying a stick (instead of an ashplant) and seeking their alter egos.'[27] But a key feature of Marcel's and Stephen's characters is their formidable erudition. Similarly, Beckett's characters are beneficiaries of *Bildung*. They are all, in one sense or another, overeducated: Murphy an ex-theology student, Watt 'probably university educated', the narrators of the trilogy fastidious writers of one sort or another. Yet all have turned 'from the loutishness of learning', as Richard Coe remarks:

> The main theme of [Beckett's] work is impotence, of mind just as much as of body. All Beckett's tramps are erstwhile scholars, but, like Vladimir and Estragon, they 'have waived their rights', and their scholarship, like Winnie's 'classics', belongs irrevocably to the past.[28]

What characterises Beckettian man then, in a second humanist transvaluation, is really two types of infirmity: physical decay, most obviously, but also intellectual atrophy. The endless permutations of objects and relationships could be seen as a singular form of pedantry, the intellectual exercise of the overeducated; or as a version of neoscholasticism, brought to bear not on theological conundrums (though there is a series of them at the end of *Molloy*, which reads like a Dada commentary), but on the logistics of a closed field of objects or actions. The quintessential Beckettian voice with its terse syntax, bitter rejoinders and remorseless logic suggests a mind stocked with learning and armed with linguistic adeptness and philosophical dexterity.

This foregrounds a further, third aspect of Beckettian dehumanisation. Learning has been fundamental to humanism since Greek *paideia* and Roman *humanitas*, the tradition of liberal education based on the classics. This discipline inaugurated 'one of the great assumptions of Western civilization – that it is possible to mould the development of the human personality by education'.[29] And yet, Beckettian man is in the mess he is to a large extent because of his erudition. Learning is not merely 'loutish', as Beckett asserts in 'Gnome', but also insidious and mind-addling. Recapitulating its own processes in an endless cogitative frenzy, the Beckettian narrator dwindles until he is reduced, in J. D. O'Hara's striking phrase (borrowed from Yeats), to 'a mind sick with thought and fastened to a dying animal'.[30]

The train of endlessly banal itemisations and numerisations has far-reaching consequences. The *Bildungsroman* was begotten by C. M. Wieland to evade the antinomies of dualism. But rather than 'resolving' dualism, this literary form sublimated it; hence it contains, as we have seen, an abiding tension. Defying the *Bildungsroman*'s insistence that subjectivity is narrative-shaped, Beckett produces not so much antinar-ratives as anti-*Bildungsromans*. *Lord Jim*, *Sons and Lovers* and *Mrs Dalloway* each offered challenges to the form and strategies for resisting it, but it is in the Beckett's trilogy that it finally comes apart; Beckett, even more than Woolf, ushers in its dissolution. Attached to story-structures by the slenderest of threads, Beckett's novels operate at the very limits of narra-tivity – most strikingly in the quasi-cacophany of *The Unnamable*, forever on the verge of complete narrative exhaustion and linguistic meltdown. Narrativised subjectivity is wrenched out of its human-shaped literary vessel and transplanted to something inhuman.

## II *MALONE DIES:* FAILED ACTS OF BIRTH AND DEATH

### *Agitating the calmative*

Beckett's writing reveals a compulsive absorption with the processes of birth and death. Both take place on cusps, at either end of 'life'; Beckett divests both of their surety. Death is made ambiguous and indistinct, and part of the mode of its virtuality is that birth, too, assumes an in-determinacy. (One cannot die without first being properly born.)[31] This is Beckett's most disquieting uncertainty, implanted at the deepest onto-logical level.

Just as the trilogy's individual parts take liberties with genre, so does the trilogy as a whole. Leslie Hill notes that it 'is constructed like a mock dynastic novel, following its story through, as it were, from one gener-ation to the next'; it resembles, in this sense, 'an obsessive genealogical fable'.[32] Such a portrayal evokes the structure of *The Rainbow*, with its successive unfolding of generations of lives. The two works part com-pany, however, in their different narrative procedures. As Chapter 3 demonstrated, Lawrence's 'duology' translates birth and death into lit-erary form: in *The Rainbow*'s rendering of narrative-as-parturition, with its tropes of cyclical renewal; and in *Women in Love*'s portrait of a gener-ation at the end of time and the end of narrative, its protagonists finally opting for posthuman transcendence over further human narrative. In Beckett's trilogy parturition and transcendence are both severely inhib-ited. Birth is either a failed event at some point in the past, or yet to be achieved in the future. Far from miming the process of a woman's labour, '[b]irth, in the trilogy, is an event without issue and an act that happens in reverse'.[33] Equally, the impossibility of transcendence ensures the durability of narrative, in one form or another. It must be wrestled with, distended, problematised – but not abandoned outright. Beckett's narrators are stuck fast within its airtight confines.

The portentous question raised in Chapter 2 – can the human mind master what the human mind has made? – demands further entreaty. For if the narrator's birth has been 'botched', the narrative he is spinning cannot but lose its human-shaped countenance. Hence there are two kinds of parity at work in *Malone*. The first is between birth and death, which are regarded as isomorphs rather than opposites – an extension of *Godot*'s diagnostic aperçu (spoken by Pozzo) that we 'give birth astride of a grave'.[34] Here, birth and death are simultaneous occurrences, separated only by what Schopenhauer called 'the momentary intermezzo of an ephemeral existence' (*W2* 466), in which 'everything lingers only for a moment, and hurries on to death' (478).

The second case of parity is a reciprocity between philosophical reflection on uncertainty (birth and death made virtual) and the formal anomalies whereby it is conveyed. Hence Beckett's prolonged attempt at performing failure is conveyed not just through failed acts of birth and death, but also through equally fallible structures of narrative supporting them. Integral to this is the recognition that narrative is a 'calmative'. As the narrator in the story of the same name (written late in 1946, immediately before the trilogy) avers: 'I'll tell myself a story, I'll try and tell myself another story, to try and calm myself...'[35] But this function of narrative – the power of form to console[36] – is what Beckett repudiates. A chief means of his resistance, in the fiction, is an emphasis on the gap between intended and unintended consequences of his narrator's actions.

Within this gap epistemological difficulties proliferate, for Beckett's narrators are set against their own narratives. If Lawrence urges that we trust the tale, not the teller,[37] Beckett evinces a bipartisan scepticism, an equal distrust of both.[38] These acts of sabotage amount to a dehumanisation of narrative, a prising apart of tale and teller: 'Beckett's narrators are constantly taken aback by the alienness of their own narratives, by the otherness of the narrator whom they must take none the less to be themselves.'[39] The ontological uncertainties that beset Molloy, discussed in Part 1, are thus echoed in the narrators' questionable ability to narrate.

The question of doubt conjoins with reflection on death in Malone's project. He recounts how once he was content to submit to boredom, 'until someone was kind enough to come and coffin me'. He says of being born: 'That's the brainwave now... live long enough to get acquainted with free carbonic gas, then say thanks for the nice time and go' (51). And his train of thought is interrupted by the desire to 'leave these morbid matters and get on with my demise' (63). If these remarks fall short of celebrating oblivion, it is because of the notes of doubt that surround them. Scepticism, that is to say, saves Beckett's morbid humour from pure nihilism. His savage wit is tempered by agnostic relativism – not the brutal certitude of denial, but a more congenial engagement with possibility.

Malone's scepticism leads him to regard life and death as indistinct analogues: 'There is another possibility that does not escape me, though it would be a great disappointment to have it confirmed, and that is that I am dead already and that all continues more or less as when I was not' (45). It makes explicit the fearful ambiguity of *Malone*'s opening sentence: 'I shall soon be quite dead at last in spite of all' (1). The word 'quite' highlights Malone's great dread that maximal death, the death of release and relief, the death that the voice of the Unnamable hopes will be 'a change', will turn out to be compromised death, a partial decease or demise in which the painful attributes of life persist.[40] The same notion informs Malone's conception of reincarnation, which he ponders in passing: 'You begin to wonder if you have not died without knowing and gone to hell or been born again into an even worse place than before' (53). If life and death are not such different states of being, then the much-anticipated acquittance of death is as black a joke as the agony of being among the living.

Beckett echoes Conrad's lament (itself an echo of Schopenhauer) that we are 'utterly out of [life]'[41]. Conrad blamed this estrangement on consciousness ('What makes mankind tragic is not that they are the victims of nature, it is that they are conscious of it').[42] Beckett also asserts our estrangement from life: we give birth astride of a grave and we come and go, as incapable of being properly born as of truly dying. Relief is nowhere at hand; there is nothing for the human to partake of (life, power, being), nor even limitedly to possess. In depicting life as an existential realm detached from human being, Beckett might seem not so different from Nietzsche who excoriated the human disposition to abjure life for 'antilife' – slave morality, bad conscience, *ressentiment*. But for Nietzsche life, or its correlate, power, nevertheless possesses inherent value, which it clearly does not in the Beckettian estimate (where the correlate for life is not power but impotence). If, then, it is only by fully inhabiting life that we can do more than 'come and go', i.e., be a being capable of escaping from birth into life and having that life consumed by death, then Beckett's bitterest irony is that life itself is uninhabitable. Human existence is a constant punishment, an empty tract of gloom between two significant – yet not, for all that, very different – occurrences. If birth and death are not dissimilar, then they are not unique events, not definitive 'cusp' experiences at all. To be human, in Beckett's world, means to undergo slow suffocation in the amniotic fluid of being, an unwitting and unwilling accessory in a process that resembles a prolonged miscarriage.

### Falling in and out of nature

Beckett's catalogue of woe is, at this point, quite extensive: body is decrepit, mind struggles to stave off atrophy, narrators cannot control and are estranged from their narratives, and human existence is denied participation in the (putative) powers of regeneration and revivification conventionally ascribed to 'life'. This dolour points to a more pervasive condition of decrepitude, a state of permanent lapsarian calamity. Frank Kermode writes: 'Beckett's decaying figures, lying on the ground, sitting in dustbins, groaning along the road to nowhere, inhabit a world in which there has certainly been a Fall, but just as certainly no Redemption.'[43] Yet Beckett's foreclosure of any potential for transcendence has an implication for its other, fallenness: the impossibility of envisaging a *pre*lapsarian state. Steven Connor is closer to the mark: 'If being is impure, if there are irresolvable contradictions in human existence, then this, for Beckett, is not to be explained as a fall from grace, a disturbance or complication of original simplicity or unity.'[44] Thus if we must speak of a fall, it can be conceived, paradoxically, only as an immediate, eventless condition, without a differential. It is a world always already exhausted, not even comparable (in *Endgame*'s caustic aside) to a poorly made pair of trousers;[45] and yet, astonishingly, running down still further.

In the couple of consciousness and life, or the human and the natural, both sides of the dichotomy are problematic. But this is a human-inflicted condition: our frailties are so determining that when we anthropomorphise – as we do, compulsively – we cannot help but project human imperfection on to nonhuman nature. This tendency is acutely examined in the trilogy. While the various devices for dehumanisation confound the lines of narrative continuity, a curious reversal is taking place in other parts of the text. As Moran's leg begins to give out on him, he sits down to observe the dawn: 'The sky sinks in the morning, this fact has been insufficiently observed. It stoops, as if to get a better look. Unless it is the earth that lifts itself up, to be approved, before it sets out' (*M* 192).

This anthropomorphisation continues in *Malone*. The cabman's horse is as deliberately described as the dawn of Moran's reverie:

It spends most of its time standing still in an attitude of dejection . . . But when the shafts tilt up . . . then it rears its head, stiffens its houghs and looks almost content . . . And each one has his reasons . . . for going where he is going rather than somewhere else, and the horse hardly less darkly than the men, though as a rule it will not know where it is going until it gets there, and not always even then. (57–8)

The most sustained passage of anthropomorphic detail comes at the end of *Malone*. Like Moran, Malone watches the day breaking, and sees a 'rack of tattered rainclouds stampeding'. Turning back to the Macmann narrative, he gives us such details as 'the great black gesticulating pines' and 'the shivering poplars' (104). Macmann and Lemuel, we learn, often heard 'the sea when it was high enough to make its voice heard'. And the 'English park' they visit contains 'trees at war with one another, and the bushes and the wild flowers and weeds, all ravening for earth and light' (106), and birds that 'wheeled long in the cruel air, screeching with anger, then settled on the grass or on the house-tops, mistrustful of the trees' (107).

These details are in bold contrast to the anomalies and discrepancies of the Molloy/Moran narratives, and to the ragged intermittences of Macmann's story. Which is to say that Beckett's narrator anthropomorphises nature, the realm of fact, at the same time as he *de*anthropomorphises the human and narratorial, the realm of value (in the narrators' astonishment at the otherness of their own narratives). Why is he doing this? Anthropomorphisation could be seen as consoling, a way of asserting control. Narrative, however, cannot be controlled; it is so deeply mired in human practice that something is bound to break down. Andrew Gibson writes:

Beckett has sometimes thought of narrative as resembling the organic. But he has usually likened it to organisms troubled by disorders or sickness, by cancers or plagues. His narrators may sometimes abruptly lose the use of certain faculties, just as Molloy and Moran may lose the use of a limb. Narratives may suddenly develop peculiar traits, as the figures they refer to develop growths or diseases.[46]

Beyond simply saying that 'life is meaningless', or 'existence is purposeless', what this suggests is that human ways of finding meaning and purpose – i.e., as embodied in practices of narrative – are as imperfect as human beings. But turning to the natural world and endowing it with anthropic properties degrades that world, too. The sky 'stoops', the cabman's horse stands in 'an attitude of dejection', rainclouds are 'tattered', trees are 'at war', and the air is 'cruel'. Incorporating these details into anthropic activity has contaminated them, has robbed them of their potentially redemptive qualities. Anthropomorphisation cannot provide consolation, it can serve only to foreground the brute facticity of the natural world. There is, then, a *double* fall: the eventless lapsarian condition that is a given; and (further) degradation wrought by anthropomorphic activity. Thus the discontinuity of the human and the natural, of man and life, is constantly being reiterated and replayed. By not moving beyond this, Beckett evades the exigencies of transcendence that inhere, as possibility, whenever fallenness is evoked.

### Intermezzo: a poetics of impotence

Every relationship in Beckett is discontinuous, as I stated earlier. There is an intractable dissociation of mind from body, human from natural, self from world. Paradoxically, however, this also gives rise to a kind of creeping homogeneity, an indistinctness that makes comparable the elements of those relations: mind is as atrophied as body, human and natural realms are both disabled, self is as unstable and fluctuant as world. There is, therefore, a kind of homology between drifting bones, disordered consciousness and dismantled world. Similarly, although tale and teller are prised apart by their individual alterities, this tends also to produce a *re*binding, a commensurability of the two. As the Unnamable expounds at one point: 'I [am] still the teller and the told' (30). Eric Levy outlines the Unnamable's dilemma: 'How can he transform himself into a story that ends if there was never a genuine separation between himself and his narration in the first place?'[47]

This commensurability yields a conception of the human as a purely 'facted' creature. For if Beckett's domain is, as we have seen, a domain of stark facticity, then the surfeit of ambiguous parity cited above makes this as applicable to its denizens as to its topography. That is why, finally, Beckett's narrators cannot be properly born – because they can never establish sufficient difference or distance from the conditions that have produced them. Transcendence is so unrealisable in Beckett that his characters are always (already) connected, umbilically, to infirmity and decrepitude, possessing them as a birthright. And if birth has never been completed – is in fact uncompletable – then death, too, fades into the ragged tapestry of being. The human as a creature of value depends on being properly born; failure to be born means escaping value inscription. Similarly, with death comes the passing, the surrendering, of value. A corpse, like an aborted foetus, is a 'fact'. And even though Beckettian man cannot fully inhabit this state, his consistently corpselike demeanour places him between the living and the dead – on a redemptionless, purgatorial plane, denied oblivion and stripped of value.

Like the Heideggerian assault on the metaphysics of subjectivity, Beckett identifies the key aspects sustaining the humanist tradition – humour, learning, narrative, postlapsarian redemption – and turns them inside out, revealing their inhuman otherness. But Heidegger's alternative, his fundamental ontology of Dasein, is a mere displacement of mastery, a relocation from human to nonhuman sources; as Emmanuel Levinas perceptively noted, it is a 'philosophy of power'. The Beckettian disposition is the opposite, a poetics of impotence. Anthropological mastery is not translated into 'ontological imperialism';[48] instead, it is recast as anthropological *non*mastery. As with the philosophy of being, so with the philosophy of life. To say that 'life appears to be more active and more productive than consciousness' (in Hannah Arendt's characterisation) is not to dissolve value but, again, to reassign it to a nonhuman locus.[49] Beckett also abjures this move; life is seen as no more *inherently* valuable than *anthropos*. He dissolves, in other words, the distinction between the human and its others. The natural, the bodily and the nonmetaphysical are not elevated above their anthropological counterparts. Nor does he rely on a fall, or antitranscendence, a postlapsarian paradigm antecedent to a future transcendence. In Beckett's work translation of the human from value into fact is more deftly and convincingly staged than the philosophies of either life or being could manage.

III *THE UNNAMABLE:* TWO SURFACES AND NO THICKNESS

In the trilogy so far, we have seen uncertainty manifested as comical discrepancy, as discontinuity (itself made uncertain, by the abovementioned homogeneity), and as virtuality (birth and death incompletion). Amid this sea of doubt there is but one guaranteed surety: the inevitability of failure. Unlike uncertainty, though, this does not have to be 'won': failure inheres structurally in the work's characteristics, in its 'impossibility'. As Richard Coe has observed, the human condition, for Beckett, was 'literally and logically impossible. And in this central concept of "impossibility", his thought has most of its origins – as does also his art.' If art sets out to elucidate the impossible then it cannot succeed, and is doomed to fail.[50]

'Impossibility', however, is only one component of the Beckettian temper, which persistently lapses (or collapses) into aporia. The Unnamable frames the situation: 'The only problem for me was how to continue, since I could not do otherwise' (44–5). It is this conjoining of the impossible with the inescapable or necessary that more accurately defines Beckett's disposition. Simple discontinuity is wrenched into the aporia of 'necessity' and 'impossibility', where two things that cannot be thought together cannot *not* be thought together, either. The impossible and the necessary are both unswerving conditions, both grounded in surety; in combination, however, they produce uncertainty.

### Descartes's dream revisited

As already noted, Beckett's trilogy narrators are both in retreat and engaged upon quests. It is in the third part of the trilogy that this contradiction becomes most problematic.[51] *The Unnamable* marks a further withdrawal, from the mind into the mind's acute sense of its fragility and tenuousness, a precognitive uncertainty that can only be disclosed through performance.

Descartes's night of turmoil and dream-abundance is a scenario that prefigures Beckett's forays into darkness and meaninglessness. The fitful sleeper becomes a paradigm for the permutations of consciousness and the possibility of slippage between states, without a humanistic, reflexive tribunal (i.e., a *cogito*) to legislate between these states. In addition, the Cartesian dream-narrative is a humanist narrative. It has the shape of a redemptive report: beginning in torment, undergoing grave mistrust and uncertainty, finally being steered towards confidence by the placating force of cogitation. It is also, in another sense, a self-reflective fable, a parable conveying its own authority to tell an exemplary story. The might of rational reassurance helped Descartes overcome his demons of scepticism and revealed to him his method – itself an elevation of the power of self-present cognition. Such a fable is as salutary as it is humanising.

Beckett's knowledge of Descartes was wide, thorough and precocious. Reference to the night of 10 November 1619 appears amid the biographical clutter of *Whoroscope* (lines 45–51):

> A wind of evil flung my despair of ease
> against the sharp spires of the one
> lady:
> not once or twice but . . .

(kip of Christ hatch it!)
in one sun's drowning
(Jesuitasters please copy).[52]

The notes appended to the poem refer to these lines as Descartes's 'vision', the dream-images that haunted him as he drifted in and out of sleep.[53] There is also a fundamental kinship between Beckettian fiction and Cartesian biography: Malone in bed evokes Descartes in the same place, pursuing his speculations without reference to the world of experience.[54] Let us assume, then, that Beckett did not just know enough about the night of dreams to versify it, but also that it touched him deeply. His response was to take it and, in Alvarez's account of the Beckettian method, 'pare away the inessentials, freeze the action, and reach down into that black core of boredom and despair that was the centre of all his work'.[55] In short, he has taken this humanising tale and dehumanised it, in two different ways.

First, there is no enlightenment for the waking dreamer. Descartes awoke, and found certainty; Beckett's Unnamable, his most tenacious narrator, is unable to distinguish between waking and dreaming. He is delivered not into certainty but into a miasma of contingency, where he must make do with hypothesis and supposition. Yet without any compensating clarity, this can only precipitate further conjecture. The humanising, consolatory climax of Descartes's ordeal – the orientation towards the 'method' that will ground Western philosophy for the next 300 years – has been excised, and in its place is the voice-filled void, a world of pure speculation. Beckett 'inherits all of the embarrassments of Cartesian dualism with none of the benefits'.[56] The assured foundationalism of the *cogito* is sundered by the symmetrical uncertainties of bodily decay and mental atrophy. Thus the Unnamable declares his double dispossession: 'I'm the partition, I've two surfaces and no thickness, perhaps that's what I feel, myself vibrating, I'm the tympanum, on the one hand the mind, on the other the world, I don't belong to either . . . ' (134). (Earlier, he indicated the opposite: 'Two holes and me in the middle, slightly choked'; 94.)

The other, more general way Beckett dehumanises the Cartesian anecdote is by blocking its path of self-assurance. When it functions most efficaciously, a narrative act is an act of confidence. It works in part by totalising, by convincing us that contingency can be transformed into necessity. This is the ideological substratum of narrative dynamics, the appearance that everything has been accounted for and is inevitable, that all contingencies have been (or will be) superseded by necessities. But as Francis Mulhern has observed, 'the work of narrativity is always an opening and a closing, a loosening and a rebinding of sense. All but the most sedate or the most forensic narratives are in some degree unsettling.'[57] Although narratives tend to totalise, they contain within them the promise of *non*totality, the disquieting intimation that something has been left out.[58] This is the shadowy underside of the Unnamable's endless production of proto-narratives. Which is to say that Beckett removes the veil of totality from narrative and exposes its ideological underpinnings. The Unnamable's stories are not only denatured and incomplete, with vague, intensely problematic beginnings and endings; they are also compulsively produced. Amid the linguistic haemorrhage are clots of narrative, providing temporal identity and nuance. And their prodigality – 'the stories go on, it's stories still' (*U* 137) – indicates the contingent character of all narratives. With Beckett narrative confidence is curbed to such a degree that narrative is made to *doubt*.

This goes some way to answering the question of why Beckett should have worked within narrative structures, when they appear anathema to his literary concerns. By doing so he could reveal the inhuman potential for narrative. In Beckett's work uncertainty is discontinuity, all relationships are broken. This means, from the point of view of narrative, that every ravelling is also an unravelling. The movement from contingency to necessity is never completed – nor even begun. Beckettian narrative remains resolutely in the mode of the aleatory, perpetually on the edge of outright dissolution. The paradigm for discontinuity, for a process that cannot be bound by 'necessity' into a narrative schema, is Darwinian natural selection. In this version, evolutionary change does not 'unfold' because it never assumes the immanent structure granted by hindsight. Its consecutive ordering is propelled by chance rather than inevitability. Narrative order, consequently, remains in an impasse. Beckett avoids this impasse by enlarging the inhuman potential of narrativity, and in doing so takes narrative deformation as far as it can go in anthropometric thought.

### *From obligation to compulsion: taking the measure*

> Possessed of nothing but my voice, the voice, it may seem natural, once the idea of obligation has been swallowed, that I should interpret it as an obligation to say something.
>
> Samuel Beckett (*U* 31)

A passage from *Women in Love*, part of Birkin's courtship of Ursula, serves as a surrogate credo for the Lawrentian transcendent:

'There is,' he said, in a voice of pure abstraction, 'a final me which is stark and impersonal and beyond responsibility. So there is a final you. And it is there that I would want to meet you – not in the emotional, loving plane – but there beyond, where there is no speech and no terms of agreement. There we are two stark, unknown beings, two utterly strange creatures, I would want to approach you, and you me. – And there could be no obligation, because there is no standard for action there, because no understanding has been reaped from that plane. It is quite inhuman . . . ' (146)

Beyond responsibility and understanding, where 'there could be no obligation': this denotes the Lawrentian inhuman. At the other end of the scale is humanist obligation, the responsibility that human beings have for one another's welfare: the automatic, nonnegotiable imperative that is the moral law. Between the two extremes of human and inhuman is Beckettian obligation.

In the first of his *Three Dialogues with George Duthuit*, Beckett intones a much-quoted statement that has come to stand for his artistic anticredo: 'The expression that there is nothing to express, nothing with which to express, nothing from which to express, no power to express, no desire to express, together with the obligation to express.'[59] This obligation to express – 'the only positive element left in this sea of Negativity'[60] – is raised again in the third dialogue, ostensibly about the painter Bram van Velde:

BECKETT: The situation is that of him who is helpless, cannot act, in the event cannot paint, since he is obliged to paint. The act is of him who, helpless, unable to act, acts, in the event paints, since he is obliged to paint.
DUTHUIT: Why is he obliged to paint?
BECKETT: I don't know.[61]

Beckett's narrators, it need hardly be said, seem obliged to narrate. The Unnamable announces that Mahood's voice 'will disappear one day, I hope, from mine, completely. But in order for this to happen I must speak, speak' (29). And later: 'Strange notion in any case, and eminently open to suspicion, that of a task to be performed, before one can be at rest. Strange task, which consists in speaking oneself' (31).

In Beckett's utterance about 'the obligation to express', Martin Esslin sees a 'moral minimalism' that is a 'residue of virtue', and 'that minimal assertion of the dignity of consciousness'.[62] But Beckett also alludes to helplessness, which casts doubt on obligation. The Unnamable exemplifies this: 'Having nothing to say, no words but the words of others, I have to speak. No one compels me to, there is no one, it's an accident, a fact. Nothing can ever exempt me from it . . . ' (36). The Beckettian narrator is not obliged to narrate, he is driven to do it, to become a narrative-producing machine. He tells stories not as 'calmatives', or to partake in a process of human self-identification, but because he has no other choice. Beckett's people cannot renounce writing, narrative or life, and they discharge narrative almost effortlessly ('I'll let down my trousers and shit stories on them,' snaps the Unnamable; 130).

We saw in *Nostromo* how obsession turns man into machine, through the fanatical desire for, and relentless pursuit of, the spoils of the San Tomé mine. Beckettian obligation, which appears to be desireless, points beyond these. Which is to say that obligation's shadow is *compulsion*, a form of the inhuman. In terms of Beckett's mastertheme of relentless self-doubt, compulsion does not dissolve scepticism, it braces it. It prevents scepticism from becoming either the tool of humanist enquiry that can yield knowledge, or a basis for the antihumanist affirmation of endless free play. Perhaps most significantly, it is the element that prevents humour, learning and narrative from being recuperated into the cathartic, the therapeutic, the redemptive. Obligation to the other, as a primordial responsibility, is thus transformed into the compulsive stirrings of consciousness, susceptible to the vicissitudes of the inhuman.

A similar form of compulsion is evident in the Schopenhauerian will. To recapitulate Lawrence's debt to Schopenhauer, it lies in the concordance between inner and outer, between the endogenous soul and the exogenous metasoul or source. Which is to say that it is through the inhuman category of the transcendent that Lawrence's residual Schopenhauerianism (via Hardy) becomes manifest. Beckettian compulsion, by contrast, in its relentless narrative production and machinelike insistence, evokes the category of the mechanical – another attribute of the Schopenhauerian will, refigured as Conradian obsession. We might also point to Schopenhauer as a paradigm for the radical doubt that pervades Beckett's work (just as Lawrence, too, discovered his own profound scepticism from reading Schopenhauer).[63]

I have argued earlier for the Schopenhauerian influence on literary modernism as both immediate (Conrad and Lawrence encountering his writing at formative phases of their careers) and secondary (refracted through the works of Maupassant and Anatole France, and of Thomas Hardy). Beckett, too, experienced both types of contact, but in such a way as to make them inseparable. For behind his *Proust* essay lurks the figure of the German pessimist, giving definition to Beckett's understanding of Proust as much as he shaped the lineaments of *A la recherche*.[64] In fact, in Beckett's essay the figure of Schopenhauer is superimposed over that of Proust; much of the text comes directly from *The World as Will and Representation*, with very little distortion.[65] Beyond *Proust*, Schopenhauer tends to fade from the Beckett canon.[66] Yet there is one particular, proto-Schopenhauerian aspect of Beckett's thought dominating the trilogy, which I will call the principle of noncancellation.

The trilogy is riven with conflicting pairs of propositions and retractions, where assertion and denial operate simultaneously. The net effect, however, is not neutralisation. Language, in the form of statement, conveys an intrinsic positivity, it is always assertive: 'It cannot actually negate anything. The closest you can get to negating something is not to say it, rather than to say and deny it.'[67] The 'double utterance' regulates the Unnamable's discourse, from the first passages: 'There must be other shifts. Otherwise it would be quite hopeless. But it is quite hopeless' (3–4); 'I shall not be alone, in the beginning. I am of course alone' (4); 'The best would be not to begin. But I have to begin. That is to say I have to go on. Perhaps in the end I shall smother in a throng. Incessant comings and goings, the crush and bustle of a bargain sale. No, no danger. Of that' (5).

All Beckett's monologists issue utterances in pairs, a proposition followed by its qualification, or (attempted) negation – only there is no negation. Utterances operate not as either/or, but as both/and. Furthermore, aporia, in its scepticism and irresolution, does not permit one term to eclipse the other; there is neither negation nor the Hegelian outcome of supersession, of syncretic harmony. Like the inevitability of failure, the principle of noncancellation is as close as Beckett comes to certainty: something cannot be, and then not be; or better, something cannot not be, having already been.

Schopenhauer dismissed the will to live (the impetus to 'go on') as a 'a delusion . . . a blind urge, an impulse wholly without ground or motive' (*W2* 357). Once a being has been called forth to be born, it becomes part of the closed field of existence, and cannot work its way back to what Schopenhauer called 'the lost paradise of non-existence' (466–7). As Malone realises, there is no way back: 'I too must have lived, once, out there, and there is no recovery from that' (47). The Unnamable, in its post-Worm guise near the end, declares: 'I'm looking for my mother to kill her, I should have thought of that a bit earlier, before being born' (146). This is pure Schopenhauer: better never to have been, because one cannot be and then not be. For to be, i.e., to be called forth by existence, is to feed the rapacious appetite of the cosmic will, to abet its proliferation. Likewise 'to be', for Beckett, is to leave an ineliminable mark on existence, a mark resistant to retrospective eradication; once the silence has been stained, it is permanently tainted.

In Beckett will begins as obligation but congeals into compulsion – sourceless causeless and desireless. It is the urge to speak, to write, to conjecture about present conditions, to generate narrative, to permutate series, to produce macabre comedy, and it brings to a halt many of the 'humanising' aspects that have defined humour, narrative, *et al.* throughout history. *The Unnamable* is, finally, a book-length reflection on compulsion. Or, more accurately, it is an aporetic enactment of this quest, since the more compulsive the enquiry becomes, the less freedom there is to reflect upon it.

### *Dehumanising narrative: the voice-machine*

The basal characteristics of narrative, which I have termed voice and machine, can also be seen as the play between 'difference' and 'sameness'. David Watson describes the typical Beckettian narrative as a violation of this convention. There is difference without sameness (enormous digressions and apparently insignificant details), and sameness without difference (mathematical permutations).[68] Watson's description explains how narrative is able to contain the ambiguous play of discontinuities that abound within homogeneous parity, where every unravelling is also a ravelling, every severance a rebinding, etc. Within the flurry of discontinuities is a collapsing of distinctions: 'In the title *L'Innommable*, distinctions between human and non-human, character and narrative voice are under threat of collapsing, leaving behind them an indeterminate flux of words in which all naming becomes impossible.'[69] Like 'teller' and 'told', voice and machine collapse into one another: *The Unnamable*, in fact, presents us with a singular hybrid, a performative example of voice *as* machine. This is one particular terminus for the problem of the philosophical unconscious, immanent to the *Bildungsroman* throughout almost 200 years of literary production. The sublimation of the incompatibility of *res extensa* and *res cogitans*, which created the unconscious in the first place, is dissolved by the voice-machine characterising Beckettian monologue.

Narrative, as we have seen, never stops for Beckettian man. It is possible, then, that he tells stories so unstoppably because it is a way of locating the 'human' – under the unavailing belief that narrative is human-shaped, so by finding this shape, by sculpting the unstoppable drone of language into anthropic modalities, relief and stillness can be sought. Necessity, in *The Unnamable*, is the compulsion to narrate; impossibility is making narrative cohere, making it resemble what it (ostensibly) already is: human-shaped. This is impossible because narrative is voice *and* machine, its human countenance is complicated by a nonhuman infrastructure. The voice-machine adds further complexity; is the compulsive outpouring of linguistic uncertainty an expression of humanity or inhumanity?

Beckettian compulsion is commingled with a disavowal, a refusal 'to accept as assured...the competence and mastery, the humanity, even, of the narrating voice'.[70] In cleaving to narrative Beckett exposes its impotence, and reveals the inhuman underside that is the voice-machine. And by doing so, in the teeth of its minatory otherness, Beckett demonstrates a refusal of solace.[71] Thus the singular hybrid that is the voice-machine, the mechanical impetus that the narrative voice cannot cast off, signifies Beckett's loss of faith in the human; his remaining unconsoled is indemnified, as it were, by his apostasy. For as interminably as the voice-machine disgorges language in narrative-shaped clusters, apostasy is loss without redemption, without the confidence that surety lies elsewhere and that the present loss will expedite its recovery. A true apostate experiences loss of faith as a constant depletion of confidence and belief; he cannot allow this to harden into alternative belief, but must remain implicated in a process of constant reiteration.

A key example of the voice-machine appears in the trilogy's denouement, perhaps the most contentious part of the Beckett corpus. It also illustrates the relentless, performative, iterative loss of faith and refusal of consolation: an eruption of broken clauses that becomes a syntactical seizure, bringing *The Unnamable* to an abrupt halt with the words: 'I can't go on, I'll go on.' The orthodox humanist reading sees these clauses as chronological, the second cancelling the first, ending in triumph.[72] Alvarez, by contrast, contends that the finale 'sounds less like an affirmation than a threat'.[73] If we consider the far-reaching overhauls that Beckett has performed on humour, on learning, on narrative and narration, and on obligation, we can only question what it might actually *mean* to 'go on'. Is this really giving voice to an affirmative humanism, an equivalent of Molly Bloom's final 'yes', an escape from aporia? In keeping with the present line of thought, 'I'll go on' can only mean 'I will continue to generate narrative', continue to be enslaved by compulsion and bound to the aporetic.

Rather than chronological, the two clauses are better seen as simultaneous. Simultaneity pervades *The Unnamable* through aporia: the bondage of the necessary ('You must go on') and the impossible ('I can't go on'). It is coded into the textual fabric through the whole double-utterance structure of proposition and retraction. Though presented consecutively, the effect of this propositional structure is one of simultaneity; each proposition begins to take on the cast of its opposite even before that opposite has (inevitably) been uttered. 'Beckett's prose conjures up a world in which the written word can be the ultimate non-committal medium.'[74] *The Unnamable*'s denouement exemplifies the refusals, confusions, denials and contradictions that persist through the extraordinary narrative apparatus that is the voice-machine.

## BECOMING HUMAN: THE DIFFERENCE OF 'HUMAN-NESS'

In literary and philosophical antihumanism, a differential operates between the human and its others. Animalisation and mechanisation of the human, which appeal to prehuman and parahuman realms, attempt to break the stranglehold of anthropological mastery. Such moves herald, however, not an annulment of mastery but a transference – from the anthropological to the nonanthropological (i.e., nature and machine technology). In other words, sovereignty is still extant, but it is shifted from the human to its others. In Beckett's texts there is no human–other differential. The human *is* its others, to the extent that it, that they, are discontinuous and deformed. And so impotent is the human mind that it is incapable of mastering anything, even its own (imperfectly begotten) creations. The radical discontinuities of body, mind and world are brought into alignment with each other through a shared condition of mutual dereliction.

We are, in short, born disabled, and the world we are born into is also disfigured and incomplete, lacking in all key respects. Like this world, we have insufficient resources to overcome our deficiencies. We possess too few reserves to bind our fragments into wholeness, our disabilities into identity, our provisional frailties into a self. As I have suggested, in Beckett's work there is a kind of negative link between the human and the natural: both are bad jobs, running down and bound for oblivion. In the absence of any human–nonhuman differential, and in the face of the uninhabitability of life, can the leap from 'fact' to 'value' still be made?

A fundamental discontinuity asserts itself above all other discontinuities: a severance of the human from any humanism. Since all that the senses report is a negative reciprocity between self and world, human and natural, Beckett's quest is for *difference*, something that might separate the human from its others, at the same time as denying much of what has been claimed for it by 'humanism'.[75] In addition, we have seen Beckett dismiss with implacable astringency humour, learning, narrative and redemption, all of which claim a special relation to being human, as do the 'heroic' qualities often associated with quests, with modernism, and with humanism *per se*. Beckett's relentless searching for difference is reflected in his clinging to narrative, even after showing its vertiginous otherness; he makes neither the Lawrentian move to the posthuman, nor the Woolfian shift into ahumanist hybridity. But if human existence is always already mired in lapsarian woe, and there is no diachronic difference to enable recuperation, we might wonder what exactly is the *point* of Beckett's work, and why it is fastened so resolutely to the chimerical.

Beckett's people, as we saw, are compelled to seek certainty, and to embark on quests. But behind the pursuit of mothers and derelicts, of maximal death and consummate stillness, is a quest for the greatest, least ascertainable entity of all: the human. It cannot be located because it does not appear to exist, yet the search is continuous and neverending, and it is through it that value is precipitated. It is not the goal that matters but its pursuit, the performance of the quest for the authentic, yet phantasmal. In undertaking this 'impossible' search, something comes fleetingly into being, only to wink out once the search is abandoned, or suspended: not the human but 'humanness'. This is separate from humanism as a core set of beliefs, and (necessarily grounding those beliefs) the human as a stable, fully self-present entity. Andrew Gibson describes it as Beckett's turn 'away from human to "human-ness"', where the latter is conceived 'not as a fixed state of being, but as a constant process of becoming'.[76] Human beings are always tied to process, to performing their selves – which flicker briefly into momentary, unified life – rather than to being their selves. The self that comes to life creates the illusion of an immanent, substantive entity, which seems to abide in absence of its being performed. Beckett foregrounds the illusion, the ephemerality of the self – dehumanising, in effect, humanism itself. His alternative 'humanness' could be described as apostasised humanism, a humanism that cannot believe in the human. Regarded in this way, the impossible and the necessary become the impossibility of being human and the necessity of practising humanness.

There is an encroaching homology in Beckett's world, and even though elements of that world remain permutatable, radical rearrangement cannot hide their gathering bankruptcy, their resistance to singularity. Beckett's quest for the human, then, is a quest for what resists homogeneity, and for what cannot be permutated. Existence, we have seen, is a bad lot; we are born crippled into a disabled world. But what is still worse, and must be resisted at any cost, is to surrender our humanness to compulsion. The particular form of Beckett's resistance was aesthetic insurrection fastened to unblinking severity – engaging in 'a massive and unrelenting critique and dismantling of the illusoriness of what passes for life'.[77] But only by exposing this illusion for what it is, i.e., anthropocentric mastery, and without recourse to *non*anthropocentric mastery, can the potentiality for value be renewed.

Transcendence, or the ability to evade compromise and contingency, becomes in Beckett's world the desire to escape from the homologising effect that holds mind, body and world in the same tight clench. This 'escape' is the search for the human. *Finding* the human is transcending the inhuman, the infirm, the decrepit. And yet this is scarcely tenable, as the human appears to be phantasmal. *Seeking* the human, on the other hand, betokens a different kind of transcendence – a more circumspect, tentative, provisional overcoming of homologous conditions. The voice-machine that iterates and reiterates, that issues propositions and withdraws them in the same movement, that mounts a concerted strike against consolation: this provides the textual frame for Beckettian overcoming and reassertion of value renewal. For the possibility of value renewal is inextricable from struggle, the struggle with discontinuity, uncertainty and apostasy. The fact of struggle – another unshakable fact in Beckett – must be performed, without it becoming a form of compulsion. For then it is no longer struggle, but mechanical reaction.

Beckettian struggle is a struggle between the animal and the mechanical. A passage in *The Unnamable* links the two categories:

The only problem for me was how to continue, since I could not do otherwise, to the best of my declining powers, in the motion which had been imparted to me. This obligation, and the quasi-impossibility of fulfilling it, engrossed me in a purely mechanical way, excluding notably the free play of the intelligence and the sensibility, so that my situation rather resembled that of an old broken-down cart or bat-horse unable to receive the least information either from its instinct or from its observation as to whether it is moving towards the stable or away from it, and not greatly caring either way. (44–5)

Animal and mechanical are merged, invoking obligation and the spectre of aporia ('how to continue, since I could not do otherwise'). The struggle in Beckett, therefore, is the struggle of an obligation animal, resisting becoming what it may already be: a compulsion machine. This resistance is the kernel of Beckettian humanness – a minimal, *performative* affirmation, restoring the possibility of value.

# *Humanness unbound*

[T]he meaning of humanity is not exhausted by the humanists, nor immune to a slippage that is at first imperceptible but can ultimately prove fatal. Is there a fragility to humanity in this humanism? Yes . . . in spite of all its generosity, Western humanism has never managed to doubt triumph or understand failure or conceive of history in which the vanquished and the persecuted might have some value.

Emmanuel Levinas[1]

The anthropometric era, as I have defined it, covers little more than a hundred years, or from the 1850s to the 1950s. In the late 1850s Darwin's 'dangerous idea' took hold of the scientific and lay mind alike, and Schopenhauer's philosophical system, after decades of neglect, began its reign over European letters and European thought generally. At the other end of the period, the 1950s, Beckett's trilogy of prose works appears as a culminating point in literary reflection on the human, situated in a precarious zone between humanist self-aggrandisement and anti-humanist censure.

As I have argued, at some time in the middle of the nineteenth century a seismic shift occurred in Western thought, an alteration in how the human was understood. The faultline spread through a number of cultural domains, changing human self-understanding within natural science, technology, philosophy, literature and literary criticism. The chief consequence of this change was that conceptions of the 'human' became decoupled from beliefs in 'humanism', the one no longer presupposing (or indemnifying) the other. The particular cast of thought or mode of praxis resulting from this has been designated the anthropometric turn: a turn away from the human as a *given* towards the human as a *problem*. Such a turn is manifested in the various attempts to take the measure of the human, and in the different modes of anthropocentrism and its others that have proliferated through late modernity. The human becomes a perplexing issue in ways, and to a degree, it has not previously enjoyed.

Concurrent with this complexification of the human, narrative has been subjected to relentless pressure. To tell a story, to narrativise an event-series, is no longer a pellucid, self-apparent undertaking. The causal–linear axis of narrative, and the somewhat 'occult' effects it produces, are now regarded with suspicion and circumspection; the anthropometric turn is thus also a turn away from narrative. Resistance to narrativisation cuts across the domains. Animal–human evolutionism, human–mechanical interactivity, human–transcendent overcoming: narrative cannot be compelled into supplying the structures needed to make these convergences fully humanised. It cannot provide this because narrative is *itself* partly 'inhuman', partly mechanical; if there were nothing machinelike about narrative formations, they would not possess us the way they do. Each individual narrative cannot be responded to afresh. It requires something familiar for support, something habitual for the functions of mutual implication, immanent structure *et al.* to be efficacious. The literary modernist effort to undermine humanist certitude and self-confidence – where the death of God had hastened the birth of Man – made visible the underlying codependency of the human and narrative. Regarding *both* as products of anthropological self-aggrandisement, modernist writing sought to align formal literary experimentation with counterhumanist critique.

In the course of the preceding chapters, loss of the conditions necessary for narratability has become evident. 'Metaphysical' evolutionism resists narrativisation; Darwin prised narrative out of nature, Nietzsche evacuated it from philosophy; the Schopenhauerian will invokes the atemporal, the ahistorical, the unnarratable; and Heidegger cleaved to certain narrative conventions, only to perform drastic alterations on them. In the literary domain the realist narratives of Conrad and Lawrence were shown to be pocked with meditative forays into existentialist tragedy and posthumanist transcendence, respectively. Woolf's intense explorations of inner experience, on the other hand, though nominally engaged with processes of human interiority, reveal these processes as providing short-cuts to the nonhuman world. Through all these changes the *Bildungsroman*, that quintessentially humanist novel form, is adumbrated, modified and finally revoked.

The limits of narrativity probed by earlier modernist forays might be seen as the starting point for Beckett's trilogy of novels. Whether a *roman fleuve* mutation or a *Bildungsroman* evisceration, these works abandon the routine landmarks of family, social register and subjective evolution. The seeds of destruction inherent in the *Bildungsroman* – the attempt to escape the philosophical intractability of *res cogitans* and *res extensa*, by demonstrating the growth of subjectivity – are brought to their fullest, deadliest bloom by Beckett's monologists. The *Bildungsroman* is buried where the Beckettian voice-machine is born.

These writers afford different responses to that most fundamental question of ethical humanism: what value, if any, is to be found in human beings? For both Conrad and Lawrence human beings are real but their value is questionable. Conrad, in the Schopenhauerian mode, devalues the human because its realm is a vale of tears. Without the serene self-regard of his German forebear, Conrad questions the wisdom and purpose of existence amid so much anguish. His use of the machine motif – the contraption that knits us in and out of existence, the field of obsession that possesses and 'mechanises' the will – suggests that to survive in Conrad's world one must become inhuman. This is not as difficult as it sounds, because nature has already done half the job anyway. Yet there is, nonetheless, only minimal value to be salvaged from the endless gloom of actuality.

Lawrence also questions the wisdom of existence. But his devaluation of the human is wedded to an agonistic overcoming, a grasping after the fleeting form of the transcendent posthuman. The human individual may be degraded and unhealthy, he or she may be little more than a squanderer of the sacred lifeforce, but for Lawrence there is an alternative, as there is not for Conrad: the flux of being, accessed through nature, offering glimpses of a beyond. Lawrence's devaluation of the human centres on what man has *wrought*, rather than what he *is*, on what civilisation has delivered via industrialisation, modernisation and democratisation. The body, the biological vessel of the human, is a source of value just as surely as man's social being is a source of endless disgust.

For Woolf the human has value to the extent that it can negotiate inconstancy and change. But this, in itself, does not secure its separateness; to the contrary, it makes legible the proximity of human life to forms of animal and plant life. Yet even without these sudden accesses of otherness, the polyphonies of perspective, nervous rhythms of recollection, and different temporal zones peculiar to each character describe a world where intersubjective contact is a precarious and effortful undertaking. That communicative action is unstable, ironised and crosspurposed makes individuals as out of synch with each other as they are with external time. Caught between mutability and isolation, human being is as provisional as the condensations of experience clouding its interior world.

Of the four, Beckett is the most generously disposed towards the human – at least in theory. It is not the posthuman or the nonhuman that is the object of Beckett's quest, but the human. The problem with Beckett's generosity (and why it cannot move beyond the theoretical) is that the human does not appear to exist. Valuation is postponed because there is an ephemerality about the human that disables its actuality. Beckettian compulsion, the irrevocable urge to go on, closes the gap between the virtualised human and the nonagency or automatistic demeanour associated with the animal or the mechanical. One of Moran's reveries shows what is at stake, and the paralysing uncertainty of being: 'And what I saw was more like a crumbling, a frenzied collapsing of all that had always protected me from all I was condemned to be. Or it was like a kind of clawing towards a light and countenance I could not name, that I had once known and long denied' (*M* 203). Behind the human is something atrophied, a being permanently unsure of its ontological status and beset by the sensations of physical and mental decomposition.

Beckett's relentless scepticism gives him, more than his modernist forebears, a pivotal position in the genealogy of anthropometric thought. I began by identifying doubt as the central feature of Beckett's writing, whose prevalence even undoes the notion of 'centrality'. In practice, the work actuates a series of switches, shuttling back and forth between human and inhuman, narrative and antinarrative, at the vanishing point of their convergence yet unable wholly to occupy either one. Beckett, as it were, uses narrative in such a way as to provide the tools to implement its abolition. Framing this is the movement from obligation into compulsion, a movement that Beckett struggles to resist. It takes place in the space where human gives way to inhuman, where elective obligation becomes mechanical compulsion. Beckett reveals the inhuman potential of narrative, its machinelike qualities. So narrative is both cleaved to and demolished, the human is acknowledged as both an obligation animal and a compulsion machine, and humanism is both refigured (into 'humanness') and apostasised. Placing itself at a distance from both Conrad's tragic antihumanism and Lawrence's agonistic posthumanism, and pressing further than Woolf's metamorphic ahumanism, Beckett's cryptohumanist writing reopens the possibility of value renewal, but without giving in to the temptations of an affirmatory, overconfident critical orthodoxy.

Beckett illuminates, through his sceptical prism, the lineaments of the 'humanless' human: the being unable to inhabit its own humanity, the entity as fact and not value. I have designated Beckett's position as apostasised humanism – a humanism not based on, but in pursuit of, something recognisably human. The potential nonexistence of this being prevents it becoming a foundation or ground (which would reassert the preanthropometric human-humanism collocation). Equally, its potential existence enables certain claims, always provisional, to be made on its behalf. In a sceptical age an apostasised humanism must suffice, as a means of negotiation between an outmoded metaphysics and a toothless relativism. Beckett recognised the tension between these two positions, and sought to escape their limitations. Rather than abandon narrative procedures outright, he probed their counterhuman qualities of mechanisation, simultaneously exploiting narrative order and seeking to escape its compelling gravitational pull. Having done so, the master of scepticism issued a critical strike, a thoroughgoing denunciation of the myriad forms of humanist self-aggrandisement.

### Beckett's theoretical inheritors

Insofar as Beckett can be said to have 'counterparts' in postwar cultural theory – and allowing for the obvious disparity between different literary forms[2] – I will suggest two possible analogues.[3] Needless to say, this can only be a brief sketch of what is really a much broader thesis (and enlarged still further in the next section). Still, even a condensed outline can give some indication of where the argument running steadily through the preceding chapters – the effect of the counterhumanist struggle of modernist narrative forms on our contemporary discourse of the inhuman – has been heading.

That destination is the 'postnarrative' attitude that has determined the seditious temper and formal difficulty of much postwar theory. In terms of publishing history, the years 1961–2 are the watershed: a mere matter of months saw the appearance of Levinas's *Totalité et infini* (1961), Foucault's *Folie et déraison* (1961) and Deleuze's *Nietzsche et la philosophie* (1962). I propose to discuss the first two figures as theoretical counterparts to Beckett. In doing so, the practice of earlier chapters is continued. Rather than attempting a 'Beckettian' reading by matching up specific traits, I attend to the commonality of their concerns, showing how they are manifested in certain attitudes and orientations.

In the first case, the cardinal issue is Beckett's suspension between narrative fixation and narrative demolition, which, in tandem with the undecidable nature of the human (as obligation animal and compulsion machine), situates him in a precarious, limbolike zone. In postwar philosophical writing the ethical reflections of Emmanuel Levinas have carved out a similar space between humanism and antihumanism. Levinas's writing has performed reclamations of metaphysics, transcendence and *subjectum*, yet has studiously avoided the foundational support of the Western tradition.

Levinasian thought might be seen as another instance of a 'humanism without the human'. It begins with an exorbitant question: how can the other be shielded from the totalising dominion of the same? Through 'transcendence', declares Levinas – although the term undergoes a drastic modification. Because it is used to signify pure alterity, it cannot be associated with self, individual or One. It is an ur-transcendence of the *other*, and it takes place prior to anything recognisably 'human'. The other must *transcend*, in this primal moment of encounter, this ur-anteriority, in order to safeguard its status as other. Furthermore, it is from this transcendence-dependent encounter that the 'human' is formed. The crucial factor is its incontestably ethical nature, 'giving value to the relation of infinite responsibility which goes from the I to the Other'. Such respect 'imposes itself on thought with the power of primordial coordinates'.[4]

For Levinas, then, the human's other is the transcendent. The human becomes human through encounter with the other, and it is this encounter that constitutes transcendence; and it is pure transcendence, absolute alterity, rather than sublation. Unlike the transcendence of Heidegger's *das Man*, the same cannot contaminate the other, lest it become not transcendence but appropriation. For the other is an abstraction prior to such conceptions as 'fellow human being' or 'neighbour'. 'Transcendence is only possible with the Other, with respect to whom we are absolutely different, without this difference depending on some quality.'[5]

John Llewelyn adroitly describes this as an 'alter-humanism',[6] a humanism of the other:

Levinas would point to a humanism of the other man, of man whose selfhood is distinguished by his being addressed. Man can call himself man only because he is called by his neighbour. The human being is human and capable of sympathy only because his humanity is responsible being for the other, only because responsibility for the freedom of the Other is anterior to freedom in myself, only because no one is willingly good.[7]

Levinasian alter-humanism is not concerned with stripping the 'human' from the human. The 'human' is always already human in that pre-conscious moment of encounter, before the assumption or taking on of metaphysical subjectivity and the reflective ego. Levinas's 'humanism without the human' is, then, a humanism *prior to* the human, prior to the peremptory demands of subjectivity and consciousness.[8]

The resistance described above to the totalising discourse of the 'same' has thoroughgoing consequences for narrative. Mutual implication of narrative events, causal relations and a culminating immanent structure all serve to *totalise* narrative's elements into a seamless, purposive and necessary whole. Perhaps most objectionably, there is the notion that in the beginning is the end, but it is not revealed *until* the end. Contingency is displaced by necessity, and the causal network and immanent structure of the whole become apparent. As we saw in Chapter 1, this is an intrinsic part of Hegelian narrative dynamics in the *Phenomenology*. It is hardly surprising, then, that Levinas has issued harsh warnings about Hegelian totality.[9] But is there any alternative to the narrative mechanics cited above, short of outright abandonment?

Like the modernist novel, Levinas's major work *Totality and Infinity* problematises narrative in extreme ways, without letting go of it altogether. As Colin Davis has shown, the central difficulty concerns the textual reproduction of Levinas's central philosophical concern, alterity, in patterns that both belie temporal order (alterity as a fundamental state) and enact it (alterity as a fundamental event). Davis writes:

The drama of *Totality and Infinity* lies in its struggle with the linguistic resources available to it. This is particularly the case in its use of the language of origins and the chronological narratives that are implied by it. [ . . . ] *Totality and Infinity* gets tangled up in the difficulties of giving a narrative form to a fundamental state.[10]

Levinas's chief problem, then, is how to convey the unfamiliar that is otherness, in the familiar form that is narrative – without the latter, and its secretion of sameness, appropriating the former. More specifically, the conflict could be seen in 'intranarrativistic' terms: how to maintain the potential alterity of 'voice', without its absorption into the familiar processes and structures of 'machine'? *Totality and Infinity* returns, insistently and aporetically, to this fundamental dilemma. In cleaving to subjectivity by seeking a narrative form for it, and simultaneously problematising narrative, Levinas's project can be seen as the mutant progeny of the *Bildungsroman*. He is wresting subjectivity from its deep-seated entanglements in narrative – entanglements perhaps congenital, if subjectivity really is narrative-shaped – yet without abandoning narrative form altogether. '[A]ll the speculative restlessness and conceptual energy of *Totality and Infinity* are deployed on the edge of a semantic abyss into which the whole text might collapse.'[11] This predicament is, of course, irresoluble, but it takes place in the space that will come to be occupied by a new generation of theoreticians.

In the very year when Levinas's heroic but doomed attempt to unite antinomies was published, the first fully realised postnarrative work also appeared: Michel Foucault's *Folie et déraison*.[12] Instead of wrestling with the fraught dilemmas of narrative, Foucault's text abandoned them outright. George Levine has suggested that Foucault disrupted the Darwinian vision of history and creation, in such a way as to reenact Darwin's contestation of earlier beliefs in coherence and continuity.[13] The means whereby he did this, I would argue, lie in the modernist transformation of storytelling mechanism – particularly as manifested in the work of Beckett. Foucault's approach to historical narrative formation might therefore be seen as a variation on, and extension of, Beckett's approach to fictional narrative formation. Which is to say that just as Beckett's fictions disable the belief in necessity, 'Foucault's histories aim to show the contingency – and hence surpassability – of what history has given us'.[14]

If Levinas's key tropes are 'totality and infinity', Foucault's are 'totality and discontinuity'. In *The Archaeology of Knowledge* he outlines his principles as 'discontinuity, rupture, threshold, limit, series, and transformation', and declares:

[I]f it is true that these discursive, discontinuous series have their regularity, within certain limits, it is clearly no longer possible to establish mechanically causal links or an ideal necessity among their constitutive elements. We must accept the introduction of chance as a category in the production of events.[15]

Conventional history is preoccupied with major changes, which it seeks to explain. It does so by seeking hidden continuities in the form of 'historical laws'. These, in turn, imply obedience to regularities and, ultimately, the discovery of causes. Historical explanation is thus causal explanation. By contrast, Foucault's use of discontinuity dispenses with causality, with both the primacy of origins and the mechanics of change.

Foucault's strategies include the following: 'discrete' periodisation (Renaissance, Classical Age, Modern Age); rejection of historicist notions of continuity (cause, influence, development, teleology, and so on); antiessentialist treatment of authors, works or entities; and rejection of unified history or unities of 'truth'.[16] Conventional historical orderings of same and other, present and past, familiar and strange, are thus eroded by Foucault's discontinuous, antidialectical, nonnarratable counterhistory. Frank Lentricchia summarises this as 'Foucault's project of introducing the forbidden concepts of rupture and discontinuity as antidotes to traditional reliance on the grand humanist assumptions of the narrative unity of history'.[17] The 'consolation of form', the potential of narrative to pacify, is spurned. Even more so than Darwinian discontinuity, which is random, unpredictable and nonnarratable, yet ultimately *explicable* (which is to say, meaningful) in terms of 'fit' between organism and environment, historical discontinuity – 'that most perplexing of Foucault's ideas'[18] – defies elucidation.

Foucault's texts are 'postnarrative' works in the sense that the form of historiography being undermined is the form that owes most to the novel. As Edward Said has noted of Foucauldian counterhistory, 'the novelistic model of successive continuity is rejected as somehow inappropriate to the reality of contemporary knowledge and experience'.[19] Instead, Foucault ventured outside historiography's enslavement to the novel form. Hayden White remarks:

Foucault rejects the authority of both logic and conventional narrative. His discourses often suggest a story, but they are never about the same characters, and the events that comprise them are not linked by laws that would permit us to understand some as causes and others as effects. Foucault's 'histories' are as fraught with discontinuities, ruptures, gaps, and lacunae as his arguments.

Similarly for Foucault's construction, in *The Order of Things*, of the 'episteme'. His development of this concept indicates that he 'refuses to see these four epochs as acts of a drama of development, or as scenes of a narrative . . . Foucault's book thus appears to have a theme, but no plot.'[20]

Foucault, then, with his postnarrative method, is returning phenomena to their nonhuman origins, making them strange again. In demonstrating how potentially 'alien' man is (i.e., the human without the 'human'), and how aleatory, recalcitrant and refractory the past is, he succeeds in making separate what has been hitherto inseparable: the human-narrative coupling. In this sense, he completed what the modernist transformation began, as the next section outlines.

### *Modernism by other means*

Writing in 1923 on 'The Future of the Novel', D. H. Lawrence remarked: 'It seems to me it was the greatest pity in the world, when philosophy and fiction got split. They used to be one, right from the days of myth . . . The two should come together again, in the novel.'[21] I suggest that it is in contemporary theoretical reflection that the two are reunited. It is here that the counterhumanist concerns of the modernist novel are allied with paraliterary practices that continue, and extend, the effort to decompose narrative form. In other words, the connections outlined above between Beckett's writing and that of Levinas and Foucault are mere local instances of a broader, more far-reaching nexus.

The proposition itself was announced by Terry Eagleton in 1983:

It is, in fact, the literary movement of modernism which brought structuralist and post-structuralist criticism to birth in the first place. Some of the later works of Barthes and Derrida are modernist literary texts in themselves, experimental, enigmatic and richly ambiguous.[22]

The influence of Eagleton's bestselling *Literary Theory* can account in part for the currency of this thesis in the 1980s. It has been used by both liberal humanist polemicists to blow the whistle on 'theory', for contributing to the atrophy of our cultural and academic institutions;[23] and by Marxisant thinkers to criticise the political apathy of antirealist thinking.[24]

From a more sympathetic perspective, Andrew Ross makes the case most cogently:

Poststructuralism is the critical revolution that was delayed: it is the continuation of modernism by other means. In *theory*, its genealogical origins (in fact, all of its important 'breaks') have been traced to Marx, Freud, Nietzsche, and, in a more instrumental way, to Saussure. In *practice*, its tribute to uncertainty was fulfilled in the historical tradition of the European avant-garde. As an *institution* of critical and theoretical practice, it earned its radical credentials in the wake of the more broad-based challenge to academic process and discipline that was mounted in the late sixties.[25]

I suggest that not only is theory a 'continuation of modernism by other means', but that these different means are necessary precisely because of the difficulties posed for modernism by narrative, and that these means represent the elimination of narrative from modernism. Theory is not just an application of modernist techniques; it bears the particular form it does because narrative has been cleared from the modernist horizon.

Narrative, as Roland Barthes remarked, is that 'great catalogue of the continuous'.[26] Theoretical antihumanism, by contrast, strives to find a form for the *dis*continuous – a form that is neither philosophy nor fiction, but works in stylistically self-reflexive (*écriture*) and performative ways, as many modern fictions do. Like the modernist novel's uniquely miscegenated nature, the typical theoretical text is a *sui generis* assimilation of fiction, philosophy, history, sociology, etc. into a striking new brand of mythography. Eagleton's remark on poststructuralism *tout entier* holds good for the more rarefied domain of 'theory': 'There is no clear division for post-structuralism between "criticism" and "creation": both modes are subsumed into "writing" as such.'[27]

Theory accomplishes what Conrad, Lawrence and Woolf (but not Beckett) were unable to do: reworking narrative logic in order to expedite cultural renewal. Conrad's proto-existentialist tragedy, Lawrence's metaphysical posthumanism and Woolf's metamorphic ahumanism were unable to separate narrative orientations from their human and humanist associations. They reacted to the modernist demand for a postnarrative fiction, yet were unable either to escape it by turning to more or less conventional realism (as, say, E. M. Forster did), or to satisfy it with a radically new form (Beckett's 'narratives against narrative'), and so the human-narrative doublet remained intact. Following in Beckett's wake, French theoreticians grasped the inhuman underside of narrative and understood its allure for those earlier novelist-critics of the human. It was this understanding that enabled them to break with narrative yet still maintain the modernist unmasking of anthropological self-aggrandisement, of the 'human' and its doctrinal codification as a form of interference.

Theoretical antihumanism strives to obtain, through the static, a glimpse of the human within the 'human'.

This brings us back to the complicated link between the human and narrative – a link that resolves into a chiasmus. In the modernist novel the struggle with narrative (which is never completed) is really a struggle with the human. In theoretical antihumanism the struggle with the human is really a struggle with narrative – a successful struggle, this time, that culminates in the formation of a 'postnarrative' technique. The reason for the latter's success is its recognition of the true nature of the symbiotic narrative-human relationship, and the necessity of forging a new literary form to break the congenital link that thwarted its predecessor. If the 'human' is narrative-shaped, then dispensing with narrative is a way of coming closer to the *human*. Storytelling is always interventional, interposing itself between *human* and 'human'. The paraliterary prose forms of theory are as eclectic as the modernist novel, but untroubled by the need to marshall that eclecticism into narrative shape. The postnarrative method of contemporary theory can treat dispersion *as* dispersion without the 'rage for order', the compulsion to find a more rarefied pattern of meaning for its allusive, performative fragments of critique.

To summarise: the relationship between modernist narrative form and counterhumanist critique, i.e., the way in which narrative deformation has contributed to antihumanist discourse, turns on three points. Firstly, theoretical antihumanist writing is a kind of 'critical modernism', a renascence of the modernist temper after its exhaustion. Secondly, theory abandons narrative form and adopts instead a 'postnarrative' method, which enables it to make cultural analyses, whether diachronic or synchronic, without the need for conventional storytelling apparatus. And thirdly, there is a chiasmus between modernism and theory, in which counterhumanist critique is secreted within narrative disruption (in the modernist novel); and then narrative abandonment provides the formal vehicle for the discourse of theoretical antihumanism.

The words 'human' and 'inhuman' imply strict categories of meaning, filled with assumptions about political and/or ethical activity or beliefs. What must be recognised, therefore, is how *in*human the human really is, and the importance of inventing new ways of being human that might reflect this. The doctrinal limitations and self-deceptions of vulgar humanism fail to acknowledge that the human has not been annihilated or superseded, but has become contingent rather than essential. The anthropometric turn, the difficulty of finding the measure of man, is concomitant with the recognition that the human's others are not only closer to hand than we realise, but that their otherness is as contingent as our humanness. When the human *is* its others – whether it be a rational animal, an affective machine, or an overcoming entity – the human-other differential no longer pertains. We must make do, it would seem, not with essences of humanity but with contingencies of humanness; and become accustomed, if we are not already, to *performing* our humanness, rather than to *possessing* it. What is contingently human comes to life as the human merges with, and emerges from, its inhuman others.

# Notes

PREFACE

1 T. Pynchon, *V* (London: Pan, 1975), p. 332.
2 I. Kant, *Practical Philosophy* (Cambridge: Cambridge University Press, 1996), p. 18.
3 Z. Bauman, *Modernity and the Holocaust* (Cambridge: Polity Press, 1989), p. 13.
4 E. Levinas, *Difficult Freedom* (Baltimore: Johns Hopkins University Press, 1990), p. 272.
5 M. Norris, *Beasts of the Modern Imagination: Darwin, Nietzsche, Kafka, Ernst, and Lawrence* (Baltimore: Johns Hopkins University Press, 1985), p. 4.
6 *Ibid.*, p. 222.


INTRODUCTION

1 I. Watt, *The Rise of the Novel* (Harmondsworth: Penguin, 1983), p. 35.
2 'It would appear, then, that the function of language is much more largely referential in the novel than in other literary forms; that the genre itself works by exhaustive presentation rather than by elegant concentration . . . . [which is] why the novel has less need of historical and literary commentary than other genres – its formal convention forces it to supply its own footnotes.' Watt, *The Rise of the Novel*, p. 30.
3 *Ibid.*, pp. 13, 15.
4 H. Kenner, *The Stoic Comedians* (London: University of California Press, 1962), pp. 69–70.
5 A. Bullock, *The Humanist Tradition in the West* (London: Thames and Hudson, 1985), p. 99.
6 M. Swales, *The German Bildungsroman from Wieland to Hesse* (Princeton: Princeton University Press, 1978), pp. 14–15.
7 J. H. Buckley, *Season of Youth* (Cambridge, Mass.: Harvard University Press, 1974), p. 18.
8 G. Lukács, *The Theory of the Novel* (London: Merlin, 1978), p. 132.
9 S. Howe, *Wilhelm Meister and his English Kinsmen* (New York: Columbia University Press, 1930), p. 6.

10 M. Beddow, *The Fiction of Humanity* (Cambridge: Cambridge University Press, 1982), p. 6.

11 F. Moretti, *The Way of the World* (London: Verso, 1987), p. 5.

12 *Ibid.*

13 Lukács, *The Theory of the Novel*, p. 148.

14 A. Danto, *Narration and Knowledge* (New York: Columbia University Press, 1985), p. 359.

15 E. Said, *Beginnings: Intention and Method* (London: Granta, 1997), p. 374.

16 H. White, 'The Value of Narrativity in the Representation of Reality', in W. J. T. Mitchell (ed.), *On Narrative* (Chicago and London: University of Chicago Press, 1980), p. 1.

17 R. Etlin, *In Defense of Humanism* (Cambridge: Cambridge University Press, 1996), p. 37.

18 S. Freud, in J. Strachey (ed.), *The Complete Psychological Works of Sigmund Freud*, vol. XVI (London: Hogarth Press, 1963), p. 285.

19 R. C. Solomon, *History and Human Nature: A Philosophical Review of European Philosophy and Culture, 1750–1850* (Brighton, Sussex: Harvester Press, 1979), p. 358.

20 M. Heidegger, *Basic Writings* (London: Routledge, 1993), pp. 249, 250.

21 For a succinct discussion of the difference, see T. Eagleton, *The Illusions of Postmodernism* (Oxford: Basil Blackwell, 1996), pp. 128–30.

22 J. P. Sartre, *Being and Nothingness* (London: Routledge, 1969), pp. 51.

23 J. Lacan, *Ecrits* (London: Tavistock, 1977), p. 160.

24 T. Carlyle, 'Signs of the Times', in *A Carlyle Reader* (Cambridge: Cambridge University Press, 1984), pp. 31–54. First published in 1829.

25 See B. Mazlish, *The Fourth Discontinuity* (New Haven and London: Yale University Press, 1993).

26 T. E. Hulme, *Speculations* (London: Routledge & Kegan Paul, 1987), pp. 255, 32.

27 C. Nash, *Narrative in Culture* (London: Routledge, 1990).

28 S. Rimmon-Kenan, *Narrative Fiction: Contemporary Poetics* (London: Routledge, 1983), p. 18.

29 S. Chatman, *Story and Discourse: Narrative Structure in Fiction and Film* (Ithaca: Cornell University Press, 1978), p. 47.

30 R. Scholes and R. Kellogg, *The Nature of Narrative* (New York: Oxford University Press, 1966), p. 238.

31 White, in 'The Value of Narrativity', p. 19.

32 F. Kermode, *The Sense of an Ending* (New York: Oxford University Press, 1967), p. 45. Hereafter '*SE*'.

33 P. Brooks, *Reading for the Plot* (Cambridge, Mass.: Harvard University Press, 1984), p. 3.

34 D. O'Hara, 'Class', in F. Lentricchia and F. McLaughlin (eds.), *Critical Terms for Literary Study* (Chicago and London: University of Chicago Press, 1995), p. 415.

35 Said, *Beginnings*, pp. 140–1.

36 *Ibid.*, p. 315.
37 P. de Man, *Allegories of Reading* (New Haven and London: Yale University Press, 1979), p. 18.
38 H. Bloom, *Poetry and Repression: Revisionism from Blake to Stevens* (New Haven and London: Yale University Press, 1976), p. 21.
39 W. Chafe, 'Some Things That Narratives Tell Us About the Mind', in B. K. Britton and A. D. Pellegrini (eds.), *Narrative Thought and Narrative Language* (Hillsdale, N. J.: Lawrence Erlbaum Associates, 1990), p. 83.
40 D. A. Miller, *Narrative and Its Discontents: Problems of Closure in the Traditional Novel* (Princeton: Princeton University Press, 1981), pp. xiii–xiv.
41 M. Bradbury, *No, Not Bloomsbury* (London: André Deutsch, 1987), p. 89.
42 Chatman, *Story and Discourse*, p. 48.
43 B. Brecht, *Brecht On Theatre* (New York: Hill and Wang, 1964), p. 37.
44 J. L. Austin, *How to Do Things with Words* (London: Oxford University Press, 1962), p. 5.
45 J. Butler, *Gender Trouble* (New York and London: Routledge, 1990), p. 140.
46 *Ibid.*, p. 139.
47 J. H. Miller, *Tropes, Parables, Performatives* (Hemel Hempstead: Harvester Wheatsheaf, 1990), p. ix.
48 M. Heidegger, *Being and Time* (Oxford: Basil Blackwell, 1962), p. 102.
49 *Ibid.*, p. 103.
50 This does not refer to the stylistic analysis of such devices as rhetoric and metaphor, demonstrating how a philosophical text undermines itself with its own figurations. Jacques Derrida and his followers have produced countless readings along these lines. What I *am* suggesting is what it might mean broadly to apply a critical literary eye to a philosophical work. A fine example of the latter is Genevieve Lloyd's *Being In Time: Selves and Narrators in Philosophy and Literature* (London and New York: Routledge, 1993).
51 Said, *Beginnings*, pp. 93–4.
52 For political readings of modernism, see R. Williams, *The Politics of Modernism: Against the New Conformists* (London: Verso, 1996) and P. Bürger, *Theory of the Avant-Garde*, trans. by M. Shaw (Minneapolis: University of Minnesota Press, 1985). For the politics of publishing modernist writing, see L. Rainey, *Institutions of Modernism* (New Haven: Yale University Press, 1999). For social readings of modernism, see J. Carey, *The Intellectuals and the Masses* (London: Faber and Faber, 1992) and P. Brantlinger, *Bread and Circuses: Theories of Mass Culture as Social Decay* (Ithaca: Cornell University Press, 1983). For conceptual histories of modernism, see A. Berman, *Preface to Modernism* (Urbana and Chicago: University of Illinois Press, 1994) and A. Eysteinsson, *The Concept of Modernism* (Ithaca: Cornell University Press, 1992).
53 For narrative and history, see H. White, *Metahistory: The Historical Imagination in Nineteenth-Century Europe* (Baltimore and London: Johns Hopkins University Press, 1973) and *Tropics of Discourse: Essays in Cultural Criticism* (Baltimore and London: Johns Hopkins University Press, 1978); and

H. Kellner, *Language and Historical Representation* (Madison, Wis.: University of Wisconsin Press, 1989). For narrative and ideology, see F. Jameson, *The Political Unconscious: Narrative as a Socially Symbolic Act* (London: Methuen, 1981). For narrative and philosophy, see J. Rée, *Philosophical Tales: An Essay on Philosophy and Literature* (London: Methuen, 1987) and P. Ricoeur, *Time and Narrative*, 3 vols. (Chicago: Chicago University Press, 1984–8) (see discussion below). For narrative and psychoanalysis, see P. Brooks, *Reading for the Plot: Design and Intention in Narrative* (Cambridge, Mass.: Harvard University Press, 1984).

54 I am indebted to David Trotter for making this suggestion. For a masterly survey of the interactions between modernism and the popular novel, see his *The English Novel in History 1895–1920* (London: Routledge, 1993).

55 For examples of the latter, see Huxley's *Point Counter Point* (London: Chatto & Windus, 1974; first published 1928) and *Eyeless in Gaza* (London: Chatto & Windus, 1955; first published 1936); and Wells's *Ann Veronica* (London: Dent, 1943; first published 1909), *The History of Mr Polly* (Harmondsworth: Penguin, 1946; first published 1910) and *The New Machiavelli* (Harmondsworth: Penguin, 1946; first published 1911).

56 Most famously, Michel Foucault's ominous assertion at the end of *The Order of Things* (London: Routledge, 1970) that man's days are numbered: 'If those arrangements were to disappear as they appeared, if some event of which we can at the moment do no more than sense the possibility [were to occur] . . . then one can certainly wager that man would be erased, like a face drawn in sand at the edge of the sea' (p. 387). Perry Anderson considers the apocalyptic announcement of the dissolution of man to be 'the slogan of the decade'. See P. Anderson, *In the Tracks of Historical Materialism* (London: Verso, 1983), p. 37.

57 Theorists have tended to favour the *sui generis*: either eccentric, 'misfit' writers such as Alfred Jarry, Antonin Artaud and Raymond Roussel – theorists *avant la lettre*, in other words – or towering figures such as Mallarmé, Joyce and Proust, who are exceptional in other ways (and regarded as such in more traditional accounts of modernism). Beckett might be seen as a successor to these latter writers, but Conrad, Lawrence and Woolf are neither as 'eccentric' as the first group nor as imposing as the second. Placing them with Beckett is thus a way of rethinking the literary genesis of our contemporary discourse of the inhuman.

58 The natural world is not, of course, 'produced' by human effort in this sense. But the domination and appropriation of natural resources effectively bring them under instrumental command, and confer a sense of 'ownership'. The urge to make the nonhuman seem like a human production is evident in Conrad's *Nostromo*, in the example of the San Tomé mine. See the discussion in Chapter 2.

59 J. Rajchman, 'Foucault, or the Ends of Modernism', in *October* 24 (1983), p. 41.

60 P. Ricoeur, *Time and Narrative*, vol. III (Chicago and London: University of Chicago Press, 1988), p. 241.

61 *Ibid.*

62 For Ricoeur's discussion of the *Bildungsroman*, see *Time and Narrative*, vol. II (Chicago and London: University of Chicago Press, 1985), *passim*.

63 Ricoeur, *Time and Narrative*, vol. III, pp. 270–3.


I


1 H. E. Gruber, *Darwin on Man: A Psychological Study of Scientific Creativity* (London: Wildwood House, 1974), p. 331.

2 F. Nietzsche, *Thus Spoke Zarathustra* (Harmondsworth: Penguin, 1969), p. 61.

3 L. Ferry, *The New Ecological Order* (Chicago and London: University of Chicago Press, 1995), p. 80.

4 See A. Lovejoy, *The Great Chain of Being* (Cambridge, Mass.: Harvard University Press, 1936).

5 Aristotle, *Politica*, in *The Works of Aristotle*, vol. X (Oxford: Clarendon Press, 1921), p. 1254a–b.

6 *Ibid.*, p. 1256b.

7 C. Singer, *A Short History of Anatomy from the Greeks to Harvey* (New York: Dover, 1957), p. 24.

8 K. Thomas, *Man and the Natural World* (London: Allen Lane, 1983), p. 124.

9 S. Baker, *The Postmodern Animal* (London: Reaktion, 2000), p. 94.

10 I should point out that Baker is basing his argument on the visual rather than the literary arts, and he declares: 'there was no modern animal, no "modernist" animal [ . . . ] The animal is the very first thing to be ruled out of modernism's bounds' (Baker, *ibid.*, p. 20). A very different case obtains in modernist literature. Lawrence and Beckett depict animals in 'nonhierarchical terms', and Woolf has a whole menagerie of zoomorphic creatures – human beings reimagined as dogs, horses, sealions and a myriad of different birds. See Chapter 4.

11 T. Mann, *Essays of Three Decades* (London: Secker & Warburg, 1947), p. 154.

12 H. White, 'The Value of Narrativity in the Representation of Reality', in W. J. T. Mitchell (ed.) *On Narrative* (Chicago and London: University of Chicago Press, 1980), p. 6.

13 S. Schama, *Landscape and Memory* (London: HarperCollins, 1995), p. 61.

14 K. Marx, *Early Writings* (Harmondsworth: Penguin, 1975) p. 328. Hereafter '*EPM*'.

15 J. O'Neill, 'Humanism and Nature', in *Radical Philosophy* 66 (1994), p. 24.

16 O. Wilde, *Selected Works* (London: William Heinemann, 1946), p. 47. Hereafter '*DL*'.

17 O. Wilde, *De Profundis and Other Writings* (Harmondsworth: Penguin, 1986), p. 22.

18 K. Soper, *What is Nature?* (Oxford: Basil Blackwell, 1995), p. 46.

19 L. Danson, *Wilde's Intentions* (Oxford: Clarendon Press, 1997), p. 42.

20 O'Neill, 'Humanism and Nature', p. 27.

21 C. Taylor, *Sources of the Self* (Cambridge: Cambridge University Press, 1989), p. 347.

22 R. Tallis, *The Explicit Animal* (Basingstoke: Macmillan, 1991), p. 162.

23 C. Darwin, *The Descent of Man* (London: John Murray, 1901), p. 231. Hereafter '*DM*'.

24 See P. Singer, *Animal Liberation* (London: Pimlico, 1995), Chapter 2.

25 I. Kant, *Lectures on Ethics* (Indianapolis, Ind.: Hackett, 1979), pp. 240, 241.

26 H. G. Wells's *The Island of Dr Moreau* (Harmondsworth: Penguin, 1967; first published 1896) – 'one of the great modern myths in the tradition of Faust and Frankenstein', writes Roslyn Haynes – is a fictional extrapolation of Darwinist principles, appearing at the dawn of modernism. Exiled on his island, Moreau the scientist undertakes experiments that effectively deconstruct the human being/animal being aporia. On the one hand, he uncovers the innate 'bestiality' of man, his incomplete transcendence of animality; and on the other, he raises up beasts to be 'remade' in human form. Moreau's invocation of the laws of evolution – which proceed via randomness, accident and contingency – overrides the moral law, dissolving the aporetic bind otherwise associated with vivisection. See R. D. Haynes, *From Faust to Strangelove: Representations of the Scientist in Western Literature* (Baltimore and London: Johns Hopkins University Press, 1994), p. 154.

27 T. Radford, 'It's Life But Not As We Know It', in *London Review of Books* 13 (1997), p. 16.

28 M. Midgley, *Beast and Man* (London: Routledge, 1995), p. 29.

29 F. Nietzsche, *Beyond Good and Evil* (Harmondsworth: Penguin, 1973), p. 162.

30 Yet Darwin's caution helped, too: he excluded man almost entirely from *The Origin of Species*, then devoted a separate work to him twelve years later, in *The Descent of Man* (1871).

31 Not, however, in its entirety. For although Darwin declared, in a letter to Charles Lyell, 'I never saw a more striking coincidence. if Wallace had my M. S. sketch written out in 1842 he could not have made a better short abstract!', he added: 'Though my Book, if it will ever have any value, will not be deteriorated; as all the labour consists in the application of the theory.' See C. Darwin, *Charles Darwin's Letters: A Selection 1825–1859* (Cambridge: Cambridge University Press, 1996), p. 188.

32 A. Desmond and J. Moore, *Darwin* (Harmondsworth: Penguin, 1991), pp. 467–70.

33 Desmond and Moore, *ibid.*, pp. 477, 488.

34 F. Nietzsche, *Unfashionable Observations* (Stanford, Calif.: Stanford University Press, 1995), p. 174.

35 Gruber, *Darwin on Man*, p. 281.

36 G. Beer, *Darwin's Plots* (London: Ark, 1985), pp. 7, 8.

37 Midgley, *Beast and Man*, pp. 145, 149.

38 E. Mayr, *One Long Argument* (Harmondsworth: Allen Lane, 1992), p. 44.

39 *Ibid.*, pp. 93–4.

40 Beer, *Darwin's Plots*, p. 25.

41 Gruber, *Darwin on Man*, pp. 196, 197.

42 Tallis, *The Explicit Animal*, p. 207.

43 Midgley, *Beast and Man*, p. 217.

44 *Ibid.*, p. 254.

45 See, for example, T. H. Huxley, *Man's Place in Nature* (New York and London: D. Appleton and Company, 1929), pp. 150–1, 155–6.

46 Alternative juxtapositions of narrative and transcendence are explored at length in Chapter 3.

47 J. Rée, *Philosophical Tales* (London: Methuen, 1987), p. 10. This narrative, outlined in the *Discourse On Method*, is supplemented by a mythographical internarrative that documents Descartes's inner turmoil, first given biographical moment in Adrien Baillet's effort of 1680. See A. Baillet, *La Vie de Monsieur Descartes* (Paris: Daniel Horthemels, 1691). This will be addressed in Chapter 5, in relation to Beckett.

48 G. Deleuze, *Nietzsche and Philosophy* (New York: Columbia University Press, 1983), p. 8.

49 S. K. Padover (ed.), *The Letters of Karl Marx* (New Jersey: Prentice-Hall 1979), pp. 156–158. See also Beer, *Darwin's Plots*, p. 58.

50 J. Wallace, 'Introduction: Difficulty and Defamiliarisation – Language and Process in *The Origin of Species*', in D. Amigoni and J. Wallace (eds.), *Charles Darwin's* The Origin of Species: *New Interdisciplinary Essays* (Manchester and New York: Manchester University Press, 1995), p. 9.

51 *Ibid.*, p. 21. Adapting Thomas Kuhn, Wallace asserts: 'the *Origin* is neither a realist novel nor a romantic poem, though it does have affinities with each, and a fascinating organisational logic'. See T. Kuhn, *The Structure of Scientific Revolutions* (Chicago: University of Chicago Press, 1970), p. 172.

52 N. Gillespie, *Charles Darwin and the Problem of Creation* (Chicago and London: University of Chicago Press, 1979), p. 3.

53 F. Nietzsche, *The Gay Science* (New York: Random House, 1974), p. 305. Hereafter '*GS*'.

54 G. W. F. Hegel, *The Phenomenology of Spirit* (Oxford: Oxford University Press, 1977), p. 50.

55 T. Pinkard, *Hegel's* Phenomenology (Cambridge: Cambridge University Press, 1994), p. 17.

56 M. H. Abrams, *Natural Supernaturalism* (New York: Norton, 1971), p. 228.

57 Rée, *Philosophical Tales*, pp. 63–4.

58 H. Sussman, 'The Metaphor in Hegel's *Phenomenology of Mind*', in J. O'Neill (ed.) *Hegel's Dialectic of Desire and Recognition* (Albany, N.Y.: State University of New York Press, 1996), p. 306.

59 Rée, *Philosophical Tales*, pp. 92, 93.

60 Abrams, *Natural Supernaturalism*, pp. 228, 229.

61 Abrams describes this as 'the most consequential pun since Christ said, "Thou art Peter, and upon this rock I will build my church." ' See Abrams, *ibid.*, p. 230.

62 R. Gooding-Williams, 'The Drama of Nietzsche's Zarathustra', in *International Studies in Philosophy* 20/2 (1988), p. III.

63 K. A. Pearson, *Viroid Life: Perspectives On Nietzsche and the Transhuman Condition* (London: Routledge, 1997), p. 86.

64 F. Nietzsche, *The Will to Power* (New York: Random House, 1967), p. 363.

65 F. Nietzsche, *On the Genealogy of Morality* (Cambridge: Cambridge University Press, 1994), p. 61. Hereafter '*GM*'.

66 Nietzsche, *Unfashionable Observations*, pp. 209–10.

67 *Ibid.*

68 Nietzsche, *Beyond Good and Evil*, p. 14.

69 For discussions of Nietzsche as narrative philosopher, albeit one concerned with local narratives rather than metanarratives, see G. Shapiro, *Nietzschean Narratives* (Bloomington, Indianapolis: Indiana University Press, 1989) and J. C. Pettey, *Nietzsche's Philosophical and Narrative Styles* (New York: Peter Lang, 1992).

70 See A. Nehamas, *Nietzsche: Life as Literature* (Cambridge, Mass.: Harvard University Press, 1985), p. 171.

71 M. Heidegger, *Basic Writings* (London: Routledge, 1978), p. 302.

72 F. Nietzsche, *Thus Spoke Zarathustra*, p. 138.

73 J. P. Stern notes: ' "Life", accordingly, appears as an amorphous, inchoate thing which must have a direction and purpose imposed on it.' See J. P. Stern, *Nietzsche* (London: Fontana, 1978), p. 80.

74 See R. Ellmann, *Yeats: The Man and the Masks* (London: Macmillan, 1949), p. 74.

75 F. Nietzsche, *Basic Writings of Nietzsche* (New York: Modern Library, 1968), p. 550.

76 Nehamas, *Nietzsche*, p. 79.

77 Pearson, *Viroid Life*, pp. 99–100.

78 Nietzsche, *Gay Science*, pp. 240, 232. Nehamas observes: 'Nietzsche always depended on literary and artistic models for understanding the world.' Indeed, 'like an artwork, the world requires reading and interpretation', it is a text to be deciphered. See Nehamas, *Nietzsche*, pp. 194, 91.

79 See A. Megill, 'Nietzsche as Aestheticist', in *Philosophy and Literature* 5/2 (1981), p. 217.

80 R. Descartes, *Discourse on Method and the Meditations* (Harmondsworth: Penguin, 1968), p. 65.

81 H. E. Rollins (ed.), *The Letters of John Keats*, vol. II (Cambridge, Mass.: Harvard University Press, 1958), p. 102.

82 M. Foucault, *Discipline and Punish: The Birth of the Prison* (Harmondsworth: Penguin, 1991), p. 295.

83 S. R. L. Clark, 'The Moral Animals', in *The Times Literary Supplement* 4875 (1996), p. 26.

84 J. Passmore, *Man's Responsibility for Nature* (London: Duckworth, 1980), p. 84.

85 Beer, *Darwin's Plots*, p. 53.

86 See E. Benton, 'Science: Ideology and Culture: Malthus and *The Origin of Species*', in Amigoni and Wallace, *Charles Darwin's* The Origin of Species, p. 73.

87 Interview with Foucault in H. Dreyfus and P. Rabinow, *Michel Foucault: Beyond Structuralism and Hermeneutics* (Brighton: Harvester, 1982), p. 187.

88 L. Hutcheon, *A Poetics of Postmodernism: History, Theory, Fiction* (London and New York: Routledge, 1988), p. 51.

89 T. Eagleton, *The Illusions of Postmodernism* (Oxford: Basil Blackwell, 1996), p. 73.

2

1 F. Karl and L. Davies (eds.), *The Collected Letters of Joseph Conrad*, vol. II (Cambridge: Cambridge University Press, 1986), pp. 94–5.

2 L. Trilling, *Sincerity and Authenticity* (Cambridge, Mass.: Harvard University Press, 1972), p. 124.

3 K. Tester, *The Inhuman Condition* (London: Routledge, 1995), p. vii.

4 *Ibid.*, p. xi.

5 K. Marx, *Early Writings* (Harmondsworth: Penguin, 1975), p. 327. Hereafter '*EPM*'.

6 Trilling, *Sincerity and Authenticity*, p. 124.

7 H. Arendt, *The Human Condition* (Chicago: Chicago University Press, 1958), pp. 121–2.

8 Tester, *The Inhuman Condition*, p. 14.

9 L. Marx and M. R. Smith, 'Introduction', in L. Marx and M. R. Smith (eds.), *Does Technology Drive History?* (Cambridge, Mass.: MIT Press, 1994), p. ix.

10 Arendt, *The Human Condition*, p. 11.

11 B. Williams, 'Making Sense of Humanity', in J. Sheehan and M. Sosna (eds.), *The Boundaries of Humanity* (Berkeley and Los Angeles: University of California Press, 1991), pp. 13, 15.

12 L. Mumford, *Technics and Civilization* (London: Routledge, 1946), p. 10.

13 M. Midgley, *Beast and Man* (London: Routledge, 1995), p. 235, n. 51.

14 R. Hahn, 'The Meaning of the Mechanistic Age', in Sheehan and Sosna (eds.), *The Boundaries of Humanity*, p. 154.

15 E. J. Dijksterhuis, *The Mechanization of the World Picture* (Oxford: Clarendon Press, 1961), p. 1.

16 See L. Winner, *Autonomous Technology: Technics-out-of-control as a Theme in Political Thought* (Cambridge, Mass.: MIT Press, 1977), p. 192.

17 Tester, *The Inhuman Condition*, p. 14.

18 *Ibid.*, p. 15.

19 Marx and Smith, 'Introduction', p. xii.

20 This refers to the second edition. See C. Darwin, *The Descent of Man* (London: John Murray, 1881), p. 586.

21 See B. Magee, *The Philosophy of Schopenhauer* (Oxford: Clarendon Press, 1997), p. 288.

22 A. Schopenhauer, *The World as Will and Representation*, vol. I (New York: Dover, 1966), p. 23. Hereafter '*W1*'.

23 A. Schopenhauer, *The World as Will and Representation*, vol. II (New York: Dover, 1966), p. 204. Hereafter '*W2*'.

24 C. Janaway, 'Schopenhauer', in K. Thomas (ed.), *German Philosophers* (Oxford: Oxford University Press, 1997), p. 262.

25 A. Schopenhauer, *On the Basis of Morality* (Indianapolis and New York: Bobbs-Merrill, 1965), p. 192.

26 Magee, *The Philosophy of Schopenhauer*, p. 199.

27 F. Nietzsche, *Human, All Too Human* (Harmondsworth: Penguin, 1994), pp. 17–18.

28 F. Nietzsche, *Ecce Homo* (Harmondsworth: Penguin, 1979), p. 132. Nietzsche refers to Schopenhauer's animadversions on pity as the source of all morality as 'nonsense'. See *The Gay Science*, p. 153.

29 T. Mann, *Essays of Three Decades* (London: Secker & Warburg, 1947), pp. 395, 394.

30 Janaway, 'Schopenhauer', p. 227.

31 J. Snow, 'Schopenhauer's Style', in *International Philosophical Quarterly* 33/4 (1993), p. 408.

32 M. A. Wollaeger, *Joseph Conrad and the Fictions of Skepticism* (Stanford, Calif.: Stanford University Press, 1990), pp. 34–5.

33 A. Schopenhauer, *Parerga and Paralipomena*, vol. II (Oxford: Clarendon Press, 1974), p. 440.

34 Magee, *The Philosophy of Schopenhauer*, p. 12.

35 A. Lovejoy, 'Schopenhauer as an Evolutionist', in B. Glass, O. Temkin and W. L. Straus, Jnr (eds.), *Forerunners of Darwin: 1745–1859* (Baltimore: Johns Hopkins University Press, 1959) p. 415.

36 W. Paley, *Natural Theology* (London: R. Faulder, 1802), p. 449.

37 The ramifications of this are explored at length in Chapter 4.

38 I. Kant, *Critique of Judgment* (Indianapolis, Ind.: Hackett, 1987), pp. 99–100.

39 E. Said, *The World, the Text and the Critic* (London: Vintage, 1983), p. 92.

40 Wollaeger, *Joseph Conrad*, p. xvii.

41 See E. Said, *Culture and Imperialism* (New York: Vintage, 1994), p. 273.

42 A. White, *Joseph Conrad and the Adventure Tradition* (Cambridge: Cambridge University Press, 1993), p. 5.

43 A. Hunter, *Joseph Conrad and the Ethics of Darwinism* (London and Canberra: Croom Helm, 1983), p. 1.

44 J. Galsworthy, *Two Essays on Conrad* (Cincinnati: Freelands, 1930), p. 52.

45 Y. Hervouet, *The French Face of Joseph Conrad* (Cambridge: Cambridge University Press, 1990), pp. 263–4, n. 17.

46 Wollaeger, *Joseph Conrad*, p. 31.

47 Z. Najder, *Joseph Conrad: A Chronicle* (Cambridge: Cambridge University Press, 1983), p. 220.

48 F. Karl and L. Davies (eds.), *The Collected Letters of Joseph Conrad*, vol. I (Cambridge, Cambridge University Press, 1983), p. 425.

49 J. Norbury, 'A Note on Knitting and Knitted Fabrics', in C. Singer, E. J. Holmyard, A. R. Hall and T. Williams (eds.), *A History of Technology*, vol. III (Oxford: Clarendon Press, 1957), p. 185.

50 *Ibid.*

51 Hunter, *Joseph Conrad*, p. 12.

52 G. Levine, *Darwin and the Novelists* (Cambridge, Mass.: Harvard University Press, 1988), pp. 308–9, n. 24.

53 E. Said, *Joseph Conrad and the Fiction of Autobiography* (Cambridge, Mass.: Harvard University Press, 1966), p. 33.

54 M. Seltzer, *Bodies and Machines* (New York and London: Routledge, 1992), pp. 103–4.

55 *Ibid.*, p. 95.

56 *Ibid.*, p. 96.

57 F. Karl, *Joseph Conrad: The Three Lives* (London: Faber and Faber, 1979), p. 368.

58 J. Conrad, *Lord Jim* (Harmondsworth: Penguin, 1986), p. 204. Hereafter '*LJ*'.

59 See I. Sadoff, 'Sartre and Conrad: Lord Jim as Existential Hero', in *Dalhousie Review* 49/4 (1969–70), p. 523. André Gide, who first formulated the *acte gratuit*, considered *Lord Jim* one of the supreme literary achievements. See J. Batchelor, *The Life of Joseph Conrad: A Critical Biography* (Oxford: Basil Blackwell, 1994), p. 194.

60 J. H. Stape, 'Lord Jim', in J. H. Stape (ed.), *The Cambridge Companion to Joseph Conrad* (Cambridge: Cambridge University Press, 1996), p. 67.

61 *Ibid.*, p. 63.

62 L. Orr, 'The Semiotics of Description in Conrad's *Nostromo*', in T. Billy (ed.), *Critical Essays on Joseph Conrad* (Boston, Mass.: G. K. Hall & Co., 1987). p. 115.

63 T. E. Jackson, 'Turning into Modernism: *Lord Jim* and the Alteration of the Narrative Subject', in *Literature and Psychology* 32/4, 1993, p. 78.

64 See S. Raval, 'Narrative and Authority: Conrad's Art of Failure', in H. Bloom (ed.), *Joseph Conrad's* Lord Jim (New York, New Haven and Philadelphia: Chelsea House, 1987), p. 90.

65 See J. H. Buckley, *Season of Youth* (Cambridge, Mass.: Harvard University Press, 1974), p. 18.

66 Mumford, *Technics and Civilization*, p. 158.

67 J. Conrad, *Nostromo* (Harmondsworth: Penguin, 1990), p. 95. Hereafter '*N*'.

68 I. Howe, *Politics and the Novel* (London: Stevens & Sons, 1961), p. 108.

69 *Ibid.*, p. 106.

70 F. Jameson, *The Political Unconscious* (London: Methuen, 1981), p. 227.

71 See A. Fogel, 'Silver and Silence: Dependent Currencies in *Nostromo*', in H. Bloom (ed.), *Joseph Conrad* (New York and Philadelphia: Chelsea House, 1986), p. 221.

72 Hunter, *Joseph Conrad*, p. 203.
73 J. Baines, *Joseph Conrad: A Critical Biography* (Harmondsworth: Penguin, 1960), p. 362.
74 *Ibid.*, p. 373.
75 Howe, *Politics and the Novel*, p. 55.
76 A. Davidson, *Conrad's Endings* (Ann Arbor, Mich.: UMI Research Press, 1984), pp. 52–3.
77 Said, *Beginnings: Intention and Method* (London: Granta, 1997), p. 118.
78 *Ibid.*, p. 133.
79 S. Butler, *Erewhon* (Harmondsworth: Penguin, 1985), p. 221.
80 Levine, *Darwin and the Novelists*, p. 267.
81 W. Heisenberg, *Physics and Philosophy* (Harmondsworth: Penguin, 1989), p. 15.
82 Butler, *Erewhon*, p. 223.
83 P. Virilio, *Open Sky* (London and New York: Verso, 1997), p. 11.
84 Arendt, *The Human Condition*, p. 313.
85 Karl and Davies (eds.), *Collected Letters*, vol. II, pp. 16–17.
86 *Ibid.*, p. 30.

3

1 D. H. Lawrence, *Study of Thomas Hardy and other Essays* (Cambridge: Cambridge University Press, 1985), p. 43.
2 L. Ferry and A. Renaut, *Heidegger and Modernity* (Chicago and London: University of Chicago Press, 1990), p. 17.
3 This pertains even though, as elaborated in Chapter 2, the proliferation of machine technology in the anthropometric era also had the opposite effect – hence 'man is no longer man', etc. This antinomical aspect of transcendence is crucial for the antihumanists discussed in this chapter, as will be made apparent.
4 Perhaps the archetype for this is the figure of the Byronic Hero, as exemplified in Byron's *Manfred*.
5 See T. Carlyle, *On Heroes, Hero-Worship and the Heroic in History* (London: Chapman and Hall, 1907).
6 F. Nietzsche, *The Gay Science* (New York: Random House, 1974), p. 305.
7 G. Steiner, *Heidegger* (London: Fontana, 1992), p. 149. See also M. Bell, *D. H. Lawrence: Language and Being* (Cambridge: Cambridge University Press, 1992).
8 F. Becket, *D. H. Lawrence: The Thinker as Poet* (Basingstoke: Macmillan, 1997), pp. 191, 195.
9 A. Fernihough, *D. H. Lawrence: Aesthetics and Ideology* (Oxford: Clarendon Press, 1993), p. 10. See also M. M. Brunsdale, *Utah Studies in Literature and Linguistics* (Berne: Peter Lang, 1978).
10 *Ibid.*, p. 40.
11 *Ibid.*, p. 25.

12 P. Bourdieu, *The Political Ontology of Martin Heidegger* (Cambridge: Polity Press, 1991), p. 27.

13 C. B. Guignon, 'Introduction' in C. B. Guignon (ed.), *The Cambridge Companion to Heidegger* (Cambridge: Cambridge University Press, 1993) p. 41. Guignon adds: 'that Heidegger saw himself in protest against mainstream Christendom is evident in such remarks as his 1928 reference to "the enormously phony religiosity of the times".' (*Ibid.*)

14 J. van Buren, 'Martin Heidegger, Martin Luther', in T. Kisiel and J. van Buren (eds.), *Reading Heidegger from the Start* (Albany, N.Y.: State University of New York, 1994), p. 160.

15 Quoted in van Buren, *ibid.*, p. 160.

16 J. van Buren, *The Young Heidegger* (Bloomington and Indianapolis: Indiana University Press, 1994), p. 147.

17 Van Buren, 'Martin Heidegger', pp. 171–2.

18 Steiner, Heidegger, p. xvi.

19 See H. T. Moore, *The Priest of Love: A Life of D. H. Lawrence* (London: Heinemann, 1974).

20 I. Watt, *The Rise of the Novel: Studies in Defoe, Richardson and Fielding*, (Harmondsworth: Penguin, 1983), p. 85

21 See, for example, A. Burns, *Nature and Culture in D. H. Lawrence* (Basingstoke: Macmillan, 1980), *passim*; D. Schneider, *D. H. Lawrence: The Artist as Psychologist* (Kansas: University Press of Kansas, 1984), pp. 45–56; C. Milton, *Lawrence and Nietzsche* (Aberdeen: Aberdeen University Press, 1987); and more recently, R. E. Montgomery, *The Visionary D. H. Lawrence* (Cambridge: Cambridge University Press, 1994), Chapter 3.

22 D. H. Lawrence, *The White Peacock* (Oxford: Oxford University Press, 1997), p. 90.

23 E. Delavenay, *D. H. Lawrence: The Man and his Work* (London: Heinemann, 1972), p. 47.

24 Montgomery, *The Visionary D. H. Lawrence*, p. 45.

25 Lawrence, *Study of Thomas Hardy*, pp. 28–9.

26 M. Heidegger, *Being and Time* (Oxford: Basil Blackwell, 1962), p. 244. Hereafter '*BT*'.

27 S. Mulhall, *Heidegger and* Being and Time (London: Routledge, 1996), p. 111.

28 T. Davies, *Humanism* (London: Routledge, 1997), p. 131.

29 M. Heidegger, *Basic Writings* (London: Routledge, 1993), p. 304.

30 M. Heidegger, *Nietzsche*, vol. IV (San Francisco: Harper & Row, 1982), p. 28.

31 M. Haar, *Heidegger and the Essence of Man* (Albany, N.Y.: State University of New York Press, 1993) pp. 59.

32 See *ibid.*, p. 113.

33 F. Dastur, *Death: An Essay on Finitude* (London and Atlantic Highlands, N.J.: Athlone Press, 1996), p. 43.

34 Heidegger, *Basic Writings*, p. 431.

35 Even though, as has been well documented, the stated subjects have been addressed in various other Heidegger texts. See Mulhall, *Heidegger*, p. 28.

36 J. Hodge, *Heidegger and Ethics* (London: Routledge, 1995), p. 168.

37 See *Being and Time*, p. 32.

38 Ferry and Renaut have argued, however, that there is an undecidability in Dasein's fallenness, an aporetic divide between 'structural' fall and 'historical' fall. See *Heidegger and Modernity*, pp. 33–9.

39 J. Young, *Heidegger, Philosophy, Nazism* (Cambridge: Cambridge University Press, 1997), p. 66.

40 See T. Eagleton, *The Ideology of the Aesthetic* (Oxford: Basil Blackwell, 1990), p. 304.

41 Mulhall, *Heidegger*, p. 69.

42 Haar, *Heidegger*, p. 184.

43 *Ibid.*, pp. 63–4.

44 Heidegger, *Basic Writings*, p. 201.

45 See W. Lewis, *Time and Western Man* (Santa Rosa: Black Sparrow, 1993) pp. 15–16; T. S. Eliot, 'The Metaphysical Poets', in *Selected Essays* (London: Faber and Faber, 1950), pp. 281–91; and T. E. Hulme, *Speculations* (London: Routledge & Kegan Paul, 1987), p. 116 and *passim*.

46 Patrick McHugh alludes to a 'metaphysical shortfall' in *Women in Love*. See 'Metaphysics and Sexual Politics in Lawrence's Novels', in *College Literature* 20/3 (1993), p. 83.

47 F. R. Leavis, *D. H. Lawrence: Novelist* (London: Chatto & Windus, 1962), pp. 17, 303,18.

48 *Ibid.*, p. 15.

49 G. Lloyd, *The Man of Reason* (London: Routledge, 1984), p. 101.

50 K. Soper, *What is Nature?* (Oxford: Basil Blackwell, 1995), p. 71.

51 L. Nead, *The Female Nude* (London: Routledge, 1992), p. 23.

52 Soper, *What is Nature?*, p. 100.

53 *Ibid.*, p. 126.

54 Fiona Becket writes: 'Lawrence's task in the books on the unconscious was in part to establish his own meanings, so that the word "unconscious" would make sense on his own terms.' Becket, *D. H. Lawrence*, p. 5.

55 D. H. Lawrence, *Sons and Lovers* (Harmondsworth: Penguin, 1994), p. 24. Hereafter '*SL*'.

56 M. Steig, *Stories of Reading* (Baltimore: Johns Hopkins University Press, 1989), p. 198.

57 P. J. Whiteley, *Knowledge and Experimental Realism in Conrad, Lawrence, and Woolf* (Baton Rouge: Louisiana State University Press, 1987), p. 109.

58 Buckley, *Season of Youth*, p. 206.

59 Lawrence, *Study of Thomas Hardy*, p. 28.

60 D. H. Lawrence, *Phoenix II* (Harmondsworth: Penguin, 1978), p. 377.

61 Earl G. Ingersoll reads this passage in terms of a metaphorical overabundance, confirming his Lacanian reading of Paul's development. See *Midwest Quarterly* 37/4 (1996), pp. 434–47.

62 Lawrence, *Phoenix II*, p. 368.

63 Nicole Ward Jouve details Lawrence's relationship to the womb as a riposte to his overwrought 'phallic consciousness'. See 'D. H. Lawrence: Womb Envy or A Womb of his Own?', in N. W. Jouve, *Female Genesis: Creativity, Self and Gender* (New York: St Martin's Press, 1998), pp. 103–18.

64 Lawrence, *Phoenix II*, p. 227.

65 *Ibid.*, p. 622.

66 See K. E. Ferguson, *The Man Question* (Berkeley and Los Angeles: University of California Press, 1993), p. 38.

67 See S. Freud, *The Standard Edition of the Complete Psychological Works of Sigmund Freud*, vol. XX (London: Hogarth Press, 1959), pp. 59–60; and vol. XXII (London: Hogarth Press, 1964), p. 107.

68 D. H. Lawrence, *Psychoanalysis and the Unconscious* and *Fantasia of the Unconscious* (New York: Viking, 1960), p. 14.

69 *Ibid.*, p. 15.

70 See C. Lewiecki-Wilson, *Writing Against the Family: Gender in Lawrence and Joyce* (Carbondale and Edwardsville: Southern Illinois University Press, 1994), p. 17.

71 L. Fraiberg, 'The Unattainable Self', in E. W. Tedlock, Jnr, *D. H. Lawrence and Sons and Lovers: Sources and Criticism* (New York: New York University Press, 1965), p. 235.

72 D. H. Lawrence, *Phoenix* (New York, Viking, 1968), p. 715; *Phoenix II*, pp. 420–1.

73 P. Middleton, *The Inward Gaze* (London: Routledge, 1992), p. 77.

74 E. Abel, M. Hirsch and E. Langland, 'Introduction', in *The Voyage In: Fictions of Female Development* (Hanover and London: University Press of New England, 1983), p. 5.

75 K. Millett, *Sexual Politics* (New York: Doubleday, 1970), pp. 257–8.

76 A comparable literary example might be Joyce's 'Oxen of the Sun' chapter in *Ulysses*, where the timescale is further skewed in both directions – the sprawling development of the English literary canon made to resemble a woman's labour – to produce a comic discrepancy.

77 T. Pinkney, *D. H. Lawrence* (London: Harvester Wheatsheaf, 1990), p. 94.

78 D. H. Lawrence, *The Rainbow* (Harmondsworth: Penguin, 1989), p. 397. Hereafter '*R*'.

79 C. M. Kaplan, 'Totem, Taboo, and *Blutbrüderschaft* in D. H. Lawrence's *Women in Love*', in C. M. Kaplan and A. B. Simpson (eds.), *Seeing Double* (Basingstoke: Macmillan, 1996), p. 14.

80 F. Kermode, *Lawrence* (London: Fontana, 1973), pp. 63–4.

81 J. C. Oates, 'Lawrence's *Götterdämmerung*: The Tragic Vision of *Women in Love*', in *Critical Inquiry* 4 (1978), p. 561.

82 D. H. Lawrence, *Women in Love* (Harmondsworth: Penguin, 1995) p. 253. Hereafter '*WL*'.

83 Terry Eagleton writes: 'If [Birkin's] position is not to be taken as wholly Lawrentian, it is not on account of other viewpoints in the novel which

might challenge it: no such alternatives are available.' See T. Eagleton, *Exiles and Emigrés: Studies in Modern Literature* (London: Chatto & Windus, 1970), p. 208.

84 Lawrence, *Phoenix*, p. 541.

85 *Ibid.*, p. 540.

86 Kermode, *Lawrence*, pp. 63–5.

87 J. Worthen, *D. H. Lawrence and the Idea of the Novel* (Basingstoke: Macmillan, 1979), pp. 95–6.

88 See R. Kiely, *Beyond Egotism* (Cambridge, Mass.: Harvard University Press, 1980), pp. 158–9.

89 Burns, *Nature and Culture*, p. 87.

90 *Ibid.*

91 G. J. Zytaruk and J. T. Boulton (eds.), *The Letters of D. H. Lawrence*, vol. II (Cambridge: Cambridge University Press, 1981), pp. 182–3.

92 Ursula's imagining is hinted at in an earlier episode: 'She knew [humanity] could not disappear so cleanly and conveniently. It had a long way to go yet, a long and hideous way.' See Lawrence, *Women in Love*, p. 128.

93 G. J. Zytaruk and J. T. Boulton (eds.), *The Letters of D. H. Lawrence*, vol. I (Cambridge: Cambridge University Press, 1979), p. 256.

94 Barbara Schapiro explicates 'fusion' in terms of preoedipal object relations, basing her argument on the theories of Nancy Chodorow and Dorothy Dinnerstein. See *Soundings* 69/3 (1986), p. 356.

95 Lawrence, *Phoenix*, p. 541.

96 See H. M. Daleski, *The Forked Flame* (London: Faber and Faber, 1965) pp. 164–5.

97 For a 'thermodynamic' reading of *Women in Love*, which considers energy exchanges in terms of a gender binary – women as 'energy receptors', men as 'energy reservoirs' – see M. Wutz, 'The Thermodynamics of Gender: Lawrence, Science and Sexism', in *Mosaic* 28/2 (1995), pp. 83–108.

98 C. Nixon, *Lawrence's Leadership Politics and the Turn Against Women* (Berkeley and Los Angeles: University of California Press, 1986), p. 170.

99 On this point Marion Shaw suggests that Lawrence's 'retreat into male supremacism' was precipitated by suspicion and disappointment. See 'Lawrence and Feminism', in *Critical Quarterly* 25/3 (1983), p. 24. Margaret Storch uses Kleinian theory to uncover, in *Women in Love*, 'a shift in the acceptance of female dominance'. See M. Storch, *Sons and Adversaries: Women in William Blake and D. H. Lawrence* (Knoxville: University of Tennessee Press, 1990), p. 117.

100 A. Gramsci, *The Modern Prince and Other Writings* (New York: International Publishers, 1957), p. 79.

101 D. Allbright, *Personality and Impersonality* (Chicago and London: University of Chicago Press, 1978), p. 22.

102 Lawrence, *Study of Thomas Hardy*, p. 26.

4

1 V. Woolf, *Collected Essays*, vol. III (London: Hogarth Press, 1967), p. 224.

2 S. Freud, *The Standard Edition of the Complete Psychological Works of Sigmund Freud*, trans. J. Strachey, vol. XVI (London: Hogarth Press, 1963), p. 285.

3 I. Kant, *Critique of Pure Reason* (New York: Willey Book Co., 1943), pp. 30, 33.

4 I. Watt, *The Rise of the Novel: Studies in Defoe, Richardson and Fielding* (Harmondsworth: Penguin, 1983), p. 13.

5 H. Bergson, *Time and Free Will* (London: Allen & Unwin, 1971), p. 220.

6 I. Kant, *Critique of Practical Reason*, trans. T. K. Abbott (Amherst, N.Y.: Prometheus, 1966), p. 156.

7 Bergson, *Time and Free Will*, p. 98.

8 An exception is Gilles Deleuze's *Bergsonism*, trans. H. Tomlinson and B. Habberjam (New York: Zone Books, 1991). More recently, Keith Ansell Pearson has focused intently on both figures. See K. A. Pearson, *Germinal Life* (London: Routledge, 1999).

9 See P. Douglass, *Bergson, Eliot and American Literature* (Lexington, Ky.: University Press of Kentucky, 1986).

10 See M. A. Gillies, *Henri Bergson and British Modernism* (Montreal and Kingston: McGill-Queen's University Press, 1996).

11 W. Lewis, *Time and Western Man* (Santa Rosa: Black Sparrow, 1993), p. 132.

12 *Ibid.*, p. 162.

13 *Ibid.*, p. 200.

14 W. Lewis, *Men Without Art* (New York: Russell & Russell, 1964), pp. 168, 169.

15 V. Woolf, *Collected Essays*, vol. II (London: Hogarth Press, 1966), p. 106.

16 *Ibid.*, pp. 105, 106.

17 V. Woolf, *Mrs Dalloway* (Harmondsworth: Penguin, 1992), p. 31. Hereafter '*MD*'.

18 V. Woolf, *To the Lighthouse* (Harmondsworth: Penguin, 1992), p. 87. Hereafter '*TL*'.

19 Kermode, *Sense of an Ending*, p. 45.

20 Watt, *The Rise of the Novel*, p. 35.

21 V. Woolf, *A Writer's Diary* (London: Hogarth Press, 1953), p. 139.

22 E. M. Forster, *Howard's End* (Harmondsworth: Penguin, 1961), p. 174.

23 *Ibid.*, pp. 174–5.

24 Lewis, *Men Without Art*, p. 158.

25 L. Marcus, *Virginia Woolf* (London: Northcote House, 1997), p. 66.

26 Woolf, *Essays*, vol. II, p. 107.

27 J. H. Miller, *Fiction and Repetition* (Oxford: Basil Blackwell, 1982), p. 181.

28 V. Woolf, *A Room of One's Own* and *Three Guineas* (Oxford: Oxford University Press, 1992), pp. 130–1.

29 H. E. Gruber, *Darwin on Man: A Psychological Study of Scientific Creativity* (London: Wildwood House, 1974), p. 197. Gillian Beer has outlined Darwinian influences on several of Woolf's novels. See G. Beer, *Virginia*

*Woolf: The Common Ground* (Edinburgh: Edinburgh University Press, 1996), pp. 13–20.

30 See, for example, E. Abel, M. Hirsch and E. Langland (eds.), *The Voyage In: Fictions of Female Development* (Hanover and London: University Press of New England, 1983); and E. Labovitz, *The Myth of the Heroine: The Female Bildungsroman in the Twentieth Century* (New York: Peter Lang, 1986).

31 E. Abel, 'Narrative Structure(s) and Female Development: The Case of *Mrs Dalloway*', in Abel, Hirsch and Langland, *The Voyage In*, p. 161.

32 D. Allbright, *Personality and Impersonality: Lawrence, Woolf and Mann* (Chicago and London: University of Chicago Press, 1978), p. 96.

33 E. Labovitz, *The Myth of the Heroine* (New York: Peter Lang, 1986), p. 214.

34 Miller, *Fiction and Repetition*, p. 178.

35 *Ibid.*, p. 182.

36 *Ibid.*, p. 181.

37 V. Woolf, *The Diaries of Virginia Woolf Vol. II: 1920–1924* (London: Hogarth Press, 1978), p. 263.

38 E. Bishop, *Virginia Woolf* (New York: St Martin's Press, 1991), p. 49.

39 P. Ricoeur, *Time and Narrative*, vol. II (Chicago: Chicago University Press, 1986), trans. K. McLaughlin and D. Pellauer, p. 104.

40 Woolf, *Diary*, p. 139.

41 Ricoeur, *Time and Narrative*, vol. II, pp. 104–5

42 Gillian Beer remarks that Woolf's awareness of the Darwinian world – the persistence in the present day of prehistoric nature and human animality – absolved her 'from the causal forms she associates with nineteenth-century narratives'. See Beer, *Virginia Woolf*, p. 17.

43 E. Auerbach, *Mimesis: The Representation of Reality in Western Literature* (Princeton, N.J.: Princeton University Press, 1968), p. 536. Although this phrase pertains to his reading of *To the Lighthouse*, it can just as readily be applied to the earlier novel.

44 N. Page, *Speech in the English Novel* (Basingstoke: Macmillan, 1988), p. 45.

45 Woolf, *Essays*, vol. II, p. 224.

46 Woolf, *Diary*, p. 139.

47 R. A. Brower, 'The Novel as Poem: Virginia Woolf Exploring a Critical Metaphor', in M. W. Bloomfield (ed.), *The Interpretation of Narrative: Theory and Practice* (Cambridge, Mass.: Harvard University Press, 1970), p. 246.

48 M. A. Leaska, *The Novels of Virginia Woolf: From Beginning to End* (New York: John Jay Press, 1972), p. 132.

49 R. Bowlby, *Virginia Woolf: Feminist Destinations* (Oxford: Basil Blackwell, 1988), p. 64.

5

1 S. Beckett, *The Unnamable* (New York: Grove Press, 1958), p. 179. Hereafter 'U'.

2 S. Beckett, *Nohow On* (London: Calder, 1989), pp. 5–7.

3 See J. Maritain, *The Dream of Descartes* (Port Washington, N.Y.: Kennikat Press, 1969), pp. 13–29; and G. Sebba, *The Dream of Descartes* (Carbondale and Edwardsville: Southern Illinois University Press, 1987).

4 S. Gaukroger, *Descartes: An Intellectual Biography* (Oxford: Clarendon Press, 1995), pp. 110–11.

5 S. Beckett, *Our Exagmination Round His Factification For Incamination of* Work in Progress (London: Faber and Faber, 1972), p. 15.

6 P. Faulkner, *Humanism in the English Novel* (London: Elek/Pemberton, 1976), p. 6.

7 A. Gibson, *Reading Narrative Discourse: Studies in the Novel from Cervantes to Beckett* (London: Macmillan, 1990), p. 160.

8 See D. Bair, *Samuel Beckett: A Biography* (London: Vintage, 1990), pp. 367–403. See also J. Knowlson, *Damned to Fame: The Life of Samuel Beckett* (London: Bloomsbury, 1996), pp. 356–93.

9 S. Beckett, in an interview with T. Driver in 'Beckett by the Madeleine', in *Columbia University Forum* 4 (1961), p. 24. Reprinted in L. Graver and R. Federman (eds.), *Samuel Beckett: The Critical Heritage* (London: Routledge & Kegan Paul, 1979), p. 220.

10 Quoted in R. Ellmann, *a long the riverrun* (Harmondsworth: Penguin, 1989), p. 235.

11 J.-M. Rabaté, foreword to C. Wulf, *The Imperative of Narration* (Brighton: Sussex Academic Press, 1997), p. vi.

12 M. Gurewitch, *Comedy: The Irrational Vision* (Ithaca: Cornell University Press, 1975), p. 181.

13 H. Bergson, *Laughter* (New York: Macmillan, 1911), p. 2. Hereafter '*L*'.

14 See John Morreall, 'Introduction', in J. Morreall (ed.) *The Philosophy of Laughter and Humor* (Albany, N.Y.: State University of New York Press, 1987), pp. 3–4.

15 C. Baudelaire, *Selected Writings on Art and Literature* (Harmondsworth: Penguin, 1972), p. 143. Hereafter '*SW*'.

16 P. Davies, *The Ideal Real* (London and Toronto: Associated University Presses, 1994), p. 24.

17 Gurewitch, *Comedy*, p. 178.

18 S. Beckett, *Molloy* (New York: Grove Press, 1955), p. 47. Hereafter '*M*'.

19 Gibson, *Reading Narrative Discourse*, p. 142.

20 E. P. Levy, *Beckett and the Voice of Species* (Dublin: Gill and Macmillan, 1980), p. 55; and A. Kennedy, *Samuel Beckett* (Cambridge: Cambridge University Press, 1989), p. 106.

21 See E. Amiran, *Wandering and Home: Beckett's Metaphysical Narrative* (University Park, Penn.: Pennsylvania State University Press, 1993).

22 T. G. Pavel, 'Naturalizing *Molloy*', in J. Phelan and P. J. Rabinowitz (eds.), *Understanding Narrative* (Columbus, Ohio: Ohio State University Press, 1994), pp. 195, 194.

23 Levy, *Beckett and the Voice of Species*, pp. 55–6.

24  D. Hayman, 'Molloy or the Quest of Meaninglessness', in M. J. Friedman (ed.), *Samuel Beckett Now* (Chicago and London: University of Chicago Press, 1970), p. 140.

25  P. Alden, *Social Mobility in the English Bildungsroman* (Ann Arbor, Mich.: UMI Research Press, 1986), p. 130.

26  S. Beckett, *Collected Poems: 1930–1978* (London: John Calder, 1984), p. 7.

27  R. Begam, *Samuel Beckett and the End of Modernity* (Stanford: Stanford University Press, 1996), p. 6.

28  R. Coe, *Beckett* (Edinburgh and London: Oliver and Boyd, 1964), p. 11.

29  A. Bullock, *The Humanist Tradition in the West* (London: Thames and Hudson, 1985), p. 11.

30  J. D. O'Hara, 'Introduction', in J. D. O'Hara (ed.), *Twentieth-Century Interpretations of* Molloy, Malone Dies, The Unnamable (Englewood Cliffs, N.J.: Prentice-Hall, 1970), p. 3; and W. B. Yeats, 'Sailing to Byzantium', in *The Poems* (London: Everyman, 1992), p. 240.

31  See *All That Fall*: 'The trouble with her was she had never really been born!' S. Beckett, *Collected Shorter Plays* (London: Faber and Faber, 1985), p. 36.

32  L. Hill, *Beckett's Fiction: In Different Words* (Cambridge: Cambridge University Press, 1990), p. 80.

33  *Ibid.*, pp. 88, 102.

34  S. Beckett, *Waiting for Godot* (London: Faber and Faber, 1965), p. 89.

35  S. Beckett, 'The Calmative', in *Collected Shorter Prose 1945–1980* (London: John Calder, 1984), p. 35.

36  F. Kermode, *The Sense of an Ending: Studies in the Theory of Fiction* (New York: Oxford University Press, 1967), p. 151.

37  D. H. Lawrence, *Studies in Classic American Literature* (Harmondsworth: Penguin, 1971), p. 8.

38  R. Kearney, *The Wake of Imagination* (London: Hutchinson, 1988), p. 308.

39  Gibson, *Reading Narrative Discourse*, p. 153.

40  See C. Ricks, *Beckett's Dying Words* (Oxford: Clarendon Press, 1993), p. 131.

41  F. Karl and L. Davies (eds.), *The Collected Letters of Joseph Conrad*, vol. II (Cambridge: Cambridge University Press), p. 16.

42  *Ibid.*, p. 30.

43  F. Kermode, in Graver and Federman, *Samuel Beckett*, p. 201.

44  S. Connor, *Samuel Beckett: Repetition, Theory and Text* (Oxford: Basil Blackwell, 1988), p. 44.

45  S. Beckett, *Endgame* (London: Faber and Faber, 1958), pp. 21–2.

46  Gibson, *Reading Narrative Discourse*, p. 154.

47  Levy, *Beckett and the Voice of Species*, p. 58.

48  E. Levinas, *Totality and Infinity: an Essay on Exteriority*, trans. Alphonso Lingis (The Hague: Martinus Nijhoff, 1979), pp. 46, 44.

49  H. Arendt, *The Human Condition* (Chicago: Chicago University Press, 1958), p. 313.

50  Coe, *Beckett*, p. 2.

51 Catharina Wulf notes the 'inward turn' in the trilogy's previous part: 'As *Malone Dies* focuses on the narrator's withdrawal from the external world into the mind, the process of gradual physical decline is less relevant.' See C. Wulf, *The Imperative of Narration*, p. 67.

52 Beckett, *Collected Poems*, p. 3.

53 *Ibid.*, p. 5. From Baillet's biographical reconstruction of this night, writes Lawrence Harvey, '[it] is not difficult to retrieve . . . the essential elements of the corresponding lines in Beckett's poem'. See L. Harvey, *Samuel Beckett: Poet and Critic* (Princeton, N.J.: Princeton University Press, 1970), p. 23.

54 H. Kenner, *Samuel Beckett: A Critical Study* (London: John Calder, 1961), p. 17.

55 A. Alvarez, *Samuel Beckett* (London: Fontana, 1973), p. 57.

56 T. Eagleton, *Crazy John and the Bishop* (Cork: Cork University Press, 1998), p. 303.

57 F. Mulhern, 'English Reading' in H. Bhabha (ed.), *Nation and Narration* (London: Routledge, 1990) p. 256.

58 J. H. Miller, 'Narration' in F. Lentricchia and T. McLaughlin (eds.), *Critical Terms for Literary Study* (Chicago and London: University of Chicago Press, 1995), p. 72.

59 S. Beckett, *Proust and Three Dialogues* (London: Calder & Boyars, 1970), p. 103.

60 M. Esslin, 'Dionysos' Dianoetic Laughter', in *As No Other Dare Fail* (London: John Calder, 1986), p. 20.

61 Beckett, *Proust*, 119.

62 Esslin, 'Dionysos' Dianoetic Laughter', p. 20.

63 See E. Delavenay, *D. H. Lawrence: The Man and his Work* (London: Heinemann, 1972), p. 47.

64 Vincent Descombes writes that Proust's narrator 'seems to have been an avid reader of Schopenhauer'. See V. Descombes, *Proust: Philosophy of the Novel* (Stanford, Calif.: Stanford University Press, 1992), p. 25.

65 J. Pilling, 'Proust and Schopenhauer: Music and Shadows', in M. Bryden (ed.), *Samuel Beckett and Music* (Oxford: Clarendon Press, 1998), p. 177. I should note that Pilling focuses on *Proust*'s coda, where Beckett *does* distort the philosophy of *The World as Will*.

66 See, for example, A. and K. Hamilton, *Condemned to Life: The World of Samuel Beckett* (Grand Rapids, Mich.: William B. Eerdmans Publishing, 1976), p. 49.

67 Davies, *The Ideal Real*, p. 71.

68 D. Watson, *Paradox and Desire in Samuel Beckett's Fiction* (Basingstoke: Macmillan, 1991), p. 13.

69 Hill, *Beckett's Fiction*, p. 56.

70 *Ibid.*, p. 59.

71 Steven Rosen notes that Beckett 'strives to remain unconsoled, to retain the integrity of a basic bitterness'. See S. Rosen, *Samuel Beckett and the Pessimistic Tradition* (New Brunswick, N.J.: Rutgers University Press, 1976), p. 21. See also Barbara Hardy, 'The Dubious Consolations in Beckett's Fiction: Art,

Love and Nature', in K. Worth (ed.), *Beckett the Shape Changer* (London and Boston: Routledge & Kegan Paul, 1975), pp. 107–38.

72 See, for example, J. Fletcher, *The Novels of Samuel Beckett* (London: Chatto & Windus, 1970), pp. 180–1; and D. Lodge, *The Art of Fiction* (Harmondsworth: Penguin, 1992), p. 222.

73 Alvarez, *Samuel Beckett*, p. 74.

74 Davies, *The Ideal Real*, p. 65.

75 See Gibson, *Reading Narrative Discourse*, p. 150.

76 *Ibid.*, pp. 151–2.

77 S. Critchley, *Very Little . . . Almost Nothing: Death, Philosophy, Literature* (London: Routledge, 1997), p. 171.

## CONCLUSION

1 E. Levinas, *Difficult Freedom* (Baltimore: Johns Hopkins University Press, 1990), pp. 281–2.

2 A remark made by Paul Davies suggests that these differences may not be so great as they first appear. He writes: 'On occasions Beckett's fiction at this period [i.e., the trilogy] reads more like essays – we have seen how academic and/or reflexive a great deal of his writing is.' In the trilogy, maintains Davies, Beckett 'is always speaking precisely as academics speak: as though he is accountable to the truthmongers whoever they are'. See P. Davies *The Ideal Real* (London and Toronto: Associated University Presses, 1994), pp. 71–2.

3 Cultural theory's engagement with Beckett dates from the mid-1980s, with two key texts: Steven Connor's *Samuel Beckett: Repetition, Theory, and Text*, which brought Beckett's writing into the theoretical domains of Deleuze and Derrida; and Leslie Hill's *Beckett's Fiction: In Different Words*, which performed a similar manoeuvre with Derrida and psychoanalysis. Subsequently, two broad streams of critical analysis can be identified. Studies indebted to Deleuze, Blanchot and Derrida are T. Trezise, *Into the Breach: Samuel Beckett and the Ends of Literature* (Princeton, N.J.: Princeton University Press, 1990); C. Locatelli, *Unwording the World* (Philadelphia: University of Pennsylvania Press, 1990); R. Begam, *Samuel Beckett and the End of Modernity* (Stanford, Calif.: Stanford University Press, 1996); and A. Uhlmann, *Beckett and Poststructuralism* (Cambridge: Cambridge University Press, 1999). Other commentaries drawing heavily on Lacan and psychoanalysis include D. Watson, *Paradox and Desire in Samuel Beckett's Fiction* (Brighton: Sussex Academic Press, 1997); C. Wulf, *The Imperative of Narration: Beckett, Bernhard, Schopenhauer, Lacan* (Brighton: Sussex Academic Press, 1997); and P. Baker, *Beckett and the Mythology of Psychoanalysis* (Basingstoke: Macmillan, 1997). Beckett's theoretical potential was given a boost by Jacques Derrida when, in an interview with Derek Attridge in 1989, he explained why he had not undertaken any theoretical analysis of Beckett's work: 'This is an author to whom I feel very close, or to whom I would like

to feel myself very close; but also too close . . . I have perhaps avoided him because of this identification.' See J. Derrida, *Acts of Literature* (New York and London: Routledge, 1992), p. 61.

4 E. Levinas, *Basic Philosophical Writings* (Bloomington and Indianapolis: Indiana University Press, 1996), pp. 22, 31.

5 *Ibid.*, p. 27.

6 J. Llewelyn, *Emmanuel Levinas: The Genealogy of Ethics* (London: Routledge, 1995), Chapter 13.

7 *Ibid.*, p. 145.

8 A clarifying note: Levinas's 'human' (as opposed to the 'disquotational' *human*) resembles Heidegger's and Nietzsche's in that it is metaphysical, 'subjectivised' and value-oriented. But these terms, like the 'human' itself, are for Levinas positive ones, not the markers of false consciousness they are for the proponents of the 'human without the "human"'. Similarly, the 'disquotational' human in Levinasian thought is not a being divested of the illusions of 'forgetfulness' and *ressentiment*, but a primal *given*, a participant in the ethical encounter that is the transcendence of the other.

9 See, for example, E. Levinas, *Difficult Freedom* (Baltimore: Johns Hopkins University Press, 1990), pp. 235–8.

10 C. Davis, *Levinas: An Introduction* (Cambridge: Polity Press, 1996), pp. 57, 59.

11 *Ibid.*, p. 60.

12 Edward Said coined the term 'postnarrative' to describe Foucault's historiographic orientation. See E. Said, *Beginninngs: Intention and Method* (London: Granta, 1997), p. 282.

13 G. Levine, *Darwin and the Novelists* (Cambridge, Mass.: Harvard University Press, 1988), p. 8.

14 G. Gutting, 'Michel Foucault: A user's manual', in G. Gutting (ed.), *The Cambridge Companion to Foucault* (Cambridge: Cambridge University Press, 1994), p. 10.

15 M. Foucault, *The Archaeology of Knowledge* (London and New York: Routledge, 1989), pp. 44, 231.

16 C. O'Farrell, *Foucault: Historian or Philosopher?* (Basingstoke: Macmillan, 1989), pp. 36–7.

17 F. Lentricchia, *Ariel and the Police* (Brighton: Harvester Press, 1988), p. 96.

18 C. C. Lemert and G. Gillan, *Michel Foucault: Social Theory as Transgression* (New York: Columbia University Press, 1982), p. 41.

19 Said, *Beginnings*, p. 282.

20 H. White, 'Michel Foucault', in J. Sturrock (ed.), *Structuralism and Since* (Oxford: Oxford University Press, 1979), p. 85.

21 D. H. Lawrence, *Study of Thomas Hardy and Other Essays* (Cambridge: Cambridge University Press, 1985), p. 154.

22 T. Eagleton, *Literary Theory* (Oxford: Blackwell, 1983), p. 121.

23 See G. Thurley, *Counter-Modernism in Current Critical Theory* (Basingstoke: Macmillan, 1980), p. 7; J. G. Merquior, 'The Modernist Invasion of Theory', in J. G. Merquior, *From Prague to Paris* (London: Verso, 1986),

pp. 209–13; and P. Washington, *Fraud: Literary Theory and the End of English* (London: Fontana, 1989), *passim.*

24 See A. Huyssen, *After the Great Divide* (Basingstoke: Macmillan, 1986).

25 A. Ross (ed.), *Universal Abandon? The Politics of Postmodernism* (Edinburgh: Edinburgh University Press, 1989), p. ix.

26 R. Barthes, *Critical Essays* (Evanston: Northwestern University Press, 1972), p. 173.

27 Eagleton, *Literary Theory*, p. 121.

# Bibliography

PRIMARY SOURCES

Beckett, S., *Molloy*, New York: Grove Press, 1955.
    *Malone Dies*, New York: Grove Press, 1956.
    *The Unnamable*, New York: Grove Press, 1958.
    *Endgame*, London: Faber and Faber, 1958.
    *Waiting for Godot*, London: Faber and Faber, 1965.
    *Proust and Three Dialogues*, London: Calder & Boyars, 1970.
    'Dante . . . Bruno. Vico . . . Joyce', in *Our Exagmination Round His Factification for Incamination of* Work in Progress, London: Faber and Faber, 1972, pp. 3–22.
    *Collected Poems 1930–1978*, London: Calder, 1984.
    *Collected Shorter Prose 1945–1980*, London: Calder, 1984.
    *Collected Shorter Plays*, London: Faber and Faber, 1985.
    *Nohow On*, London: Calder, 1989.
Baudelaire, C., *Selected Writings on Art and Literature*, Harmondsworth: Penguin 1972.
Bergson, H., *Laughter: An Essay on the Meaning of the Comic*, trans. C. Brereton and F. Rothwell, New York: Macmillan, 1911.
    *Time and Free Will*, London: Allen & Unwin, 1971.
Conrad, J., *The Collected Letters of Joseph Conrad*, Cambridge: Cambridge University Press, 1983, eds. F. Karl and L. Davies, vol. I 1861–1897.
    *The Collected Letters of Joseph Conrad*, Cambridge: Cambridge University Press, 1986, eds. F. Karl and L. Davies, vol. II 1898–1902.
    *Lord Jim*, Harmondsworth: Penguin, 1986.
    *Nostromo: A Tale of the Seaboard*, Harmondsworth: Penguin, 1990.
Darwin, C., *The Origin of Species By Means of Natural Selection*, Harmondsworth: Penguin, 1985.
    *The Descent of Man, and Selection in Relation to Sex*, London: John Murray, 1901.
    *Charles Darwin's Letters: A Selection 1825–1859*, ed. F. Burkhardt, Cambridge: Cambridge University Press, 1996.
Descartes, R., *Discourse on Method and the Meditations*, Harmondsworth: Penguin, 1968.

Foucault, M., *The Order of Things*, London: Routledge, 1970.

 *Power/Knowledge*, trans. C. Gordon, Brighton, Sussex: Harvester Press, 1980.

 *The Archaeology of Knowledge*, London and New York: Routledge, 1989.

 *Discipline and Punish: The Birth of the Prison*, trans. A. Sheridan, Harmondsworth: Penguin, 1991.

Hegel, G. W. F., *The Phenomenology of Spirit*, trans. A. V. Miller, Oxford: Oxford University Press, 1977.

Heidegger, M., *Being and Time*, trans. J. Macquarrie and E. Robinson, Oxford: Basil Blackwell, 1962.

 *Basic Writings*, ed. D. F. Krell, London: Routledge, 1993.

 *Nietzsche*, trans. F. A. Capuzzi, San Francisco: Harper & Row, 1982, vol. IV.

Kant, I., *Critique of Pure Reason*, trans. J. M. D. Meiklejohn, New York: Willey Book Co., 1943.

 *Critique of Practical Reason*, trans. T. K. Abbott, Amherst, N.Y.: Prometheus, 1966.

 *Lectures on Ethics*, Indianapolis, Ind.: Hackett, 1979.

 *Critique of Judgment*, trans. W. S. Pluhar, Indianapolis, Ind.: Hackett, 1987.

 *Practical Philosophy*, Cambridge: Cambridge University Press, 1996.

Lawrence, D. H., *Psychoanalysis and the Unconscious* and *Fantasia of the Unconscious*, New York: Viking, 1960.

 *Phoenix*, ed. E. D. McDonald, New York: Viking, 1968.

 *Studies in Classic American Literature*, Harmondsworth: Penguin, 1971.

 *Phoenix II*, eds. W. Roberts and H. T. Moore, Harmondsworth: Penguin, 1978.

 *The Letters of D. H. Lawrence*, eds. G. J. Zytaruk and J. T. Boulton, Cambridge: Cambridge University Press, 1979, vol. I.

 *The Letters of D. H. Lawrence*, eds. G. J. Zytaruk and J. T. Boulton, Cambridge: Cambridge University Press, 1981, vol. II.

 *Study of Thomas Hardy and Other Essays*, Cambridge: Cambridge University Press, 1985.

 *The Rainbow*, Harmondsworth: Penguin, 1989.

 *Sons and Lovers*, Harmondsworth: Penguin, 1994.

 *Women in Love*, Harmondsworth: Penguin, 1995.

 *The White Peacock*, Oxford: Oxford University Press, 1997.

Levinas, E., *Totality and Infinity: An Essay on Exteriority*, trans. Alphonso Lingis, The Hague: Martinus Nijhoff, 1979.

 *Difficult Freedom*, Baltimore: Johns Hopkins University Press, 1990.

 *Basic Philosophical Writings*, Bloomington and Indianapolis: Indiana University Press, 1996.

Marx, K., *Early Writings*, Harmondsworth: Penguin, 1975.

 *The Letters of Karl Marx*, trans. and ed. S. K. Padover, New Jersey: Prentice-Hall, Inc., 1979.

Nietzsche, F., *The Will to Power*, trans. W. Kaufmann and R. J. Hollingdale, New York: Random House, 1967.

    *Basic Writings of Nietzsche*, New York: Modern Library, 1968.

    *Thus Spoke Zarathustra: A Book for Everyone and No One*, trans. R. J. Hollingdale, Harmondsworth: Penguin, 1969.

    *Beyond Good and Evil: Prelude to a Philosophy of the Future*, trans. R. J. Hollingdale, Harmondsworth: Penguin, 1973.

    *The Gay Science*, trans. W. Kaufmann, New York: Random House, 1974.

    *Ecce Homo: How One Becomes What One Is*, trans. R. J. Hollingdale, Harmondsworth: Penguin, 1979.

    *Human, All Too Human: A Book for Free Spirits*, trans. M. Faber and S. Lehmann, Harmondsworth: Penguin, 1994.

    *On the Genealogy of Morality*, trans. C. Diethe, Cambridge: Cambridge University Press, 1994.

    *Unfashionable Observations*, trans. R. T. Gray, Stanford, Calif.: Stanford University Press, 1995.

Schopenhauer, A., *On the Basis of Morality*, trans. E. F. J. Payne, Indianapolis and New York: Bobbs–Merrill, 1965.

    *The World as Will and Representation*, trans. E. F. J. Payne, New York: Dover, 1966, vols. I and II.

    *Parerga and Paralipomena*, trans. E. F. J. Payne, Oxford: Clarendon Press, 1974, vol. II.

Wilde, O., *Selected Works*, London: William Heinemann, 1946.

    *De Profundis and Other Writings*, Harmondsworth: Penguin, 1986.

Woolf, V., *A Writer's Diary*, London: Hogarth Press, 1953.

    *The Common Reader, First Series*, London: Hogarth, 1957.

    *Collected Essays*, London: Hogarth Press, 1966, vol. II.

    *Collected Essays*, London: Hogarth Press, 1967, vol. III.

    *The Diaries of Virginia Woolf*, London: Hogarth Press, 1978, vol II 1920–1924.

    *Mrs Dalloway*, Harmondsworth: Penguin, 1992.

    *To the Lighthouse*, Harmondsworth: Penguin, 1992.

    *A Room of One's Own* and *Three Guineas*, Oxford: Oxford University Press, 1992.

## SECONDARY SOURCES

Abel, E., Hirsch, M. and Langland, E. (eds.), *The Voyage In: Fictions of Female Development*, Hanover and London: University Press of New England, 1983.

Abrams, M. H., *Natural Supernaturalism*, New York: Norton, 1971.

Alden, P., *Social Mobility in the English Bildungsroman*, Ann Arbor, Mich.: UMI Research Press, 1986.

Allbright, D., *Personality and Impersonality: Lawrence, Woolf and Mann*, Chicago and London: University of Chicago Press, 1978.

Alvarez, A., *Samuel Beckett*, London: Fontana, 1973.

Amigoni, D. and Wallace, J. (eds.), *Charles Darwin's* The Origin of Species: *New Interdisciplinary Essays*, Manchester and New York: Manchester University Press, 1995.

Amiran, E., *Wandering and Home: Beckett's Metaphysical Narrative*, University Park, Penn.: Pennsylvania State University Press, 1993.

Anderson, P., *In the Tracks of Historical Materialism*, London: Verso, 1983.

Arendt, H., *The Human Condition*, Chicago: Chicago University Press, 1958.

Aristotle, *The Works of Aristotle*, trans. B. Jowett, Oxford: Clarendon Press, 1921, vol. X.

Auerbach, E., *Mimesis: The Representation of Reality in Western Literature*, Princeton, N. J.: Princeton University Press, 1968.

Austin, J. L., *How to Do Things with Words*, London: Oxford University Press,1962.

Bair, D., *Samuel Beckett: A Biography*, London: Vintage, 1990.

Baillet, A., *La Vie de Monsieur Descartes*, Paris: Daniel Horthemels, 1691.

Baines, J., *Joseph Conrad: A Critical Biography*, Harmondsworth: Penguin, 1960.

Baker, P., *Beckett and the Mythology of Psychoanalysis*, Basingstoke: Macmillan, 1997.

Baker, S., *The Postmodern Animal*, London: Reaktion, 2000.

Barthes, R., *Critical Essays*, Evanston: Northwestern University Press, 1972.

Batchelor, J., *The Life of Joseph Conrad: A Critical Biography*, Oxford: Basil Blackwell, 1994.

Bauman, Z., *Modernity and the Holocaust*, Cambridge: Polity Press, 1989.

Becket, F., *D. H. Lawrence: The Thinker as Poet*, Basingstoke: Macmillan, 1997.

Beddow, M., *The Fiction of Humanity*, Cambridge: Cambridge University Press, 1982.

Beer, G., *Darwin's Plots*, London: Ark, 1985.
    *Virginia Woolf: The Common Ground*, Edinburgh: Edinburgh University Press, 1996.

Begam, R., *Samuel Beckett and the End of Modernity*, Stanford: Stanford University Press, 1996.

Beja, M. (ed.), *Critical Essays on Virginia Woolf*, Boston, Mass.: G. K. Hall & Co, 1985.

Bell, M., *D. H. Lawrence: Language and Being*, Cambridge: Cambridge University Press, 1992.

Berman, A., *Preface to Modernism*, Urbana and Chicago: University of Illinois Press, 1994.

Bhabha, H. (ed.), *Nation and Narration*, London: Routledge, 1990.

Billy, T. (ed.), *Critical Essays on Joseph Conrad*, Boston, Mass.: G. K. Hall & Co., 1987.

Bishop, E., *Virginia Woolf*, New York: St Martin's Press, 1991.

Bloom, H., *Poetry and Repression: Revisionism from Blake to Stevens*, New Haven and London: Yale University Press, 1976.
    (ed.), *Joseph Conrad*, New York, New Haven and Philadelphia: Chelsea House, 1986.
    (ed.), *Virginia Woolf*, New York, New Haven and Philadelphia: Chelsea House, 1986.

(ed.), *Joseph Conrad's* Lord Jim, New York, New Haven and Philadelphia: Chelsea House, 1987.

Bloomfield, M. W. (ed.), *The Interpretation of Narrative: Theory and Practice*, Cambridge, Mass.: Harvard University Press, 1970.

Bourdieu, P., *The Political Ontology of Martin Heidegger*, trans. P. Collier, Cambridge: Polity Press, 1991.

Bowlby, R., *Virginia Woolf: Feminist Destinations*, Oxford: Basil Blackwell, 1988.

Bradbury, M., *No, Not Bloomsbury*, London: André Deutsch, 1987.

Brantlinger, P., *Bread and Circuses: Theories of Mass Culture as Social Decay*, Ithaca: Cornell University Press, 1983.

Brecht, B., *Brecht On Theatre*, New York: Hill and Wang, 1964.

Britton B. K. and Pellegrini, A. D. (ed.), *Narrative Thought and Narrative Language*, Hillsdale, N. J.: Lawrence Erlbaum Associates, 1990.

Brooks, P., *Reading for the Plot: Design and Intention in Narrative*, Cambridge, Mass.: Harvard University Press, 1984.

Brunsdale, M. M., *Utah Studies in Literature and Linguistics*, Berne: Peter Lang, 1978.

Bryden, M. (ed.), *Samuel Beckett and Music*, Oxford: Clarendon Press, 1998.

Buckley, J. H., *Season of Youth*, Cambridge, Mass.: Harvard University Press, 1974.

Bullock, A. *The Humanist Tradition in the West*, London: Thames and Hudson, 1985.

Bürger, P., *Theory of the Avant-Garde*, trans. M. Shaw, Minneapolis: University of Minnesota Press, 1985.

Burns, A., *Nature and Culture in D. H. Lawrence*, Basingstoke: Macmillan, 1980.

Butler, J., *Gender Trouble*, New York and London: Routledge, 1990.

Butler, S., *Erewhon, or, Over the Range*, Harmondsworth: Penguin, 1985.

Carey, J., *The Intellectuals and the Masses*, London: Faber and Faber, 1992.

Carlyle, T., *On Heroes, Hero-Worship and the Heroic in History*, London: Chapman and Hall, 1907.

  *A Carlyle Reader*, Cambridge: Cambridge University Press, 1984.

Chatman, S., *Story and Discourse: Narrative Structure in Fiction and Film*, Ithaca: Cornell University Press, 1978.

Clark, S. R. L., 'The moral animals', in *The Times Literary Supplement* 4875 (1996), pp. 25–6.

Coe, R., *Beckett*, Edinburgh and London: Oliver and Boyd, 1964.

Connor, S., *Samuel Beckett: Repetition, Theory and Text*, Oxford: Basil Blackwell, 1988.

Critchley, S., *Very Little . . . Almost Nothing: Death, Philosophy, Literature*, London: Routledge, 1997.

Daleski, H. M., *The Forked Flame: A Study of D. H. Lawrence*, London: Faber and Faber, 1965.

Danson, L., *Wilde's Intentions: The Artist in His Criticism*, Oxford: Clarendon Press, 1997.

Danto, A., *Narration and Knowledge*, New York: Columbia University Press, 1985.

Dastur, F., *Death: An Essay on Finitude*, London and Atlantic Highlands, N.J.: Athlone Press, 1996.

Davidson, A., *Conrad's Endings*, Ann Arbor, Mich.: UMI Research Press, 1984.

Davies, P., *The Ideal Real: Beckett's Fiction and Imagination*, London and Toronto: Associated University Presses, 1994.

Davies, T., *Humanism*, London: Routledge, 1997.

Davis, C., *Levinas: An Introduction*, Cambridge: Polity Press, 1996.

Delavenay, E., *D. H. Lawrence: The Man and his Work*, London, Heinemann, 1972.

Deleuze, G., *Nietzsche and Philosophy*, trans. H. Tomlinson, New York: Columbia University Press, 1983.

　　　　*Bergsonism*, trans. H. Tomlinson and B. Habberjam, New York: Zone Books, 1991.

de Man, P., *Allegories of Reading*, New Haven and London: Yale University Press, 1979.

Derrida, J., *Acts of Literature*, New York and London: Routledge, 1992.

Descombes, V., *Proust: Philosophy of the Novel*, Stanford, Calif.: Stanford University Press, 1992.

Desmond, A. and Moore, J., *Darwin*, Harmondsworth: Penguin, 1991.

Dijksterhuis, E. J., *The Mechanization of the World Picture*, Oxford: Clarendon Press, 1961.

Douglass, P., *Bergson, Eliot and American Literature*, Lexington, Ky.: University Press of Kentucky, 1986.

Dreyfus, H. and Rabinow, P., *Michel Foucault: Beyond Structuralism and Hermeneutics*, Brighton: Harvester, 1982.

Eagleton, T., *Exiles and Emigrés: Studies in Modern Literature*, London: Chatto & Windus, 1970.

　　　　*Literary Theory*, Oxford: Blackwell, 1983.

　　　　*The Ideology of the Aesthetic*, Oxford: Basil Blackwell, 1990.

　　　　*The Illusions of Postmodernism*, Oxford: Basil Blackwell, 1996.

　　　　*Crazy John and the Bishop*, Cork: Cork University Press, 1998.

Eliot, T. S., *Selected Essays*, London: Faber and Faber, 1950.

Ellmann, R., *Yeats: The Man and the Masks*, London: Macmillan, 1949.

　　　　*a long the riverrun*, Harmondsworth: Penguin, 1989.

Esslin, M. 'Dionysos' Dianoetic Laughter', in *As No Other Dare Fail*, London: John Calder, 1986, pp. 15–23.

Etlin, R., *In Defense of Humanism*, Cambridge: Cambridge University Press, 1996.

Eysteinsson, A., *The Concept of Modernism*, Ithaca: Cornell University Press, 1992.

Faulkner, P., *Humanism in the English Novel*, London: Elek/Pemberton, 1976.

Ferguson, K. E., *The Man Question: Visions of Subjectivity in Feminist Theory*, Berkeley and Los Angeles: University of California Press, 1993.

Fernihough, A., *D. H. Lawrence: Aesthetics and Ideology*, Oxford: Clarendon Press, 1993.

Ferry, L., *The New Ecological Order*, trans. C. Volk, Chicago and London: University of Chicago Press, 1995.

Ferry, L. and Renaut, A., *Heidegger and Modernity*, Chicago and London: University of Chicago Press, 1990.

Fletcher, J., *The Novels of Samuel Beckett*, London: Chatto & Windus, 1970.

Forster, E. M., *Howards End*, Harmondsworth: Penguin, 1961.

Freud, S., *The Standard Edition of the Complete Psychological Works of Sigmund Freud*, trans. J. Strachey, London: Hogarth Press, 1963, vol. XVI 1916–17.

   *The Standard Edition of the Complete Psychological Works of Sigmund Freud*, trans. J. Strachey, London: Hogarth Press, 1959, vol. XX 1925–6.

   *The Standard Edition of the Complete Psychological Works of Sigmund Freud*, trans. J. Strachey, London: Hogarth Press, 1964, vol. XXII 1932–6.

Friedman, M. J. (ed.), *Samuel Beckett Now*, Chicago and London: University of Chicago Press, 1970.

Galsworthy, J., *Two Essays on Conrad*, Cincinnati: Freelands, 1930.

Gaukroger, S., *Descartes: An Intellectual Biography*, Oxford: Clarendon Press, 1995.

Gibson, A., *Reading Narrative Discourse: Studies in the Novel from Cervantes to Beckett* London: Macmillan, 1990.

Gillespie, N., *Charles Darwin and the Problem of Creation*, Chicago and London: University of Chicago Press, 1979.

Gillies, M. A., *Henri Bergson and British Modernism*, Montreal and Kingston: McGill-Queen's University Press, 1996.

Glass, B., Temkin, O. and Straus, W. L., Jnr. (eds.), *Forerunners of Darwin: 1745–1859* Baltimore: Johns Hopkins University Press, 1959.

Gooding-Williams, R., 'The Drama of Nietzsche's Zarathustra: Intention, Repetition, Prelude', in *International Studies in Philosophy* 20/2 (1988), pp. 105–16.

Gramsci, A., *The Modern Prince and Other Writings*, New York: International Publishers, 1957.

Graver, L. and Federman, R. (eds.), *Samuel Beckett: The Critical Heritage*, London: Routledge & Kegan Paul, 1979.

Gruber, H. E., *Darwin on Man: A Psychological Study of Scientific Creativity*, London: Wildwood House, 1974.

Guignon, C. B. (ed.), *The Cambridge Companinion to Heidegger*, Cambridge: Cambridge University Press, 1993.

Gurewitch, M., *Comedy: The Irrational Vision*, Ithaca: Cornell University Press, 1975.

Gutting, G. (ed.), *The Cambridge Companion to Foucault*, Cambridge: Cambridge University Press, 1994.

Haar, M., *Heidegger and the Essence of Man*, Albany, N.Y.: State University of New York Press, 1993.

Hamilton, A. and Hamilton, K., *Condemned to Life: The World of Samuel Beckett*, Grand Rapids, Mich.: William B. Eerdmans Publishing, 1976.

Harvey, L., *Samuel Beckett: Poet and Critic*, Princeton, N.J.: Princeton University Press, 1970.

Haynes, R. D., *From Faust to Strangelove: Representations of the Scientist in Western Literature*, Baltimore and London: Johns Hopkins University Press, 1994.

Heisenberg, W., *Physics and Philosophy*, Harmondsworth: Penguin, 1989.

Hervouet, Y., *The French Face of Joseph Conrad*, Cambridge: Cambridge University Press, 1990.

Hill, L., *Beckett's Fiction: In Different Words*, Cambridge: Cambridge University Press, 1990.

Hodge, J., *Heidegger and Ethics*, London: Routledge, 1995.

Howe, I., *Politics and the Novel*, London: Stevens & Sons, 1961.

Howe, S., Wilhelm Meister *and his English Kinsmen*, New York: Columbia University Press, 1930.

Hulme, T. E., *Speculations: Essays on Humanism and the Philosophy of Art*, London: Routledge & Kegan Paul, 1987.

Hunter, A., *Joseph Conrad and the Ethics of Darwinism*, London and Canberra: Croom Helm, 1983.

Hutcheon, L., *A Poetics of Postmodernism: History, Theory, Fiction*, London and New York: Routledge, 1988.

Huxley, A., *Eyeless in Gaza*, London: Chatto & Windus, 1955.
  *Point Counter Point*, London: Chatto & Windus, 1974.

Huxley, T. H., *Man's Place in Nature*, New York and London: D. Appleton and Company, 1929.

Huyssen, A., *After the Great Divide*, Basingstoke: Macmillan, 1986.

Ingersoll, E. G., *Midwest Quarterly* 37/4 (1996), pp. 434–47.

Jackson, T. E., 'Turning into Modernism: *Lord Jim* and the Alteration of the Narrative Subject', *Literature and Psychology* 32/4 (1993), pp. 65–85.

Jameson, F., *The Political Unconscious: Narrative as a Socially Symbolic Act*, London: Methuen, 1981.

Janaway, C., *Self and World in Schopenhauer's Philosophy*, Oxford: Clarendon Press, 1989.

Jouve, N. W., *Female Genesis: Creativity, Self and Gender*, New York: St Martin's Press, 1998.

Kaplan, C. M. and Simpson, A. B. (eds.), *Seeing Double: Revisioning Edwardian and Modernist Literature*, Basingstoke: Macmillan, 1996.

Karl, F., *Joseph Conrad: The Three Lives*, London: Faber and Faber, 1979.

Kearney, R., *The Wake of Imagination: Ideas of Creativity in Western Culture*, London: Hutchinson, 1988.

Keats, J., *The Letters of John Keats*, vol. II, 1814–1821, ed. H. E. Rollins, Cambridge, Mass.: Harvard University Press, 1958.

Kellner, H., *Language and Historical Representation*, Madison, Wis.: University of Wisconsin Press, 1989.

Kennedy, A., *Samuel Beckett*, Cambridge: Cambridge University Press, 1989.

Kenner, H., *Samuel Beckett: A Critical Study*, London: John Calder, 1961.
  *The Stoic Comedians*, London: University of California Press, 1962.

Kermode, F., *The Sense of an Ending: Studies in the Theory of Fiction*, New York: Oxford University Press, 1967.
  *Lawrence*, London: Fontana, 1973.

Kiely, R., *Beyond Egotism: The Fiction of James Joyce, Virginia Woolf and D. H. Lawrence*, Cambridge, Mass.: Harvard University Press, 1980.

Kisiel, T. and van Buren, J. (eds.), *Reading Heidegger from the Start*, Albany, N.Y.: State University of New York, 1994.

Knowlson, J., *Damned to Fame: The Life of Samuel Beckett*, London: Bloomsbury, 1996.

Kuhn, T., *The Structure of Scientific Revolutions*, Chicago: University of Chicago Press, 1979.

Labovitz, E., *The Myth of the Heroine*, New York: Peter Lang, 1986.

Lacan, J., *Ecrits*, trans. A. Sheridan, London: Tavistock, 1977.

Lanser, S. S., *The Narrative Act: Point of View in Prose Fiction*, Princeton, N.J.: Princeton University Press, 1981.

Leaska, M. A., *The Novels of Virginia Woolf: From Beginning to End*, New York: John Jay Press, 1972.

Leavis, F. R., *D. H. Lawrence: Novelist*, London: Chatto & Windus, 1962.

Lemert, C. C. and Gillan, G., *Michel Foucault: Social Theory as Transgression*, New York: Columbia University Press, 1982.

Lentricchia, F., *Ariel and the Police*, Brighton: Harvester Press, 1988.

Lentricchia, F. and McLaughlin, T. (eds.), *Critical Terms for Literary Study*, Chicago and London: University of Chicago Press, 1995.

Levine, G., *Darwin and the Novelists*, Cambridge, Mass.: Harvard University Press, 1988.

Levy, E. P., *Beckett and the Voice of Species: A Study of the Prose Fiction*, Dublin: Gill and Macmillan, 1980.

Lewiecki-Wilson, C., *Writing Against the Family: Gender in Lawrence and Joyce* Carbondale and Edwardsville: Southern Illinois University Press, 1994.

Lewis, W., *Men Without Art*, New York: Russell & Russell, 1964.

   *Time and Western Man*, Santa Rosa: Black Sparrow, 1993.

Llewelyn, J., *Emmanuel Levinas: The Genealogy of Ethics*, London: Routledge, 1995.

Lloyd, G., *The Man of Reason: 'Male' and 'Female' in Western Philosophy*, London: Routledge, 1984.

   *Being in Time: Selves and Narrators in Philosophy and Literature*, London and New York: Routledge, 1993.

Locatelli, C., *Unwording the World*, Philadelphia: University of Pennsylvania Press, 1990.

Lodge, D., *The Art of Fiction: Illustrated from Classic and Modern Texts*, Harmondsworth: Penguin, 1992.

Lovejoy, A., *The Great Chain of Being: A Study of the History of an Idea*, Cambridge, Mass.: Harvard University Press, 1936.

Lukács, G., *The Historical Novel*, trans. H. and S. Mitchell, London: Merlin, 1962.

   *The Theory of the Novel: A Historico-Philosophical Essay on the Forms of Great Epic Literature*, trans. A. Bostock, London: Merlin, 1978.

Magee, B., *The Philosophy of Schopenhauer*, Oxford: Clarendon Press, 1997.

Mann, T., *Essays of Three Decades*, trans. H. T. Lowe-Porter, London: Secker & Warburg, 1947.

Marcus, L., *Virginia Woolf*, London: Northcote House, 1997.

Maritain, J., *The Dream of Descartes*, trans. M. L. Andison, Port Washington, N.Y.: Kennikat Press, 1969.

Marx, L. and Smith, M. R. (eds.), *Does Technology Drive History?*, Cambridge, Mass.: MIT Press, 1994.

Mayr, E., *One Long Argument: Charles Darwin and the Genesis of Modern Evolutionary Thought*, Harmondsworth: Allen Lane, 1992.

Mazlish, B., *The Fourth Discontinuity*, New Haven and London: Yale University Press, 1993.

McHugh, P., 'Metaphysics and Sexual Politics in Lawrence's Novels', in *College Literature* 20/3 (1993), pp. 83–97.

Megill, A., 'Nietzsche as Aestheticist', *Philosophy and Literature* 5/2 (1981), pp. 204–25.

Merquior, J. G., *From Prague to Paris*, London: Verso, 1986.

Middleton, P., *The Inward Gaze: Masculinity and Subjectivity in Modern Culture*, London: Routledge, 1992.

Midgley, M., *Beast and Man: The Roots of Human Nature*, London: Routledge, 1995.

Miller, D. A., *Narrative and Its Discontents: Problems of Closure in the Traditional Novel*, Princeton: Princeton University Press, 1981.

Miller, J. H., *Fiction and Repetition*, Oxford: Basil Blackwell, 1982.
      *Tropes, Parables, Performatives*, Hemel Hempstead: Harvester Wheatsheaf, 1990.

Millett, K., *Sexual Politics*, New York: Doubleday, 1970.

Milton, C., *Lawrence and Nietzsche: A Study in Influence*, Aberdeen: Aberdeen University Press, 1987.

Mitchell, W. J. T. (ed.), *On Narrative*, Chicago and London: University of Chicago Press, 1980.

Montgomery, R. E., *The Visionary D. H. Lawrence: Beyond Philosophy and Art*, Cambridge: Cambridge University Press, 1994.

Moore, H. T., *The Priest of Love: A Life of D. H. Lawrence*, London: Heinemann, 1974.

Moretti, F., *The Way of the World: The Bildungsroman in European Culture*, London: Verso, 1987.

Morreall, J. (ed.), *The Philosophy of Laughter and Humor*, Albany, N.Y.: State University of New York Press, 1987.

Mulhall, S., *Heidegger and* Being and Time, London: Routledge, 1996.

Mumford, L., *Technics and Civilization*, London: Routledge, 1946.

Najder, Z., *Joseph Conrad: A Chronicle*, Cambridge: Cambridge University Press, 1983.

Nash, C. (ed.), *Narrative in Culture: The Uses of Storytelling in the Sciences, Philosophy and Literature*, London: Routledge, 1990.

Nead, L., *The Female Nude: Art, Obscenity and Sexuality*, London: Routledge, 1992.

Nehamas, A., *Nietzsche: Life as Literature*, Cambridge, Mass.: Harvard University Press, 1985.

Nixon, C., *Lawrence's Leadership Politics and the Turn Against Women*, Berkeley and Los Angeles: University of California Press, 1986.

Norris, M., *Beasts of the Modern Imagination: Darwin, Nietzsche, Kafka, Ernst, and Lawrence*, Baltimore: Johns Hopkins University Press, 1985.

Oates, J. C., 'Lawrence's *Götterdämmerung:* The Tragic Vision of *Women in Love*', in *Critical Inquiry* 4 (1978), pp. 559–78.

O'Farrell, C., *Foucault: Historian or Philosopher?*, Basingstoke: Macmillan, 1989.

O'Hara, J. D. (ed.), *Twentieth-Century Interpretations of* Molloy, Malone Dies, The Unnamable, Englewood Cliffs, N.J.: Prentice-Hall, 1970.

O'Neill, J., 'Humanism and Nature', *Radical Philosophy* 66 (1994), pp. 21–9.
    (ed.) *Hegel's Dialectic of Desire and Recognition*, Albany, N.Y.: State University of New York Press, 1996.

Page, N., *Speech in the English Novel*, Basingstoke: Macmillan, 1988.

Paley, W., *Natural Theology*, London: R. Faulder, 1802.

Passmore, J., *Man's Responsibility for Nature*, London: Duckworth, 1980.

Pearson, K. A., *Viroid Life: Perspectives on Nietzsche and the Transhuman Condition* London: Routledge, 1997.
    *Germinal Life*, London: Routledge, 1999.

Pettey, J. C., *Nietzsche's Philosophical and Narrative Styles*, New York: Peter Lang, 1992.

Phelan, J. and Rabinowitz, P. J. (eds.), *Understanding Narrative*, Columbus, Ohio: Ohio State University Press, 1994.

Pinkard, T., *Hegel's* Phenomenology: *The Sociality of Reason*, Cambridge: Cambridge University Press, 1994.

Pinkney, T., *D. H. Lawrence*, London: Harvester Wheatsheaf, 1990.

Pynchon, T., *V*, London: Pan, 1975.

Radford, T., 'It's life but not as we know it', *London Review of Books* 13 (1997), pp. 15–16.

Rainey, L., *Institutions of Modernism*, New Haven: Yale University Press, 1999.

Rajchman, J., 'Foucault, or the ends of Modernism', *October* 24 (1983), pp. 37–62.

Rée, J., *Philosphical Tales: An Essay on Philosophy and Literature*, London: Methuen, 1987.

Ricks, C., *Beckett's Dying Words*, Oxford: Clarendon Press, 1993.

Ricoeur, P., *Time and Narrative*, 3 vols., trans. K. McLaughlin and D. Pellauer, Chicago: Chicago University Press, 1984–8.

Rimmon-Kenan, S., *Narrative Fiction: Contemporary Poetics*, London: Routledge, 1983.

Roe, S., *Writing and Gender: Virginia Woolf's Writing Practice*, Hemel Hempstead: Harvester Wheatsheaf Press, 1990.

Rosen, S., *Samuel Beckett and the Pessimistic Tradition*, New Brunswick, N.J.: Rutgers University Press, 1976.

Ross, A. (ed.), *Universal Abandon? The Politics of Postmodernism*, Edinburgh: Edinburgh University Press, 1989.

Sadoff, I. 'Sartre and Conrad: Lord Jim as Existential Hero', in *Dalhousie Review* 49/4 (1969–70), pp. 518–25.

Said, E., *Joseph Conrad and the Fiction of Autobiography*, Cambridge:, Mass.: Harvard University Press, 1966.
    *The World, the Text and the Critic*, London: Vintage, 1983.
    *Culture and Imperialism*, New York: Vintage, 1994.
    *Beginnings: Intention and Method*, London: Granta, 1997.
Sartre, J. P., *Being and Nothingress*, London: Routledge, 1969.
Schama, S., *Landscape and Memory*, London: HarperCollins, 1995.
Schapiro, B., *Soundings* 69/3 (1986), pp. 347–65.
Schneider, D. J., *D. H. Lawrence: The Artist as Psychologist*, Kansas: University Press of Kansas, 1984.
Scholes, R. and Kellogg, R., *The Nature of Narrative*, New York: Oxford University Press, 1966.
Sebba, G. *The Dream of Descartes*, Carbondale and Edwardsville: Southern Illinois University Press, 1987.
Seltzer, M., *Bodies and Machines*, New York and London: Routledge, 1992.
Shapiro, G., *Nietzschean Narratives*, Bloomington, Indianapolis: Indiana University Press, 1989.
Sheehan, J. and Sosna, M. (eds.), *The Boundaries of Humanity*, Berkeley and Los Angeles: University of California Press, 1991.
Shaw, M., 'Lawrence and Feminism', in *Critical Quarterly* 25/3 (1983), pp. 23–8.
Singer, C., *A Short History of Anatomy from the Greeks to Harvey*, New York: Dover, 1957.
Singer, C., Holmyard, E. J., Hall, A. R. and Williams, T. (eds.), *A History of Technology*, Oxford: Clarendon Press, 1957, vol. III.
Singer, P., *Animal Liberation: A New Ethics for Our Treatment of Animals*, London: Pimlico, 1995.
Smith, A. (ed.), *Lawrence and Women*, London: Vision, 1978.
Snow, J., 'Schopenhauer's Style', in *International Philosophical Quarterly* 33/4 (1993), pp. 401–12.
Solomon, R. C., *History and Human Nature: A Philosophical Review of European Philosophy and Culture, 1750–1850*, Brighton, Sussex: Harvester Press, 1979.
Soper, K., *What is Nature?: Culture, Politics and the Non-Human*, Oxford: Basil Blackwell, 1995.
Stape, J. H. (ed.), *The Cambridge Companion to Joseph Conrad*, Cambridge: Cambridge University Press, 1996.
Steig, M., *Stories of Reading: Subjectivity and Literary Understanding*, Baltimore: Johns Hopkins University Press, 1989.
Steiner, G., *Heidegger*, London: Fontana, 1992.
Stern, J. P., *Nietzsche*, London: Fontana, 1978.
Storch, M., *Sons and Adversaries: Women in William Blake and D. H. Lawrence*, Knoxville: University of Tennessee Press, 1990.
Sturrock, J. (ed.), *Structuralism and Since* (Oxford: Oxford University Press, 1979).
Swales, M., *The German Bildungsroman from Wieland to Hesse*, Princeton: Princeton University Press, 1978.

Tallis, R., *The Explicit Animal: A Defence of Human Consciousness*, Basingstoke: Macmillan, 1991.

Taylor, C., *Sources of the Self: The Making of the Modern Identity*, Cambridge: Cambridge University Press, 1989.

Tedlock, E. W., Jnr, *D. H. Lawrence and* Sons and Lovers: *Sources and Criticism*, New York: New York University Press, 1965.

Tester, K., *The Inhuman Condition*, London: Routledge, 1995.

Thomas, K., *Man and the Natural World: Changing Attitudes in England 1500–1800* London: Allen Lane, 1983.

    (ed.), *German Philosophy*, Oxford: Oxford University Press, 1997.

Thurley, G., *Counter-Modernism in Current Critical Theory*, Basingstoke: Macmillan, 1980.

Todorov, T., *On Human Diversity: Nationalism, Racism, and Exoticism in French Thought*, trans. Catherine Porter, Cambridge, Mass., London, England: Harvard University Press, 1993.

Trezise, T., *Into the Breach: Samuel Beckett and the Ends of Literature*, Princeton, N.J.: Princeton University Press, 1990.

Trilling, L., *Sincerity and Authenticity*, Cambridge, Mass.: Harvard University Press, 1972.

    *The Last Decade*, New York: Harcourt Brace Jovanovich, 1977.

Trotter, D., *The English Novel in History 1895–1920*, London: Routledge: 1993.

Uhlmann, A., *Beckett and Poststructuralism*, Cambridge: Cambridge University Press, 1999.

Unwin, T. (ed.), *Michel Foucault Philosopher*, New York: Routledge, 1992.

Van Buren, J., *The Young Heidegger: Rumor of a Hidden King*, Bloomington and Indianapolis: Indiana University Press, 1994.

Virilio, P., *Open Sky*, trans. J. Rose, London and New York: Verso, 1997.

Washington, P., *Fraud: Literary Theory and the End of English*, London: Fontana, 1989.

Watson, D., *Paradox and Desire in Samuel Beckett's Fiction*, Basingstoke: Macmillan, 1991.

Watt, I., *The Rise of the Novel: Studies in Defoe, Richardson and Fielding* Harmondsworth: Penguin, 1983.

Wells, H. G., *Ann Veronica*, London: Dent, 1943.

    *The History of Mr Polly*, Harmondsworth: Penguin, 1946.

    *The New Machiavelli*, Harmondsworth: Penguin, 1946.

    *The Island of Dr Moreau*, Harmondsworth: Penguin, 1967.

White, A., *Joseph Conrad and the Adventure Tradition: Constructing and Deconstructing the Imperial Subject*, Cambridge: Cambridge University Press, 1993.

White, H., *Metahistory: The Historical Imgination in Nineteenth-Century Europe* Baltimore and London: Johns Hopkins University Press, 1973.

    *Tropics of Discourse: Essays in Cultural Criticism*, Baltimore and London: Johns Hopkins University Press, 1978.

Whiteley, P. J., *Knowledge and Experimental Realism in Conrad, Lawrence, and Woolf*, Baton Rouge: Louisiana State University Press, 1987.

Williams, R., *The Politics of Modernism: Against the New Conformists*, London: Verso, 1996.

Winner, L., *Autonomous Technology: Technics-out-of-control as a Theme in Political Thought*, Cambridge, Mass.: MIT Press, 1977.

Wollaeger, M. A., *Joseph Conrad and the Fictions of Skepticism*, Stanford, Calif.: Stanford University Press, 1990.

Worth, K. (ed.), *Beckett the Shape Changer*, London and Boston: Routledge & Kegan Paul, 1975.

Worthen, J., *D. H. Lawrence and the Idea of the Novel*, Basingstoke: Macmillan, 1979.

Wulf, C., *The Imperative of Narration: Beckett, Bernhard, Schopenhauer, Lacan*, Brighton: Sussex Academic Press, 1997.

Wutz, M., 'The Thermodynamics of Gender: Lawrence, Science and Sexism', in *Mosaic* 28/2 (1995), pp. 83–108.

Yeats, W. B., *The Poems*, London: Everyman, 1992.

Young, J., *Heidegger, Philosophy, Nazism*, Cambridge: Cambridge University Press, 1997.

# Index